Perspectives on Children and Young People

Volume 9

Series editors

Johanna Wyn, The University of Melbourne, Parkville, Australia
Helen Cahill, The University of Melbourne, Parkville, Australia
Hernan Cuervo, The University of Melbourne, Parkville, Australia

This series builds on the Springer Handbook on Childhood and Youth, and on the widespread interest in current issues that pertain to young people and children. The series contributes to the field of youth studies, which encompasses the disciplines of sociology, psychology, education, health, economics, social geography and cultural studies. Within these fields, there is a need to address two distinctive elements in relation to children and youth. The first of these is social change, and in particular, the risks and opportunities that are emerging in relation to the global changes to young people's lives captured by the metaphor 'the Asian Century'. The second of these is the emerging interest in building on the traditions of 'northern' theorists, where the traditions of the field of youth studies lie, through an engagement with new conceptual approaches that draw on the global south. These two elements frame the Handbook on Childhood and Youth, and in so doing, set the scene for a deeper engagement with key topics and issues through a book series. The series consists of two types of book. One is the research-based monograph produced by a sole author or a team of authors who have collaborated on a single topic. These books meet the need for deep engagement with emerging issues, including the demonstration of how new concepts are being used to understand the complexities of young people's lives. The second is edited collections that provide depth on particular topics by bringing together key thinkers and writers on that topic. The edited collections are especially relevant to new and emerging areas of youth studies where there is debate. These books are authored by a mix of established academics, mid-career academics and early career academics, ensuring that the series showcases the work of emerging scholars and offers fresh approaches and insights in the field of youth studies. While the focus is 'youth studies' this series contributes to a deeper understanding of the ways in which this field is enriched through inter-disciplinary scholarship and research, reaching across the fields of health and wellbeing, education and pedagogy, geography, sociology, psychology, the arts and cultural studies.

More information about this series at http://www.springer.com/series/13560

Rosalyn Black · Lucas Walsh

Imagining Youth Futures

University Students in Post-Truth Times

Springer

Rosalyn Black
School of Education
Deakin University
Burwood, VIC, Australia

Lucas Walsh
Faculty of Education
Monash University
Clayton, VIC, Australia

ISSN 2365-2977　　　　　　　　ISSN 2365-2985　(electronic)
Perspectives on Children and Young People
ISBN 978-981-13-6759-5　　　　ISBN 978-981-13-6760-1　(eBook)
https://doi.org/10.1007/978-981-13-6760-1

Library of Congress Control Number: 2019932599

© Springer Nature Singapore Pte Ltd. 2019
This work is subject to copyright. All rights are reserved by the Publisher, whether the whole or part of the material is concerned, specifically the rights of translation, reprinting, reuse of illustrations, recitation, broadcasting, reproduction on microfilms or in any other physical way, and transmission or information storage and retrieval, electronic adaptation, computer software, or by similar or dissimilar methodology now known or hereafter developed.
The use of general descriptive names, registered names, trademarks, service marks, etc. in this publication does not imply, even in the absence of a specific statement, that such names are exempt from the relevant protective laws and regulations and therefore free for general use.
The publisher, the authors and the editors are safe to assume that the advice and information in this book are believed to be true and accurate at the date of publication. Neither the publisher nor the authors or the editors give a warranty, expressed or implied, with respect to the material contained herein or for any errors or omissions that may have been made. The publisher remains neutral with regard to jurisdictional claims in published maps and institutional affiliations.

This Springer imprint is published by the registered company Springer Nature Singapore Pte Ltd.
The registered company address is: 152 Beach Road, #21-01/04 Gateway East, Singapore 189721, Singapore

This book is dedicated to Johanna Wyn, whose tremendous legacy has been a constant inspiration.
Rosalyn Black

This book is dedicated to Fazal Rizvi, who after 20 years is still showing me the way.
Lucas Walsh

For Jack Keating (1947–2012).
Rosalyn Black and Lucas Walsh

Acknowledgements

The authors are deeply indebted to Prof. Andrew Peterson and Dr. Sarah Pickard for their involvement in the field research underpinning this book: we are grateful beyond words. We wish to thank Joanne Gleeson for her superb research assistance. On a more personal note, we also wish to thank Rosalyn's husband, Tony, and Lucas's wife, Emma, for always being there and supporting everything we do.

Contents

1 Introduction 1
   Young Perspectives of Post-truth Times 2
   The Challenges of Uncertainty 5
   The Approach of This Book 7
   References 10

2 Setting the Scene 13
   Introduction 13
   The Research Project 14
   The Universities and Interviewees 16
   Conceptualising Youth in Changing Times 17
   Conceptualising the Young University Student 19
   The Missing Middle 20
   Inserting Time and the Imagined Future 22
   Inserting Mobility 25
   Inserting Affect 26
   Conclusion 28
   References 28

3 The Changing Promises and Prospects of Higher Education 35
   Introduction 35
   Higher Education for Individual Success 36
   To Give Us the Best Prospects 38
   The Truths and Promises of Higher Education 40
   Higher Education and Mobility 43
   Not Working but Learning: The Rise and Rise of 'Homo Economicus' 45
   What Matters Is Who I Know 48
   Conclusion 50
   References 51

4 Imagining the Family in Post-truth Times ... 57
Introduction ... 57
Reinserting the Family into Higher Education ... 58
Dreaming of Home ... 60
Leaving Home to Learn ... 63
Sharing and Supporting Hope Beyond Money and Shelter ... 65
Forming Families of Their Own ... 67
Parenting and Higher Education ... 70
Conclusion ... 71
References ... 72

5 Planning for Uncertainty: The Workforce Ahead ... 77
Introduction ... 77
The Changing Value of Higher Education Qualifications ... 78
Strategies for an Imagined Career ... 79
Work and the Massification of Higher Education ... 81
The Impact of Economic Downturns ... 84
Technology, Digital Skills and the Automation of Labour ... 85
The Emergence of the Gig Economy ... 86
Keeping Faith in the Opportunity Bargain ... 87
Conclusion ... 89
References ... 90

6 Reacting to the Future: The University Student as Homo Promptus ... 95
Introduction ... 95
   Homo Promptus Is Entrepreneurial and Strategic ... 96
   Homo Promptus Plans for the Future While Living Life in the Short-Term ... 98
   Homo Promptus Is not Tethered to a Single Place ... 101
   Homo Promptus Is Permanently in 'Situational' Mode ... 104
   Homo Promptus Lives in Waithood ... 106
Being 'Precarious People' ... 107
Conclusion ... 110
References ... 111

7 Making the Future: Homo Promptus and the Political ... 115
Introduction ... 115
The Politics of Uncertainty ... 116
Losing Trust in Politics ... 118
The Comfort of the Familiar ... 121
Homo Promptus as a Political Actor ... 123
Young Political Actors in a Post-truth World ... 126
Post-truth Politics and Affect ... 128

	Conclusion	130
	References	131
8	**Conclusion—What Is the Future of Youth?**	135
	Introduction	135
	Rethinking the Truths of Youth	137
	Engaging the Microfuture: 'My Biggest Worry … Is Outside of Myself'	140
	Imagining the Mesofuture: 'I just Don't Know What the Future Might Bring'	141
	Navigating the Macrofuture: 'There's Something Weird Happening'	143
	Imagining the Future in Post-truth Times	146
	Concluding Thoughts for a Hopeful Future	148
	References	151

About the Authors

Dr. Rosalyn Black is Senior Lecturer in Education at Deakin University. Her research interests and her previous publications meet at the intersection of the sociologies of education and youth. They include young people's experience of citizenship in socially unequal contexts.

Dr. Lucas Walsh is Professor of Education Policy and Practice, Youth Studies, and Deputy Dean of the Faculty of Education at Monash University. His research focuses on the political, economic, cultural, social, and technological dimensions of young people's participation, and the implications of these for educators and policy.

This is Rosalyn and Lucas' third book, following a 10-year collaboration.

Chapter 1
Introduction

There are quite a few new elements in the emerging human situation, which in all probability carry far-reaching moral consequences. These new elements stem from the overall tendency to dismantle, deregulate and dissipate the once solid and relatively lasting frames in which the concerns and efforts of most individuals were inscribed. Jobs, once seen as 'for life', are more often than not now temporary and may disappear virtually without notice, together with the factories or offices or bank branches which offered them. Even the skills which the jobs required are ageing fast, turning overnight from assets into obsolete liabilities. Being prudent and provident, thinking of the future, becomes ever more difficult, as there is little sense in accumulating skills for which tomorrow there may be no demand, or saving money which tomorrow may lose much of its purchasing power. At the moment young men and women enter the game of life, none can tell what the rules of the game will be like in the future. Their only certainty is that the rules will change many times over before the game is finished (Bauman 1994, p. 12).

It is almost a quarter century since Bauman made this observation, but his perspective remains alarmingly salient: the spectre of uncertainty unsettles our times in ways that have deep implications for young people and for the sociologies of education and youth. We have been researching and writing about young people's lives, both together and separately, for the last decade. Over this time, we have seen the global escalation of an environment of volatility, uncertainty, complexity and ambiguity. These concepts are popularly collected under the acronym VUCA, but this term is too closely linked to the military and business sectors to suit our purposes. Instead, we use the term 'uncertainty' across this book to represent this collection of forces and locate them within a wider social, economic and political context.

The collective effect of these forces shows itself in numerous ways. Labour markets are becoming more mutable, fluid and precarious; social fabrics are being strained, torn and reformed by unprecedented human mobility, migration and demographic change; debt crises and austerity programs are unsettling the economic landscape and disrupting individuals' hopes for a good life; deepening inequality and punitive policies are dismantling previously accepted ideas about social justice and cohesion; political orthodoxies and stabilities are being challenged and upended; planetary changes and environmental disasters are looming; and what have been seen to be the certainties of human life have been called into question, from the notion of a sustainable career to the notion of a sustainable civilisation.

This uncertainty is further reflected in the emergence of post-truth politics. Post-truth was the 2016 Oxford Dictionaries Word of the Year, defined as 'relating to or denoting circumstances in which objective facts are less influential in shaping public opinion than appeals to emotion and personal belief' (Oxford Living Dictionaries 2017). It was a *mot de jour* when we conceived the idea for this book. While acknowledging that its presence in the zeitgeist will probably be fleeting, we are deliberately provocative in its use. We have three intentions here.

The first of these is to note that the loss of influence of objective facts mentioned above has direct implications for the public and policy portrayal of young people: it encourages the use of persistent youth stereotypes ranging from 'entitled' and 'lazy' to 'wild' and even 'dangerous'. These stereotypes are not new, but their use and effects need to be seen in the context of the appeals to emotion and personal belief over evidence that have intensified in recent years. Our second intention is to evoke the economic, social and political upheaval of the current period in which the young people of this book find themselves, and the ways that these upheavals are challenging the social orthodoxies that have conventionally underpinned their lives.

Our third intention, and arguably our most important, intersects with the first two: we wish to interrogate certain 'truths of youth'. We have borrowed the phrase from Kelly's longstanding discussion (e.g. 2000, 2011) about the construction of fixed ideas or truths about young people as a cohort, truths that link young people and risk, and that are deployed to justify their regulation by government and other organisations. In this book, we use the phrase a little differently to our colleague to think about persistent assumptions that are still made about young people. These include the idea that youth is a stable category with a finite beginning and end, the promise that higher education will lead to a secure and desirable future, and the assumption that young people as a generation have become politically disenchanted and civically disengaged. We also use Kelly's phrase to reflect on what may be the untold truths about the effect of uncertainty on young people's lives. First, though, let us return to the broader meanings and implications of the post-truth era and the ways in which they are amplifying that uncertainty.

Young Perspectives of Post-truth Times

The term post-truth was allegedly first used in 1992 by Serbian-American playwright Steve Tesich, who wrote this in the Nation magazine in reference to the Iran-Contra scandal and the Persian Gulf war: 'we, as a free people, have freely decided that we want to live in some post-truth world' (in Flood 2016). Since then, the phrase has entered the common lexicon. The Oxford Dictionaries editors note that use of the term 'post-truth' increased by around 2,000% in 2016 compared to the previous year, largely sparked by the European Union (EU) membership referendum in the UK and the presidential election in the United States (US) (Flood 2016). In addition, something new may now be going on. Arguing that post-truth 'is emphatically not the same as lies, spin and falsehood', d'Ancona suggests that

> What is new is not mendacity but the public's response to it – the growing primacy of emotional resonance over fact and evidence, the replacement of verification with social media algorithms that tell us what we want to hear. Truth is losing its value as society's reserve currency, and legitimate scepticism is yielding place to pernicious relativism (2017).

In the post-truth world, normative foundations are eroded and replaced with affect or emotion and the rejection of reason. Everything from policy to personal development is prosecuted through regulatory and other mechanisms that appeal to personal subjectivities rather than community imaginaries. Particularly within what have been called 'post-fact politics', appeals are made to feelings over facts, to emotion over evidence. Davies suggests that 'the authority of facts has been in decline for quite some time', locating it in the move to big data and the oversupply of facts in the late in the 20th century (2016). This may be justified, but it does not capture the full extent of the current assault on reason and evidence.

This assault is manifest in the idea of 'fake news', which is attached in a kind of elliptic orbit to the post-truth era. It is also reflected in what The Guardian journalist Nick Enfield has called a 'suspicion of specialists and experts'. As Enfield explains:

> In our new normal, experts are dismissed, alternative facts are (sometimes flagrantly) offered, and public figures can offer opinions on pretty much anything. And thanks to social media, pretty much anyone can be a public figure. In much public discourse, identity outranks arguments, and we are seeing either a lack of interest in evidence, or worse, an erosion of trust in the fundamental norms around people's accountability for the things we say (2017).

The post-truth era has a strong affective or emotional dimension, then, one with particular implications for youth studies in particular. At the same time, the role of emotion and affect has also captured the imagination of some youth scholars as an area of research. As we will argue in Chap. 2, affect needs to be viewed as an important aspect of young people's current and imagined future lives, but it also needs to be interrogated within the context of what the evidence and what young people themselves are saying about those lives. Both facts and feelings matter. There is a need for deeper interrogation into young people's hopes, plans and concerns for their economic, political and family lives in post-truth times. There is also a need to ask whether the promises of higher education are becoming post-truth promises, the affective appeal of which is only poorly supported by fact.

Many young people are acutely aware of this post-truth climate and what it might mean for their personal and collective futures. In February 2017, *The Guardian Australia* (Adler et al. 2017) asked selected students beginning university to describe the biggest issue currently facing their home country of Australia. Their responses highlight a range of concerns about what the future holds for young people starting university today.

These concerns include what some see as the rise of the politics of fear or uncertainty, something that we discuss further in Chap. 7. Sarkis Ghattas is a student at the University of Technology Sydney. She notes that 'There is a scent of fear all around the world'. Philippa Ardler, a student of political, economic and social sciences at

Sydney University, is deeply concerned about 'the rise of conservative right politics [and] the breaking down of cohesive society as the tenuous strands holding our global community together begin to tear'. She highlights the growth of extremist right wing politics in America and its influence on the rest of the world, seeing Trump as stoking 'fear and ignorance of people who are different'. She also points to the rise of similar attitudes closer to home: 'in Australia, we are witnessing the emergence of extremist views, as rightwing politicians feel braver to express, impress and act, all behind the facade of "freedom of speech"'.

'Our society', Philippa argues, 'splits further into the disunity of "us and them", in a time where we should be standing together'. She goes on to say: 'As an Aboriginal person, I am worried for my people. As an ally of the LGBTQ+ community, I am worried for my friends. As a human being, I am scared for the world'. Annie Marsh, an Arts student at Australian National University (ANU), suggests that 'With Brexit Island and even Trumperica ahead of us, perhaps it's time to ask ourselves what we can do to ensure that in 2017, equality will no longer be forsaken for apathy'. Business and law student, Zoe Turner, expresses concern about the treatment of asylum seekers and refugees in the offshore detention centres of Nauru and Manus Island: 'Australia's own immigration policies … are clearly violating basic human rights'. Phillip Brooks, studying engineering and data, expresses similar concerns about the 'discrimination against people seeking asylum from war-torn countries in the Middle East, who are being turned away. There is discrimination against the unborn, who are being treated as subhuman organisms without the basic right to life'.

ANU student of arts and law Max Koslowski is also worried 'that Europe and USA's tsunami of far-right support will come for Australia, too. Australians, particularly the younger generation, are not immune to the forces that got Trump into office and made Brexit a reality'. Max points to a recent survey finding that 40% of Australians are not satisfied with the democratic system: 'For younger people, like myself, these levels aren't just historically low, but they are much lower than the satisfaction levels of our parents and grandparents'. He argues that young people's democratic anxieties 'are founded in the inaction and uncertainty that has come to represent Australian politics. I have grown up in a political landscape that has switched leaders five times in six years' (the Prime Minister at the time was also removed by his own party a year later). This concern is shared by Jasper Lindell, who is studying political science at the ANU. He asks:

> Who's running the show at the moment? Is it the political parties, lobbyists, faction on the fringe, newspaper columnists, the Twitterati, the left, the right or people in marginal electorates? Or is the government, the cabinet or the prime minister? It's hard to say … . Here's the problem: young people need political leadership, and quickly, before we end up in more of a disillusioned mess. But it can't be half-hearted, in some areas and not others, because then it will just be another round of political hypocrisy.

For Max, the uncertainty of the future also extends to young people's job futures:

> My peers don't know whether they will be able to get a job, because youth unemployment is above 13%, almost double what it was in 2008. They don't know whether they should go to university, because the revolving door of Australian politics might deliver them unaffordable degrees. And they don't know what to study, because they aren't sure which industries will be next in line in globalisation's conveyor belt of economic change (Adler et al. 2017).

The Challenges of Uncertainty

These testimonies show how acutely aware some young people are of recent political, economic and social developments and of the fear, concern and uncertainty that attend them. Change and uncertainty are by no means new—the concept of an uncertain world dates from the end of the Cold War—but they continue to be particularly present across the lives of many young people and are implicated in shaping their futures. As we explain shortly, our discussion across this book draws on our interviews with 30 young people in France, the UK and Australia as well as on an extensive youth studies scholarship which highlights young people's relationship to uncertainty (e.g. Antonucci et al. 2014; Bessant et al. 2017; France 2016; France and Threadgold 2016; Furlong 2016; Kelly 2016; Wyn 2016).

This relationship shows itself in multiple ways. We have touched on these earlier: let's expand on them a little further. In many western nations, economic insecurity is troubling young people's transition to the workforce. The Global Financial Crisis (GFC) of 2007–2008 impacted upon young people immediately and disproportionately in relation to older groups (OECD 2010): many lost their jobs and have faced greater precarity in the workforce ever since. In France, for example, economic growth has been slowing, with the economic policy uncertainty index recently reaching an all-time high. In both France and the UK, this insecurity has been exacerbated by the uncertainty arising from the 2016 UK referendum decision to leave the EU. At the same time, the rise of far-right political parties reflects a destabilisation of political certainties and social cohesion across many nations, while cultural and identity politics have heightened long-term challenges arising from the unprecedented levels of human mobility.

Within this landscape, the previous certainties of young people's post-education trajectories are being eroded. This is also changing the nature of normative material-life projects such as home ownership and the formation of committed relationships. Instead, young university students arguably find themselves in a post-truth world, in which even the solidity of objective facts as a basis for making decisions at personal and policy levels is being challenged. These developments have potentially profound implications for young people's sense of identity and security, and for the mobility and stability of their current and future lives. They also have implications for higher education. The challenges of uncertainty strike at the very heart of the purposes of higher education, raising questions about how well universities have adjusted to the fluid conditions of contemporary life. While much of what takes place in universities has not changed significantly during the last century, preparing young people for an increasingly post-industrial society requires new approaches grounded in a nuanced understanding of their experiences and imaginaries of employment and their attitudes to the changing world around them. This raises questions about the discourses that attend higher education as a sector and a system.

As we discuss at length in Chap. 3, higher education is imbued with the discursive promise that graduates will be able to take their place as mobile global (and globalised) citizens with broad career prospects and capacities to contribute politically, economically and socially across national and world stages. High-achieving young graduates, in particular, are encouraged to see themselves as members of a new global middle class who enjoy career and life opportunities that transcend the constraints of national boundaries (Ball 2010; Power et al. 2013). This discourse belies the mounting debt and changing prospects of many graduates. Internationally, studies show that the 'graduate earnings premium'—the income power of graduates—is largely enjoyed by those with postgraduate and professional degrees, rather than those with undergraduate qualifications. They also show that this premium is falling. In Australia, for example, it has fallen by 8% for women and 6% for men since 2006 (Bolton 2018). In its place, a generational divide is emerging that has direct implications for young graduates. On the one hand, incomes derived from graduate degrees have not kept pace with the incomes derived from postgraduate qualifications. On the other hand, we have seen the growth of billionaires since the 1980s—the 'one per cent' identified by the Occupy Movement (Côté 2014).

As we also elaborate in Chap. 3, an increase in the number of university graduates overall, combined with the greater mobility of qualified workers across countries, is intensifying competition for skilled work. Even in established economies such as France and the UK, graduates have struggled for some years to translate their qualifications into the life outcomes traditionally associated with high levels of education (Bremer 2013; Roberts and Li 2017; Vina 2016). Job prospects for Australian university graduates are also declining, with fewer finding full-time employment after completing their studies (Lamacraft 2016). At the same time, the social and economic mobility of young people from middle-class backgrounds is being challenged by the entry of professionals from emerging economies such as India. This appears to be driving 'credential inflation', which is in turn reducing the value of academic credentials over time (Ortlieb 2015). In a more competitive labour market, employers can demand higher qualifications (Foster et al. 2007; Modestino 2010). One of the more perverse outcomes of this competition is illustrated by Brown and his colleagues (2011), who note the use of the Dutch auction in parts of Europe. This sees graduates with the brightest CVs competing for jobs by offering to accept the lowest-paying wage. This is despite the fact that the current generation of European young people are the most highly educated in the continent's history (Oinonen 2018).

The 'opportunity bargain' that higher education will lead to better employment (Brown et al. 2011, p. 5) is also increasingly challenged by a globalised, technologically-disrupted job market. While technology is transforming the labour force, there are questions about whether the knowledge and skills being acquired by young people are sufficiently well aligned to this transformation (FYA 2015). This is a real concern given the prediction that technology

> will cause unprecedented disruption of global citizens' lives over the coming decades, due to: 1. Speed of change: unlike previous industrial revolutions, the labor market and society will have insufficient time to adapt to the expected pace of change. 2. Ubiquity of change: the advances talked about under the umbrella of the Fourth Industrial Revolution – 3D printing, material sciences, automated smart systems – will impact almost all sectors and levels of jobs and qualifications (Infosys 2016, p. 5).

The Approach of This Book

As we flagged earlier, we have spent the last decade working together to document young people's changing place and roles in contemporary society. We have a long-standing interest in young people's experiences in contexts characterised by escalating uncertainty as well as certain continuities. We also have a long-standing interest in the role of education policy, institutions and systems in constructing and shaping those experiences. Where our previous research focused primarily on economic and political macro-trends (e.g. Walsh and Black 2011, 2018a, b; Walsh 2016a, b), our discussion in this book seeks to provide a more intimate insight into the lives of a relatively small cohort of young people in three countries: Australia, France and the UK. We have purposely selected these three countries to represent a sliding scale of the uncertainty we have described above, with the UK at the most precarious end of the scale and Australia arguably at the other end, having experienced over two decades of unbroken economic growth.

Our discussion draws on interviews with young undergraduate or postgraduate students within one public university in each of these three countries. These interviews present a point-in-time reflection on these young people's hopes, plans and concerns for their imagined futures, how these imagined futures relate to their current experiences, and how their realisation may be supported or undermined by current socio-political climates. We also draw on a review of the recent international literature and relevant data from recent large-scale studies to highlight the relevance of this point-in-time reflection for a much wider group of young people, both now and into the future. Our discussion takes the following form.

Chapter 2 establishes the theoretical frameworks and guiding ideas of the book, through which the insights of our young interviewees will be analysed. We begin by outlining the research project that has yielded these insights and providing a brief account of the universities and contexts in which our interviews were conducted. We then discuss the conceptualisations of youth and young people that we use in the book, reflecting on the fluidity and complexity of youth as a category and the role of uncertainty in amplifying this complexity. We introduce the tripartite lens which we use across the book, which draws on Brooks' categorisations (2018) to think about young university students as family members, workers and political actors. Following this, we discuss the ideas and theorisations of time and the imagined future, mobility and affect on which we draw across the book. We also introduce our use of ideas such as push and pull factors to reflect on the ways in which family relationships, in particular, can influence young people's imagined and actual trajectories through and beyond higher education in uncertain times.

Chapter 3 then reflects on the nature of contemporary higher education and its inherent discourses about improved access to life chances. We draw on our interviews and our review of the recent international literature to consider these discourses, the promises that they communicate about young futures, and how they relate to young people's own hopes, plans and concerns in relation to their higher education and their imagined futures beyond it. Hearkening back to our discussion in this Introduction, we also consider the 'truths of youth' that are rapidly changing the nature of the educational contract between young university students, their universities and the outcomes for which they have been led to hope.

Wyn and her colleagues have mounted an argument for the reinsertion of the family into youth studies (2012). Understanding how young people imagine their future as family members brings an important dimension to their experiences of uncertainty and their responses to it. Evidence from the past decade suggests that young people face growing challenges in planning their private lives. This ranges from quotidian activities such as catching up with family and friends to larger life projects such as obtaining a home (owned or securely rented) or forming a family. Chapter 4 considers the nature and role of the family for young university students in an era when experiences of youth are increasingly protracted and prolonged. We draw on our interviews and review of the literature to critically investigate young people's current and imagined future lives as family members and how these relate to the promises of higher education and the forces of uncertainty.

Following this discussion, Chap. 5 looks at what might lie ahead for young people in changing global labour markets characterised by hyper-competition and precarity. We draw on the international literature and data to reflect on how these changing labour markets are challenging the promises of higher education in relation to work and altering post-higher education pathways for young people. We look at the nature of young people's working lives, both during and after university, and reflect our interviewees' hopes, plans and concerns for their imagined futures as workers. We also explore the impact of other developments on our interviewees and young university students in general, such as the massification of higher education, the impact of economic downturns, technology, and the emergence of the gig economy.

In Chap. 3, we suggest that the contemporary university student is less the 'homo educandus' envisioned by Kant than the 'homo economicus' described by Stuart Mill and other economic theorists. Building on this, Chap. 6 introduces our argument that what appears to be emerging from the era of uncertainty is a third youth category—*homo promptus*. We use this term to describe the individualised and entrepreneurial self that is produced by neoliberal education and labour market forces and discourses, and actively cultivated by young university students in response to these forces and discourses. In proposing this, we build on Peou and Zinn's typology, which describes the ways in which young people approach the future either in entrepreneurial mode, as something to be planned and enacted proactively, or in 'situational' mode, as something that is 'mainly unknowable' (2015, pp. 734–736). We suggest that homo promptus combines these two modes within a youth selfhood that has five dispositions or behaviours: homo promptus is entrepreneurial and strategic, is expected to constantly plan for the future while living life in the short-term, is not tethered to a single place, is permanently in 'situational' mode, and lives in waithood. Drawing on our interviews, we argue that the driving impetus for these dispositions and behaviours is the uncertainty that attends young people's current and imagined future working lives, although they also manifest themselves in young people's lives as family members and political actors.

Many of the economic trends which we discuss across the book are also entwined with political change, of which Brexit and the election of Donald Trump are two recent and seismic examples. This is adding to the destabilisation of political orthodoxies in ways that have immediate implications for the mobility and security of many young people and that exacerbate the growing distance between young people and their political representatives. The emergence of post-truth politics is further adding to this destabilisation, unsettling the very foundations of public discourse and the ability of governments (and citizens) to respond to pressing changes. In Chap. 7, we turn to the political dimension of young people's lives, drawing on our interviews and review of the literature to consider the ways in which young people's role as political actors reflects the values and behaviours of homo promptus. We consider their scepticism of conventional political processes and information sources; their preference for modes of political action that are extra-institutional, affective, flexible and personally meaningful; and their reliance on their 'gut-feelings' in navigating political discourses. We also reflect on their concerns about post-truth politics and their implications for young people's relationship to the political process.

As we will show, our interviewees' perspectives on these issues are varied, reflecting the complexities of young people's lives in general. One common theme to emerge, however, is the uncertainty and instability experienced by all. In the Conclusion, we present their responses to a final question: are the conventional truths of adulthood and youth changing? We also present a tripartite framework through which young people's imagined futures might be better understood. This framework proposes that youth futures can be understood as: microfutures, which encompass hopes and concerns about the future arising directly from young people's immediate life-worlds; mesofutures, which include events that are within the visible horizons of young people's lives but may not be within their immediate grasp; and macrofutures, which comprise more abstract forces and events such as political and economic instability and technological and climate change. We conclude with a series of reflections about what hope might mean for young people navigating the post-truth world, and how it might be sustained.

References

Adler, P., Lindell, J., Marsh, A., Gattas, S., Turner, Z., Brooks, P., et al. (2017, February 21). 'We need leadership—quickly': First-year students on the biggest issue facing Australia. *The Guardian*. Retrieved February 23, 2017, from https://www.theguardian.com/australia-news/2017/feb/21/we-need-leadership-quickly-first-year-students-on-the-biggest-issue-facing-australia.

Antonucci, L., Hamilton, M., & Roberts, S. (2014). Constructing a theory of youth and social policy. In L. Antonucci, M. Hamilton, & S. Roberts (Eds.), *Young people and social policy in Europe: Dealing with risk, inequality and precarity in times of crisis* (pp. 13–34). London: Palgrave Macmillan UK.

Ball, S. J. (2010). Is there a global middle class? The beginnings of a cosmopolitan sociology of education: A review. *Journal of Comparative Education, 69*(1), 137–161.

Bauman, Z. (1994). Alone again: Ethics after certainty. *Issues 9, Demos Papers*. London: Demos.

Bessant, J., Farthing, R., & Watts, R. (2017). *The precarious generation: A political economy of young people*. Abingdon: Routledge.

Bolton, R. (2018, September 12). Uni degrees lose some of their allure as the premium for being a graduate falls. *Australian Financial Review*. Retrieved October 4, 2018, from https://www.afr.com/news/policy/education/university-degrees-lose-some-of-their-allure-as-the-premium-for-being-a-graduate-starts-to-fall-20180912-h15an7.

Bremer, C. (2013, April 25). Rising unemployment creates France's 'Generation Slog'. *Reuters*. Retrieved September 15, 2016, from http://www.reuters.com/article/us-france-unemployed-idUSBRE93O0MA20130425.

Brooks, R. (2018). Understanding the higher education student in Europe: A comparative analysis. *Compare: A Journal of Comparative and International Education, 48*(4), 500–517. https://doi.org/10.1080/03057925.2017.1318047.

Brown, P., Lauder, H., & Ashton, D. (2011). *The global auction: The broken promises of education, jobs, and incomes*. USA: Oxford University Press.

Côté, J. E. (2014). Towards a new political economy of youth. *Journal of Youth Studies, 17*(4), 527–543. https://doi.org/10.1080/13676261.2013.836592.

d'Ancona, M. (2017, May 12). Ten alternative facts for the post truth world. *The Guardian*. Retrieved May 12, 2017, from https://www.theguardian.com/books/2017/may/12/post-truth-worst-of-best-donald-trump-sean-spicer-kellyanne-conway.

Davies, W. (2016, August 24). The age of post-truth politics. *The New York Times*. Retrieved September 18, 2017, from https://www.nytimes.com/2016/08/24/opinion/campaign-stops/the-age-of-post-truth-politics.html?mcubz=0.

Enfield, N. (2017, November 17). We're in a post-truth world with eroding trust and accountability. It can't end well. *The Guardian*. Retrieved November 19, 2017, from https://www.theguardian.com/commentisfree/2017/nov/17/were-in-a-post-truth-world-with-eroding-trust-and-accountability-it-cant-end-well.

Flood, A. (2016, November 15). 'Post-truth' named word of the year by Oxford Dictionaries. *The Guardian*. Retrieved November 16, 2016, from https://www.theguardian.com/books/2016/nov/15/post-truth-named-word-of-the-year-by-oxford-dictionaries.

Foster, S., Delaney, B., Bateman, A., & Dyson, C. (2007). *Higher-level vocational education and training qualifications: Their importance in today's training market*. Adelaide: NCVER.

France, A. (2016). *Understanding youth in the global economic crisis*. Bristol: Policy Press.

France, A., & Threadgold, S. (2016). Youth and political economy: Towards a Bourdieusian approach. *Journal of Youth Studies, 19*(5), 612–628. https://doi.org/10.1080/13676261.2015.1098779.

Furlong, A. (2016). The changing landscape of youth and young adulthood. In A. Furlong (Ed.), *Routledge handbook of youth and young adulthood* (2nd ed., pp. 3–11). London: Routledge.

References

Infosys. (2016). *Amplifying human potential: Education and skills for the fourth industrial revolution*. Retrieved May 25, 2017, from http://www.experienceinfosys.com/humanpotential.

Kelly, P. (2000). Youth as an artefact of expertise: Problematizing the practice of youth studies in an age of uncertainty. *Journal of Youth Studies, 3*(3), 301–315. https://doi.org/10.1080/713684381.

Kelly, P. (2011). Breath and the truths of youth at risk: Allegory and the social scientific imagination. *Journal of Youth Studies, 14*(4), 431–447. https://doi.org/10.1080/13676261.2010.543668.

Kelly, P. (2016). Young people and the coming of the Third Industrial Revolution: New work ethics and the self as enterprise after the GFC, after neo-Liberalism. In A. Furlong (Ed.), *Routledge handbook of youth and young adulthood* (2nd ed., pp. 391–399). Oxon and New York: Routledge.

Lamacraft, T. (2016, September 29). University graduates struggle to find full-time work as enrolments increase, study finds. *ABC News*. Retrieved February 21, 2017, from http://www.abc.net.au/news/2016-09-29/uni-graduate-job-prospects-in-decline/7890562.

Modestino, A. S. (2010). *Mismatch in the labor market: Measuring the supply of and demand for skilled labor in New England. New England Public Policy Center Research Report Number 10-2*. Boston: Federal Reserve Bank of Boston.

Oinonen, E. (2018). Under pressure to become—From a student to entrepreneurial self. *Journal of Youth Studies, 21*(10), 1344–1360. https://doi.org/10.1080/13676261.2018.1468022.

Organisation for Economic Co-operation and Development [OECD]. (2010). *Off to a good start? Jobs for youth*. Paris: Organisation for Economic Co-operation and Development. Retrieved May 1, 2015, http://www.oecd.org/els/emp/46717876.pdf.

Ortlieb, E. (2015, February 12). Just graduating from university is no longer enough to get a job. *The Conversation*. Retrieved February 16, 2015, from http://theconversation.com/just-graduating-from-university-is-no-longer-enough-to-get-a-job-36906.

Oxford Living Dictionaries. (2017). Word of the Year 2016 is ... *English Oxford Living Dictionaries*. Retrieved October 5, 2018, from https://en.oxforddictionaries.com/word-of-the-year/word-of-the-year-2016.

Peou, C., & Zinn, J. (2015). Cambodian youth managing expectations and uncertainties of the life course: A typology of biographical management. *Journal of Youth Studies, 18*(6), 726–742. https://doi.org/10.1080/13676261.2014.992328.

Power, S., Brown, P., Allouch, A., & Tholen, G. (2013). Self, career and nationhood: The contrasting aspirations of British and French elite graduates. *The British Journal of Sociology, 64*(4), 578–596. https://doi.org/10.1111/1468-4446.12048.

Roberts, S., & Li, Z. (2017). Capital limits: Social class, motivations for term-time job searching and the consequences of joblessness among UK university students. *Journal of Youth Studies, 20*(6), 732–749. https://doi.org/10.1080/13676261.2016.1260697.

The Foundation for Young Australians [FYA]. (2015). *New Work Order (excerpt)*. Retrieved April 9, 2016, from www.fya.org.au/wp-content/uploads/2015/08/The-New-Work-Order-infographic-1-overview1.png.

Vina, G. (2016, April 26). Young UK graduates struggle to find skilled work. *Financial Times*. Retrieved September 13, 2017, from https://www.ft.com/content/480d0ad6-0ba9-11e6-b0f1-61f222853ff3.

Walsh, L. (2016a). *Educating generation next: Young people, teachers and schooling in transition*. Basingstoke: Palgrave Macmillan.

Walsh, L. (2016b). *Educating for uncertainty: Ideas and challenges for schooling in a post-industrial society*. CSE Seminar Series paper 253, April 2016. Richmond: Centre for Strategic Education.

Walsh, L., & Black, R. (2011). *In their own hands: Can young people change Australia?*. Melbourne: ACER Press.

Walsh, L., & Black, R. (2018a). Off the radar democracy: Young people's alternate acts of citizenship in Australia. In S. Pickard & J. Bessant (Eds.), *Youth politics in crisis: New forms of political participation in the austerity era* (pp. 217–232). Basingstoke: Palgrave Macmillan.

Walsh, L., & Black, R. (2018b). *Rethinking youth citizenship after the age of entitlement*. London: Bloomsbury.

Wyn, J. (2016). Educating for late modernity. In A. Furlong (Ed.), *Routledge handbook of youth and young adulthood* (pp. 91–98). New York: Routledge.

Wyn, J., Lantz, S., & Harris, A. (2012). Beyond the 'transitions' metaphor: Family relations and young people in late modernity. *Journal of Sociology, 48*(1), 3–22. https://doi.org/10.1177/1440783311408971.

Chapter 2
Setting the Scene

Introduction

> The young used to be the future. They were promised a better world than their parents and grandparents. Not so anymore, at least not everywhere. Across the globe people talk about a lost generation, a jinxed generation or ant tribes. The future is not as promising as it used to be, and as a consequence, young people are losing faith in governments and institutions and many are pessimistic about their futures (Morales et al. 2013).

Despite the reference to the neologism of ant tribes, which refers to low-income university graduates living a poverty-level existence in the cities of China, warnings such as this have resounded in the public, policy and scholarly fields for many years now. Concerns about young people's 'mortgaged futures' (Kelly 2017, p. 57) were amplified in the wake of the GFC, with its grim immediate and downstream effects on young people's labour market participation, as well as on their life chances beyond that. They are now accelerating again in response to the kinds of uncertainties which we have described in the Introduction and which include mutable and precarious labour markets; strained or reformed social fabrics; unsettled economic presents and prospects; deepened inequality and threats to social justice and cohesion; the destabilisation of political orthodoxies; environmental and planetary change; and a deep challenge to the certainties of human life.

This book draws on the findings of a research project designed and conducted by the authors during 2017 and 2018 which involved interviews with 30 young university students. As we discussed in the Introduction, this project emerges from our long-standing interest in young people's experiences in contexts characterised by escalating uncertainty as well as certain continuities. It also emerges from our long-term interest in the role of education policy, institutions and systems in constructing and shaping these experiences. This book reflects our particular concern about the ways in which higher education as a system—and individual universities—discursively construct young people's current and imagined future lives as well as how they may enable young people to realise those imagined futures.

While the accounts of our interviewees provide the central focus of the following chapters, our discussion is also informed by recent thinking within the international literature as it relates to the themes of the book. In particular, it is informed by the literature of the sociology of youth, or youth studies. This chapter establishes the theoretical frameworks and guiding ideas of this book, through which the insights of our young interviewees will be analysed in the chapters to come. It discusses the conceptualisations of youth and young people that we use in the book, including the tripartite lens which draws on Brooks' categorisations (2018) to think about young university students as family members, workers and political actors. It also discusses the ideas and theorisations of time and the imagined future, mobility and affect on which we draw across the book. We begin by outlining the research project that has yielded these insights and provide a brief account of the universities and contexts in which our interviews were conducted.

The Research Project

The research project which led to this book was informed by three central questions:

1. What discursive promises about young people's current and future lives as family members, workers and political actors are fostered by public universities in nations facing the effects of uncertainty?
2. What hopes, plans and concerns do young people at such universities have for their own imagined futures?
3. How do these discursive promises and imagined futures relate to young people's current experiences? How is their realisation supported or undermined by current socio-political climates?

Our research focused on young people at one public university in each of Australia, France and the UK. We purposely selected these three nations to represent a sliding scale of uncertainty and precarity, as we explained in the Introduction, with the UK at the most precarious end of the scale and Australia arguably at the other end, having experienced relative economic prosperity compared to France and the UK.

At each university, we held individual interviews with young people between the ages of 19 and 29: eight young people from the UK, 11 from France and 11 from Australia, creating a purposive total sample of 30 interviewees. This purposive sample is intrinsic to our methodological aims in this project. Our intention has not been to make representative claims about any given cohort of young people, but rather to investigate the current experience and future hopes of particular young people in particular geographic places and at a particular historical moment, and to provide a fine-grained analysis of those young people's individual accounts (Ritchie et al. 2013). This is an approach that has been used with particular effect in other recent studies of young people's imagined futures and orientations towards higher education in various socio-geographic contexts (e.g. Allen 2016; Biasin et al. 2016; Budd 2017; Cook 2016; Forsberg and Timonen 2018).

Table 2.1 Interviewees by country of interview

France			UK			Australia		
Preferred name	Age	Country of birth	Preferred name	Age	Country of birth	Preferred name	Age	Country of birth
Grace	22	Democratic Republic of Congo	Alice	21	UK	Abi	26	Indonesia
Ines	20	France	Becky	25	UK	Alice	28	Australia
Juliane	25	Germany	Ellie	19	UK	Allysa	26	Indonesia
Juliette	24	France	Finlay	20	UK	Cynthia	19	Australia
Kim	26	Germany	George	22	UK	Irina	23	Russia
Lyr	25	France	Isabella	21	Italy	Jack	26	China
Morgane	23	France	Mark	21	UK	Jessica	22	Australia
Ninon	22	France	Tom	19	UK	Lila	24	China
Paloma	22	France				Mel	20	Australia
Sophia	21	France				Rose	27	India
Zaynab	23	France				Tyler	29	Australia

At the time of our interviews, all of our interviewees were enrolled in either undergraduate or postgraduate study. In France and the UK, the invitation to participate in the research project was circulated through a snowballing network of academics at the universities in question. In Australia, the recruitment advertisement was disseminated via online media and through a snowballing technique whereby students and academic teaching staff were asked to nominate or invite students of the appropriate age who might wish to participate in the project. Table 2.1 provides the details of the final three cohorts of interviewees.

A brief demographic survey was circulated to all interviewees before the interviews. Most of these interviews took place in person (with two conducted via the Internet communication software Skype) and averaged 90 minutes in duration. Each used a semi-structured style which reflected our desire to ensure some continuity within and across each series of interviews, while also creating the conditions under which interviewees could depart from our questions to pursue other lines of thought and discussion (Miles et al. 1994). A list of generic guiding questions and prompts drew on the ideas that we unpack in this chapter to explore how our interviewees imagine their lives in 10 years' time. While these prompts encompassed areas of our interviewees' lives that might be accompanied by normative expectations or assumptions, care was taken in each interview to avoid the imposition of normative or 'proper trajectories', 'hierarch[ies] of achievements' or 'authorised aspirations' (Allen 2016, pp. 809–810). As we explain later in this chapter, it has not been our intention either in our interviews or in this book to contain, categorise or homogenise young people's lives or the ways in which they describe those lives to us.

With the permission of our interviewees, all interviews were recorded, transcribed and subjected to a thematic analysis (Miles et al. 2014). While we allowed new themes to emerge from the data, we also paid attention to the themes described above as well as to key affective terms that might capture how the interviewees feel about their imagined future and the circumstances which may affect the unfolding of that future across time.

The Universities and Interviewees

Our French university is located in the historic heart of a major city and has its origins in the 13th century. The current institution is housed in a series of 16th century buildings that proudly communicate their cultural heritage. Our interviews took place in a café opposite one of the campuses, where our participants' stories were punctuated by the quotidian chat of patrons and tinkle of cutlery and glasses bouncing off the low beamed ceilings and thick stone walls.

The cultural resources of the city are also attractive to our interviewees. A number have chosen this university because of these resources and because of its national and global reputation. For most, however, the decision to enrol here has been a pragmatic one: most are either living in the city where the university is located or else commute from towns located within an hour from it. Only one has relocated to France (from Germany) in order to take up study at the university. The university is also attractive because it offers a unique international Masters of Journalism program, in which a number of our interviewees are enrolled, and because its tuition fees are low. In this regard, it is like most higher education institutions in France, which are funded by the state and usually charge only nominal fees. By contrast, studying at France's highly selective private *Grandes Écoles* can be an expensive proposition.

At the time of the interviews, our French interviewees were aged between 20 and 26 and all were engaged in postgraduate study. In most instances, they are French nationals, born in France of French parents. Two are German, however, and one was born in the Democratic Republic of the Congo. Some of their parents have also come to France from former French colonies such as the Democratic Republic of the Congo, Tunisia and Morocco.

Our UK university is located in a small, ancient cathedral city in regional England. While it is a relatively new university, repurposed in the 1990s from a teacher training college, its history is nonetheless an important aspect of the way in which it describes itself. The original campus was built upon land that formed the precincts of an abbey founded in the seventh century, and the famous cathedral is still a nearby presence. This is not a geographic accident: a strong moral purpose remains an important aspect of the university's public profile.

While the city itself is one of the wealthiest places in the region, unemployment across the wider region is high. The university's recent expansion to other regional cities and towns forms part of its mission to enhance accessibility to higher education for the region's more disadvantaged communities, and it actively promotes an ethic of service to the public good. For a number of our interviewees, the financial cost of higher education is clearly a burden and a source of anxiety. These young people have typically taken out government loans to cover the costs of tuition and living, which means that they may be facing debts of up 30,000 British pounds when they graduate.

All of our UK interviewees were undergraduates at the time of the interviews. As such, the cohort is a little younger on average than the French cohort, ranging from 19 to 25 but mostly clustered around 21 or 22. Like their French peers, their university's proximity to home has been a common consideration in their decision to enrol, although half have relocated from elsewhere in the country in order to do so. Unlike their French counterparts, more than half acknowledge that their ability to be accepted by the university has also been a key factor in this decision. The vast majority of these young people are UK citizens: only one was born outside the UK (in Italy), although their parents' birthplaces include Nigeria, Bulgaria, Italy and Australia.

Moving across the world to Australia's south, our Australian university has been running for over 60 years. With more than 70,000 students from over 170 countries and a number of international campuses, it is amongst Australia's largest and most highly ranked universities. In a strong echo of the UK university's credo, its current marketing campaign urges students to prepare themselves for successful lives that have the potential to benefit the community as a whole as well as to give them the global employment mobility and opportunity which is at the heart of the university's promise to its graduates.

This global focus is reflected in the demographic makeup of the young people we interviewed. Fewer than half are Australian citizens: the rest have come to Australia as international students from Indonesia, Russia, India, Malaysia and China. At the time of our interviews, most were studying at a postgraduate level and most were in their mid-20s. The university's national or global reputation has been a key factor in its choice by most of these young people, a theme to which we return in Chaps. 3 and 5.

Conceptualising Youth in Changing Times

As we have explained, our discussion in this book is centrally informed by the perspectives of 30 young university students between the ages of 19 and 29. This raises the perennial question of what youth denotes and how it should be understood. Even after so much scholarly discussion of the issue, the notion of what constitutes youth remains contested. The United Nations (2014, p. 1) provides a widely accepted definition which identifies young people as being between 15 and 24 years of age, but it also notes that 'youth is more fluid than other fixed age-groups'. Other definitions of youth include those offered by the UN-Habitat Urban Youth Fund (15–32), the United Nations Population Fund (10–24), the World Health Organization (10–29), the World Bank (15–34) and the EU (15–29) (see Commonwealth Secretariat 2016).

This variability, fluidity and complexity of youth as a category has been well recognised within youth studies. Wyn and White mounted the argument for a more nuanced and sophisticated understanding of youth back in 1997. Their seminal suggestion that 'youth and childhood have had and continue to have different meanings depending on young people's social, cultural and political circumstances' (p. 10) laid the foundation for an ongoing project that seeks to move away from static definitions of youth. Their argument that youth is, above all, a constructed relationship (Wyn and White 2015) has also informed this project. As Wyn observes, 'childhood and youth (and adulthood) are fluid relationships that are given definition and meaning by their social, cultural, political, institutional, locational, governmental, and economic contexts' (2015, p. 5). Sukarieh and Tannock describe these contexts in further detail:

> Both youth as a social category and the individual lives of young people are constantly being worked upon, molded, given form and substance – in a word, produced – by the actions of the state, schools, universities, courts, corporations, the media, churches, NGOs and other civil society organisations operating at the local, national and global levels (2014, p. 4).

One of the manifestations of this plasticity of youth as a category has been its growing complexity. Du Bois-Reymond and López Blasco suggest that 'youth is now not only conceived as a phase in the life course, but also a life condition that is marked by unpredictability, vulnerability and reversibility' (2003, p. 20). Langevang promotes a similar conceptualisation of youth when she describes it as 'both a shifting social position and a fluid process' (2008, p. 2046). Another manifestation of the plasticity of youth as a category has been its elongation or prolongation due to the deferral of what have traditionally been considered the markers of adulthood in many cultures: home ownership, family formation and the attainment of stable livelihoods. As Sukarieh and Tannock note, 'youth as a social category has spread horizontally to cover an even greater range of the world's population who are in their second and third (and even fourth) decades of life' (2014, p. 54).

Higher education has been a key factor in this prolongation and complexity: as the 'educational arms race' continues to drive the expansion and extension of young people's engagement in higher education (Sukarieh and Tannock 2014, p. 114), so too the experience of youth continues to be extended. This experience is now being prolonged into an 'extended present' (Nowotny 1994) or what Honwana characterises as 'waithood' (2014, p. 19). This waithood may last well beyond what is commonly considered young adulthood: as Honwana argues, 'some [young people] never get out of it and remain permanently in the precarious and improvised life that waithood imposes' (2014, p. 21). Growing numbers of young people are also subject to 'yo-yo transitions' (Du Bois-Reymond and López Blasco 2003): complex cycles of dependence and independence, of entering and leaving education and employment, of leaving and re-entering the parental home, which also extend and complicate their experience of youth.

This prolongation of youth is inextricably associated with uncertainty, one that affects both young people's experience of the present and the prospect of the future. A large body of youth studies has depicted this future as 'a space crowded with risks and contingencies' (Cook 2016, p. 700) which young people have to manage. Our own earlier work has been influenced by this scholarship, drawing on the work of Bauman (e.g. 2007) as well as that of leading youth scholars who have highlighted young people's relationship to the multiple risks of the contemporary era (e.g. Antonucci et al. 2014; Bessant et al. 2017; France 2016; Furlong 2016b; Kelly 2016; Wyn 2016). Given the uncertain contexts which frame our discussions in this book, this work continues to be pertinent for us.

We are mindful, however, of the longstanding warnings within youth studies against overstating the extent and impact of change on young people's lives and of the accompanying argument that young lives are also subject to the constraints of continuity (Cieslik and Pollock 2017; Roberts 2009; Woodman and Wyn 2014; Wyn and White 2015). As Hardgrove and her colleagues note, youth scholars have 'developed an eye for generational "rupture" and sharp breaks between the lived experiences and values of this generation and those of their parents and grandparents' (2015, p. 164), but there is also 'a good deal of *coherence*' between these values and experiences (2015, p. 164, original emphasis). We respect these arguments, particularly as they relate to the persistence of structural inequality and other aspects of young people's lives. We agree with Woodman and Wyn's prescription that 'understanding the dynamic between continuity and change is one of the central challenges for youth sociology today' (2014, p. 3).

We also argue in concert with such scholars as Bessant et al. (2017) and Talburt and Lesko (2015) that contemporary young people live in 'an epoch of austerity and precarity, [where] the promise of good life is increasingly difficult to attain and lives are lived seemingly out of order' (Talburt and Lesko 2015, p. 171). We agree with Leccardi that 'young people in the new century find themselves having to define their existential choices within a social landscape that is strongly characterized by the acceleration of change' (2014, p. 41). The perception that this change is accelerating emerges in the testimonies of many of our interviewees.

Conceptualising the Young University Student

We use a number of lenses to think about the perspectives of the young university students who are the major focus of this book, but we are particularly indebted to Brooks' recent work. While as she explains, 'a common-sense understanding of the university student is perhaps as a learner, an individual who is, above all else, dedicated to his or her studies' (Brooks 2018, p. 501), this construction has largely been replaced in recent decades by more complex ones. Brooks' work recognises this complexity. She has proposed a four-strand construction of the university student as a consumer of higher education, a worker, a family member and a political actor. We have adopted three of these categories to consider young people's hopes, plans and concerns for their current and imagined future lives as family members, workers and political actors. While we recognise and refer at times to the experience of young university students as consumers of higher education, this is not our primary interest here. Instead, we wish to interrogate those aspects of young people's lives that speak to how they envisage the future.

Our use of these three categories also takes up the recommendation of Wyn and her colleagues (2017). Writing from Australia, they observe that the vast majority of young people have by their late 20s completed at least their first educational qualification and are seeking two key things: to participate in the labour market and to create personal and family relationships. These things all matter, as does the relationship between them. As they note, 'the intersections of education, work and relationships are central to determining the quality of people's lives at this age' (p. 2). To this, we add the political dimension or category, in order to shed light on the wider forces that may be shaping young people's lives, and their responses and orientations to those forces.

Our use of these three categories is deliberately elastic and inclusive. It is not our intention here to categorise or homogenise young people's lives.

Our conceptualisation of young people as family members recognises that family structures and the nature of family formation is changing. It includes the fluid, complex and multidirectional relationships of the contemporary family. It also encapsulates any definition of family that our interviewees may choose to adopt. This may include their role as children of parents or carers, as parents or carers of children or other significant people, or as current or prospective partners in any form of romantic relationship, whether cohabiting or not (Berger 2017; Hakim 2018). We will explore these experiences in Chap. 4.

Our conceptualisation of young people as workers includes their involvement in a wide range of employment and career situations, including self-employment, entrepreneurial projects and start-ups, and voluntary roles. It includes their unemployment, under-employment or insecure employment. It also encompasses their need to work while studying, and the circumstances that drive that need, such as the escalation of higher education fees or debts and/or the reduction of state higher education subsidies. We will explore these and other related issues in Chap. 5.

Finally, our conceptualisation of young people as political actors includes conventional modes of political action such as their enrolment to vote and their membership or support of formal political parties. It further encompasses their participation in a wide range of alternative, 'small p' political organisations or in other modes of activism or protest. It also includes their disenchantment or disengagement from any formal or conventional political process or institution. We will explore these possibilities further in Chap. 7.

The Missing Middle

Our discussion in this book is also informed by a number of trends in youth studies. The first of these relates to what has been called the missing middle (e.g. Roberts 2013; Woodman 2013). As Cairns and his colleagues explain, 'A "missing middle" emerges when qualitatively interesting issues are prioritised in research and policy at the expense of less spectacular but quantitatively more noteworthy phenomena' (2014, p. 1047).

The relationship between education and social mobility has been a focus of sociological research since the 1950s, but there has also been a renewed interest in the role of higher education in promoting young people's social mobility and the emergence of policies designed to foster such aspirations (e.g. Boliver 2017; Finnegan and Merrill 2017; Smith 2016; Sukarieh and Tannock 2017). This interest is given fresh imperative by the uncertainty which we describe in the Introduction. As a corollary to this, much of the literature in this area has focused on the experience of working-class or otherwise marginalised young people. We are certainly concerned about the political and structural forces that shape many young people's hopes in relation to their higher education and that mediate the realisation of those hopes. We have expressed this concern in our previous work (e.g. Walsh and Black 2018a, b), as well as our concern about the experience of young people whose lives and hopes are mediated by class and/or socioeconomic forces.

In this book, however, we are more concerned with the argument within youth studies for greater attention to 'ordinary' young people and youth experiences. As Wyn and White note, it has been an orthodoxy of youth studies to assume that the voices and experiences of variously disadvantaged young people are in the greatest need of exploration and representation: 'the tendency is to "study down" rather than to "study up"' (2015, p. 37). Much of the earlier argument in favour of this research focus arose from the youth transitions literature: as Roberts points out, the previous tendency was for research to focus either on clearly successful or clearly troubled transitions to adulthood, overlooking the experience of the many young people whose transitions sit between these two ends of the spectrum (2013). Researching disadvantage continues to be an important and valuable approach within youth studies (Wyn and White 2015), but the interest in ordinary, everyday or mainstream youth experiences has grown in importance as well. It has grown to encompass an interest in young people's political participation (Harris and Roose 2013; Harris et al. 2010), educational aspiration and opportunity (Smyth and McInerney 2013; Woodman 2013), religiosity (Johns et al. 2015) and citizenship (Kallio and Häkli 2013; Spinney et al. 2015; Wood 2017).

Our discussion in the Introduction shows our interest in the dramatic scales of change associated with global uncertainty, but we are also interested in the many continuities we have acknowledged earlier. Certain aspects of young people's lives may not be changing greatly, including their hopes for a fulfilling future, and the family or parental expectations that may inform those hopes. By the same token, we are interested in 'the ordinariness and everydayness of change' (Wood 2017, p. 9) in young people's lives, as well as in the more dramatic shifts and uncertainties we have described at the start of this chapter.

Our interest in 'ordinary' youth experiences of higher education is reflected in our choice of the three universities from which our interviewees are drawn. As we have explained earlier, all three are public universities. While this means different things in different national contexts, a public university remains one that is predominantly funded by the public purse, whether through a national or subnational government.

The public university also remains the dominant form of university in each of the three nations that are the chief focus of our research project and of this book.

We recognise that the idea of the public university is problematic, and becoming more so. In the UK, for example, there is a long tradition of elite universities funded by the public purse. In Australia, escalating higher education fees and student debts are fast reducing the ideal of universal educational access and equity to an empty promise. The boundaries of the public university are shifting, with many arguably becoming public-private hybrids (Guzmán-Valenzuela 2016). Nonetheless, there is still an idea—or an ideal—of the public university as one that is part of the public sphere and that is, if only theoretically, accessible to large numbers of young people. This makes it an important context for our discussion.

Inserting Time and the Imagined Future

The second aspect of our discussion that is informed by recent thinking within youth studies is that of time, particularly in relation to the imagined future. The association between young people and the future is curiously persistent within policy and educational discourses. Young people are frequently positioned as 'seismographs' of the future, warning beacons of social and cultural change (Johansson 2017, p. 510). They are also constructed as 'a resource for others, for future economic growth and global competition, and for the maintenance of our society' (Nikunen 2017, p. 673). This latter discourse is directed with particular strength towards young university students, who are charged with the responsibility, on graduation, of contributing to—and improving—a range of social, economic and political structures and conditions (Holmes 2013).

McLeod has described time as a 'silent backdrop and organiser of structures and subjectivities' (2017, p. 14), but one that has particular implications for how young people conceptualise their lives. The extended present to which we refer earlier is one of the key temporal dimensions of young people's lives (Woodman 2011; Leccardi 2012; Woodman and Leccardi 2015). Their relationship to the imagined future is another key dimension. The association between young people and the future is a complex one, made more complex by uncertainty. As Furlong notes, this uncertainty brings young people 'new paths to freedom and space to experiment, but also the loss of a positive relation with the biological time, because of the great difficulty in looking ahead in time and controlling, at least ideally, the future' (2016a, p. 3). Partly because of this, recent years have seen a growing scholarly interest in the temporal dimensions of young lives, including the ways in which young people imagine their futures (e.g. Carabelli and Lyon 2016; Cook 2017; Gill et al. 2016; Hardgrove et al. 2015; Heggli et al. 2013; Mathisen et al. 2017; Patel 2017; Roberts and Evans 2013) and the nature of their 'future making' (Duggan 2017). This temporal turn offers a more nuanced understanding and theorisation of 'the messy, moving relations between past, present and future' (McLeod 2017, p. 13) and how young people interact with those relations.

There has been a concern that this focus on the imagined future has tended to separate that future from young people's current lives, to 'place the future in an artificial temporal and spatial suspension from the present' (Carabelli and Lyon 2016, p. 1113), a concern which some youth scholars have been keen to address. Hardgrove and her colleagues remind us that young people's transitions and navigations of the world are 'experienced in the immediate, but they are also about movement toward the future' (2015, p. 164). They go on to argue that 'we can see how they position themselves in the present by looking at how they imagine themselves positioned in the future' (p. 164). While our concerns in this book include the discursive promises about young people's future lives that are fostered by their universities, and the hopes, plans and concerns that young people have for their imagined futures, we are also concerned about how these discursive promises and imagined futures relate to their current experiences, particularly in nations facing the effects of uncertainty.

We believe that this is an important combination of foci. There is a concern within youth studies that traditional approaches to investigating young people's transitions and experience of employment has been 'wedded to a futuristic notion which views children and young people not as complete individuals now, but as future adults, citizens and workers' (Wood 2017, p. 4). Brannen and Nilsen have been calling for some years for studies of young people's hopes, aspirations and future orientations to take better account of the present contexts of their lives, including the socioeconomic and sociospatial contexts (2007).

In response, as we have flagged earlier, a large body of youth studies is seeking to refocus attention on the everyday nature of young people's experiences, on 'the daily and wayfaring roots and routes of living' (Wood 2017, p. 10). Some of this research also highlights the complex relationships between young people's present experience and imagined futures. Cuzzocrea and Mandich, for example, have made a strong argument for the power of the imagined future to shape the ways in which young people act in the present. 'Even if unrealistic', they argue, 'imagination cannot be reduced to unimportant ways of looking into the future; it does, in fact, open a space in the future, and, in doing so, ultimately defines a range of possibilities for action' (2016, p. 555). Langevang, too, argues that the imagined future represents a constructive way of understanding the complexity and fluidity of young people's lives in uncertain times and places: imagined futures, she suggests, are 'spaces of possibility, desirability or perceived danger' that guide the way that young people navigate the events of the present (2008, p. 2040). As Hardgrove and her colleagues note, 'we can see how [young people] position themselves in the present by looking at how they imagine themselves positioned in the future' (2015, p. 164).

Our discussion in this book is also informed by some of the typologies that have been developed to conceptualise young people's relationships to their imagined futures. Nilsen's typology (1999) is one of the earliest of these. It distinguishes between 'dreams' or abstract goals that are not determined by a young person's present circumstances; 'hopes' or vague goals that are nonetheless related to those circumstances; and 'plans'—made up of specific and concrete goals that are constructed in the context of those circumstances. Nilsen's work with Brannen has yielded a second and very useful typology that characterises young people's future orientation as 'deferment' (seeing the future in vague or abstract terms), 'predictability' (seeing the future as known, planned and charted) or 'adaptability' (seeing the future as malleable or contingent) (Brannen and Nilsen 2002). A third typology emerges from Peou and Zinn's work with young Cambodian people (2015). This proposes that young people in 'entrepreneurial mode' approach the future as something to be proactively planned and enacted. Those in 'traditional mode' have a 'closed future perspective' that draws on sociocultural norms and may not respond to new circumstances (p. 734). Young people in 'situational mode' see the future as 'mainly unknowable' (p. 736). Longo's work has also been helpful in proposing a fourth typology of youth temporalities in relation to their imagined future career (2018): planners, or young people who see their future career trajectory as something to be planned; executers, who see their careers as largely predetermined; dormants, whose efforts to plan and control their lives feel overwhelmed by events and circumstances; and opportunists, who see themselves as active protagonists in their careers.

Following Nilsen's lead, our interviewees have been invited to share their hopes for the future. They have also been invited to discuss the plans that they may have in place to further the realisation of these hopes as well as to consider what external circumstances may thwart or change these plans. We have drawn on Brannen and Nilsen's work to reflect on how young people imagine their futures and what external forces and discourses may shape their hopes, plans and concerns for those futures. We have also drawn on Peou and Zinn's work in Chap. 6 to reflect further on the nature of the adaptive, entrepreneurial youth selfhood that is produced and expected by education and labour market forces and discourses.

This brings us back to the question of what resources may support young people in their orientation to the future. For young people with access to socioeconomic and educational resources, for example, future uncertainty may be read as possibility or potentiality rather than as risk. In Leccardi's discussions with higher education qualified young people in Italy, the future is not seen as the predictable product of stable plans but as a flexible 'series of presents' (2005, p. 140) that can be adapted and revised as they unfold. Cook's conversations with young people in Australia suggests that some engage in extensive and confident future planning, drawing on standard institutional pathways such as higher education completion. As one of her interviewees notes, 'I probably have my whole life planned out the whole way through, and various trajectories if things go differently' (Cook 2016, p. 706).

This flexible orientation is shared by the young university students described by Brannen and Nilsen, who draw on their considerable resources to develop a sense of themselves as 'creators of their own destinies without help or hindrance from others' (2005, p. 423). Similar attitudes emerge from the socially and academically privileged young graduates interviewed by Brooks and Everett (2008), who see future planning as unnecessary—not because the future is a threatening or foreclosed space but because they possess the resources to deal with it. Cairns and his colleagues also describe the sanguine future orientations of young university students in Portugal who have been relatively immune to the effects of the economic crisis that has prevailed there since the GFC (2014). The message from studies such as these is that some young people are relatively unconcerned about the future because things have worked out well for them to date and because they see themselves as having multiple options going forward. There are also other resources on which young people may rely, a theme to which we return in Chap. 4.

Inserting Mobility

A third key theme within youth studies which informs our discussion is the geographic and mobility turn (e.g. Cuervo and Wyn 2017; Wood and Black 2018; Woodman and Leccardi 2015). We support Farrugia's call for 'a more spatialised youth sociology' (2014, p. 293), one that takes account of the localised and emplaced nature of young people's lives even in this era of flux. We also have a great deal of sympathy with Farrugia and Wood's proposal that youth is best understood as 'a collection of social processes that unfolds in place' (2017, p. 211).

At the same time, we recognise that young people's lives are increasingly characterised by mobilities between places (Skelton and Gough 2013). An escalating youth mobility—including transnational mobility—is recognised as one of the key contemporary trends affecting young people (Robertson et al. 2018; Wyn and White 2015). The new mobilities paradigm proposed by Sheller and Urry (2006, 2016) has done much to theorise this mobility as well as interrogate the discursive equations between mobility and freedom. It has also encouraged a critical questioning of the power relationships and uneven distribution of mobilities as well as their role in promoting or perpetuating various inequalities.

We are not necessarily concerned with all of these nuances in this particular book, but we are concerned with the relationship between higher education and young people's actual or imagined geographic mobility. Our discussion draws on ideas of how young people navigate uncertain times and contexts—metaphorically, affectively and geographically. It also draws on ideas such as push and pull factors that were first developed in relation to migration and mobility but that can also shed light on the complex forces underpinning young people's movements (and constraints) in pursuit of higher education and the future it promises (e.g. Lesjak et al. 2015; Mazzarol and Soutar 2002; Ojiaku et al. 2018; Roberts 2009). One of the greatest examples of these push and pull factors is the way in which family relationships influence young people's imagined and actual trajectories through and beyond higher education in uncertain times: this is something we explore in Chap. 4.

As we will discuss, higher education is a key driver of elective youth mobility (as opposed to the forced mobility experienced by so many young people globally, such as refugees). Certain discourses of higher education promote this mobility not only as a 'symbolic and material resource' (Robertson et al. 2018, p. 204) but as a 'cultural aspiration' (Skrbis et al. 2014, p. 614). International mobility, in particular, has become '*de rigueur* in order to successfully reach personal and professional goals' (Cairns 2014, p. 1, original emphasis). More than this, it has become synonymous with the adaptive, entrepreneurial youth subjectivity of neoliberal times, an attribute of the young neoliberal agent who approaches life as a project, acting both creatively and reactively and 'interpret[ing] the uncertainty of the future as a proliferation of virtual possibilities' (Leccardi 2014, p. 49). For young university students and graduates in uncertain economies, international mobility has also become 'an asset', one that can be employed to 'circumnavigate disadvantage at home' (Cairns 2012, p. 237).

We would like to pause here to clarify one thing before we continue. We make a number of references to neoliberalism across this book. Neoliberalism is based on the idea that 'the profit motive of companies, combined with consumers' ability to choose the product that suits them best, will result in the best possible social and economic outcomes' (Denniss 2018, p. 33). The concept of neoliberalism, with its emphasis on free markets, free trade and the responsibilisation of the individual for a wide range of life experiences and outcomes (Harvey 2005; Rose 1989), has been a strong presence within education and youth studies for many years. Precisely because of this, there is a concern that it has been applied too globally and too indiscriminately as a way of explaining issues ranging from inequality to the complex relationship between the individual and the state (see Rowlands and Rawolle 2013).

At the same time, there is a continuing argument for the importance of a scholarship that can critically challenge the prevalence of policies and practices within education that could be seen as neoliberal in character, and their impact on young lives (Apple 2017; Keddie 2016; Kelly and Pike 2017; Turner 2015). We support this argument: the scholarly critique of neoliberalism remains important for our analysis. We are concerned about the ways in which young people's imagined futures are shaped by neoliberal discourses that encourage them to aspire to educational and economic success, to be resilient and adaptable in the face of the forces that may hinder that success, and to forge their own solutions to uncertainty. Even where (or perhaps *particularly* where) circumstances are difficult and possibilities limited, these discourses incite young people to engage in a form of hope or optimism that one commentator has described as magical thinking: 'believing you can have everything you want if you strategise shrewdly, reinvent yourself, push upscale, stay hungry and keep the faith' (Bidisha 2015). These discourses have become so prevalent that individual responsibility has become the assumed youth response to all external difficulties, regardless of how complex or structurally constituted these may be (Leccardi 2014). In the words of one young working-class woman in the UK, 'we can get everything we want if we try hard' (Mendick et al. 2015, p. 167).

Inserting Affect

The fourth aspect of our discussion that is informed by recent thinking within youth studies relates to the affective turn in the humanities and social sciences, which has brought new attention to multiple aspects of human experience including the role of emotions and affects in shaping the individual life and the relationship between the individual and the social (see Clough and Halley 2007). The affective turn has been embraced as an opportunity to shift the focus of social science research away from 'discourse and disembodied talk and texts' (Wetherell 2012, p. 2). It has also been taken up as a means of drawing deeper attention to the 'everyday details and embodied experiences' (McLeod 2016, p. 277) of individual and collective lives. In this way, it is closely aligned to the interest of youth scholars in the everyday worlds of young people which we have discussed earlier in this chapter.

In particular, our discussion across this book takes note of a large body of recent youth studies which is concerned with young people's affective responses to uncertainty. Some of these studies have addressed young people's anxieties about the wider social and environmental future, including the future of the planet as a whole (e.g. Cook 2015; Ojala 2012; Threadgold 2012). Others, including most of those that we cited earlier in this chapter, have focused on young people's affective relationship to their personal imagined futures. Our concern in this book is primarily located within this second set of studies.

Some of these reveal the way in which the imagined future may prompt '*anticipated* future emotions', especially anxiety, as young people weigh up the options that may be available to them in the future (Pimlott-Wilson 2015, p. 290, original emphasis). Others highlight the importance of hope as an affective resource for young people (Bishop and Willis 2014; Carabelli and Lyon 2016; Heggli et al. 2013). These studies suggest that hope can be a strategy for young people dealing with present difficulties (McLeod 2015), a kind of capital where other forms of capital are limited (Grant 2017). They show how for such young people, higher education may be heavily invested with hope of avoiding 'a life of struggle and/or low paid jobs' (Leathwood and O'Connell 2003, p. 605). They also show that mobility can be a focus of such hope. One particularly poignant example comes from Cuzzocrea and Mandich's study of young people in Sardinia, where youth unemployment is high and few young people undertake higher education. For these young people, hope is all about mobility: their imagined futures depend on leaving the island. Even though it is unclear how this imagined mobility might be achieved, it serves as a form of youth agency: it is 'an entry ticket' that allows these young people 'to bypass the uncertainty associated with crude reality' (Cuzzocrea and Mandich 2016, p. 552).

Other studies highlight the effect (and affect) of present uncertainty on young people's imagined futures. Hardgrove and her colleagues describe young people in the UK who want to improve their lives in the face of unstable labour markets and challenging economic climates but who struggle to imagine the future in the specific ways that might help them realise this desire (2015). In Devadason's study of young people's orientation to the future in the UK and Sweden (2008), too, those in socioeconomically precarious Bristol are more anxious about the future than their Gothenburg peers, for whom the greater social support offered by the state makes the present a comfortable place and the future less pressing. The implications of these studies hearken back to our earlier observation that young people who feel that they have access to material and other resources may be less anxious about the future and its attendant uncertainties.

As we flagged in the Introduction, we believe that the affective dimensions of post-truth times have particular implications for the sociologies of education and youth. We believe that a focus on affect has the potential to shed light on the 'lived, embodied, visceral effects' of young people's engagement with the promises, expectations, anxieties and desires that are implicit in higher education (Fortier 2016, p. 1042). At the same time, we argue that the importance of affect as an aspect of young lives and identities needs to be tempered by evidence: as researchers and educational practitioners, we need to draw on and critically respond to what this evidence tells us about young people's current and possible future lives.

Conclusion

This chapter has introduced the theoretical frameworks and guiding ideas which will be used across this book to contextualise the insights that arise from our discussions with our 30 young interviewees and from recent thinking within the international literature. These frameworks and guiding ideas include Brooks' tripartite categorisation (2018) of young university students as family members, workers and political actors, categories that are important but that also point to the familiar dimensions and continuities of students' lives. Our use of these categories reflects our desire as youth scholars to acknowledge and draw attention to 'ordinary' young people and youth experiences as well as the more dramatic shifts, changes and uncertainties which we have begun to describe.

These themes of continuity and change are also reflected in the ideas of time and the imagined future, mobility and affect on which we draw across this book and which we use as lenses to explore how our young interviewees envisage and feel about both their current circumstances and their possible futures. Investigating young people's relationship to temporality and mobility is central to understanding how they navigate the conflicting forces of continuity and change. Investigating how young people engage affectively with these forces is central to understanding the nuanced and complex relationship which many have with the imagined future in uncertain times.

References

Allen, K. (2016). Top girls navigating austere times: Interrogating youth transitions since the 'crisis'. *Journal of Youth Studies, 19*(6), 805–820. https://doi.org/10.1080/13676261.2015.1112885.

Antonucci, L., Hamilton, M., & Roberts, S. (2014). Constructing a theory of youth and social policy. In L. Antonucci, M. Hamilton, & S. Roberts (Eds.), *Young people and social policy in Europe: Dealing with risk, inequality and precarity in times of crisis* (pp. 13–34). London: Palgrave Macmillan UK.

Apple, M. W. (2017). What is present and absent in critical analyses of neoliberalism in education. *Peabody Journal of Education, 92*(1), 148–153. https://doi.org/10.1080/0161956X.2016.1265344.

Bauman, Z. (2007). *Liquid times: Living in an age of uncertainty*. Cambridge: Polity Press.

Berger, B. (2017). *The family in the modern age: More than a lifestyle choice*. New York: Routledge.

References

Bessant, J., Farthing, R., & Watts, R. (2017). *The precarious generation: A political economy of young people*. Abingdon: Routledge.

Biasin, C., Cornacchia, M., & Marescotti, E. (2016). Expectations and young hopes: A research with graduate students in education. *Studi sulla formazione, 19*(2), 37. https://doi.org/10.13128/Studi_Formaz-20202.

Bidisha. (2015, May 27). Politicians keep using the word aspiration—But what does it mean? *The Guardian*. Retrieved June 30, 2017, from http://www.theguardian.com/commentisfree/2015/may/27/politicians-aspiration-labour.

Bishop, E. C., & Willis, K. (2014). 'Without hope everything would be doom and gloom': Young people talk about the importance of hope in their lives. *Journal of Youth Studies, 17*(6), 778–793. https://doi.org/10.1080/13676261.2013.878788.

Boliver, V. (2017). Misplaced optimism: How higher education reproduces rather than reduces social inequality. *British Journal of Sociology of Education, 38*(3), 423–432. https://doi.org/10.1080/01425692.2017.1281648.

Brannen, J., & Nilsen, A. (2002). Young people's time perspectives: From youth to adulthood. *Sociology, 36*(3), 513–537. https://doi.org/10.1177/0038038502036003002.

Brannen, J., & Nilsen, A. (2005). Individualisation, choice and structure: A discussion of current trends in sociological analysis. *The Sociological Review, 53*(3), 412–428. https://doi.org/10.1111/j.1467-954X.2005.00559.x.

Brannen, J., & Nilsen, A. (2007). Young people, time horizons and planning: A response to Anderson et al. *Sociology, 41*(1), 153–160. https://doi.org/10.2307/42856966.

Brooks, R. (2018). Understanding the higher education student in Europe: A comparative analysis. *Compare: A Journal of Comparative and International Education, 48*(4), 500–517. https://doi.org/10.1080/03057925.2017.1318047.

Brooks, R., & Everett, G. (2008). The prevalence of 'life planning': Evidence from UK graduates. *British Journal of Sociology of Education, 29*(3), 325–337. https://doi.org/10.1080/01425690801966410.

Budd, R. (2017). Undergraduate orientations towards higher education in Germany and England: Problematizing the notion of 'student as customer'. *Higher Education, 73*(1), 23–37. https://doi.org/10.1007/s10734-015-9977-4.

Cairns, D. (2012). 'I wouldn't stay here': Economic crisis and youth mobility in Ireland. *International Migration, 52*(3), 236–249. https://doi.org/10.1111/j.1468-2435.2012.00776.x.

Cairns, D. (2014). *Youth transitions, international student mobility and spatial reflexivity: Being mobile?*. Basingstoke: Palgrave Macmillan.

Cairns, D., Growiec, K., & de Almeida Alves, N. (2014). Another 'missing middle'? The marginalised majority of tertiary-educated youth in Portugal during the economic crisis. *Journal of Youth Studies, 17*(8), 1046–1060. https://doi.org/10.1080/13676261.2013.878789.

Carabelli, G., & Lyon, D. (2016). Young people's orientations to the future: Navigating the present and imagining the future. *Journal of Youth Studies, 19*(8), 1110–1127. https://doi.org/10.1080/13676261.2016.1145641.

Cieslik, M., & Pollock, G. (2017). Introduction: Studying young people in late modernity. In M. Cieslik & G. Pollock (Eds.), *Young people in risk society: The restructuring of youth identities and transitions in late modernity* (pp. 1–21). London: Routledge.

Clough, P. T., & Halley, J. (2007). *The affective turn: Theorizing the social*. Durham and London: Duke University Press.

Commonwealth Secretariat. (2016). *Global youth development index and report 2016* (Vol. 1). London: Commonwealth Secretariat.

Cook, J. (2015). Young adults' hopes for the long-term future: From re-enchantment with technology to faith in humanity. *Journal of Youth Studies, 19*(4), 517–532. https://doi.org/10.1080/13676261.2015.1083959.

Cook, J. (2016). Young people's strategies for coping with parallel imaginings of the future. *Time & Society, 25*(3), 700–717. https://doi.org/10.1177/0961463X15609829.

Cook, J. (2017). *Imagined futures: Hope, risk and uncertainty*. Cham, Switzerland: Springer.

Cuervo, H., & Wyn, J. (2017). A longitudinal analysis of belonging: Temporal, performative and relational practices by young people in rural Australia. *Young, 25*(3), 1–16. https://doi.org/10.1177/1103308816669463.

Cuzzocrea, V., & Mandich, G. (2016). Students' narratives of the future: Imagined mobilities as forms of youth agency? *Journal of Youth Studies, 19*(4), 552–567. https://doi.org/10.1080/13676261.2015.1098773.

Denniss, R. (2018). Dead right: How neoliberalism ate itself and what comes next. *Quarterly Essay, 70*. Carlton: Black Inc.

Devadason, R. (2008). To plan or not to plan? Young adult future orientations in two European cities. *Sociology, 42*(6), 1127–1145. https://doi.org/10.1177/0038038508096937.

Du Bois-Reymond, M., & López Blasco, A. (2003). Yo-yo transitions and misleading trajectories: Towards integrated transition policies for young adults in Europe. In A. López Blasco, W. McNeish, & A. Walther (Eds.), *Young people and contradictions of inclusion: Towards integrated transition policies in Europe* (pp. 19–42). Bristol: The Policy Press.

Duggan, S. (2017). Understanding temporality and future orientation for young women in the senior year. *Discourse: Studies in the Cultural Politics of Education, 38*(6), 795–806. https://doi.org/10.1080/01596306.2016.1173650.

Farrugia, D. (2014). Towards a spatialised youth sociology: The rural and the urban in times of change. *Journal of Youth Studies, 17*(3), 293–307. https://doi.org/10.1080/13676261.2013.830700.

Farrugia, D., & Wood, B. E. (2017). Youth and spatiality: Towards interdisciplinarity in youth studies. *Young, 25*(3), 209–218. https://doi.org/10.1177/1103308817712036.

Finnegan, F., & Merrill, B. (2017). 'We're as good as anybody else': A comparative study of working-class university students' experiences in England and Ireland. *British Journal of Sociology of Education, 38*(3), 307–324. https://doi.org/10.1080/01425692.2015.1081054.

Forsberg, H., & Timonen, V. (2018). The future of the family as envisioned by young adults in Ireland. *Journal of Youth Studies, 21*(6), 765–779. https://doi.org/10.1080/13676261.2017.1420761.

Fortier, A.-M. (2016). Afterword: Acts of affective citizenship? Possibilities and limitations. *Citizenship Studies, 20*(8), 1038–1044. https://doi.org/10.1080/13621025.2016.1229190.

France, A. (2016). *Understanding youth in the global economic crisis*. Bristol: Policy Press.

Furlong, A. (2016a). Foreword. In C. Leccardi & E. Ruspini (Eds.), *A new youth? Young people, generations and family life* (pp. xv–xix). London & New York: Routledge.

Furlong, A. (2016b). The changing landscape of youth and young adulthood. In A. Furlong (Ed.), *Routledge handbook of youth and young adulthood* (2nd ed., pp. 3–11). London: Routledge.

Gill, J., Esson, K., & Yuen, R. (2016). *A girl's education*. London: Springer.

Grant, T. (2017). The complexity of aspiration: The role of hope and habitus in shaping working-class young people's aspirations to higher education. *Children's Geographies, 15*(3), 289–303. https://doi.org/10.1080/14733285.2016.1221057.

Guzmán-Valenzuela, C. (2016). Unfolding the meaning of public(s) in universities: Toward the transformative university. *Higher Education, 71*(5), 667–679. https://doi.org/10.1007/s10734-015-9929-z.

Hakim, C. (2018). *Models of the family in modern societies: Ideals and realities*. Oxon and New York: Routledge.

Hardgrove, A., Rootham, E., & McDowell, L. (2015). Possible selves in a precarious labour market: Youth, imagined futures, and transitions to work in the UK. *Geoforum, 60,* 163–171. https://doi.org/10.1016/j.geoforum.2015.01.014.

Harris, A., & Roose, J. (2013). DIY citizenship amongst young Muslims: Experiences of the 'ordinary'. *Journal of Youth Studies, 17*(6), 794–813. https://doi.org/10.1080/13676261.2013.844782.

Harris, A., Wyn, J., & Younes, S. (2010). Beyond apathetic or activist youth: 'Ordinary' young people and contemporary forms of participation. *Young, 18*(1), 9–32. https://doi.org/10.1177/110330880901800103.

Harvey, D. (2005). *A brief history of neoliberalism*. Oxford: Oxford University Press.

References

Heggli, G., Haukanes, H., & Tjomsland, M. (2013). Fearing the future? Young people envisioning their working lives in the Czech Republic, Norway and Tunisia. *Journal of Youth Studies, 16*(7), 916–931. https://doi.org/10.1080/13676261.2013.766682.

Holmes, L. (2013). Competing perspectives on graduate employability: Possession, position or process? *Studies in Higher Education, 38*(4), 538–554. https://doi.org/10.1080/03075079.2011.587140.

Honwana, A. (2014). Waithood: Youth transitions and social change. In D. Foeken, T. Dietz, L. Haan, & L. Johnson (Eds.,) *Development and equity: An interdisciplinary exploration by ten scholars from Africa, Asia and Latin America* (pp. 28–40). Brill Online.

Johansson, T. (2017). Youth studies in transition: Theoretical explorations. *International Review of Sociology, 27*(3), 510–524. https://doi.org/10.1080/03906701.2016.1261499.

Johns, A., Mansouri, F., & Lobo, M. (2015). Religiosity, citizenship and belonging: The everyday experiences of young Australian Muslims. *Journal of Muslim Minority Affairs, 35*(2), 171–190. https://doi.org/10.1080/13602004.2015.1046262.

Kallio, K. P., & Häkli, J. (2013). Children and young people's politics in everyday life. *Space and Polity, 17*(1), 1–16. https://doi.org/10.1080/13562576.2013.780710.

Keddie, A. (2016). Children of the market: Performativity, neoliberal responsibilisation and the construction of student identities. *Oxford Review of Education, 42*(1), 108–122.

Kelly, P. (2016). Young people and the coming of the Third Industrial Revolution: New work ethics and the self as enterprise after the GFC, after neo-Liberalism. In A. Furlong (Ed.), *Routledge handbook of youth and young adulthood* (2nd ed., pp. 391–399). Oxon and New York: Routledge.

Kelly, P. (2017). Growing up after the GFC: Responsibilisation and mortgaged futures. *Discourse: Studies in the Cultural Politics of Education, 38*(1), 57–69. https://doi.org/10.1080/01596306.2015.1104852.

Kelly, P., & Pike, J. (2017). Is neo-liberal capitalism eating itself or its young? In P. Kelly & J. Pike (Eds.), *Neo-liberalism and austerity* (pp. 1–31). London: Springer.

Langevang, T. (2008). 'We are managing!' Uncertain paths to respectable adulthoods in Accra, Ghana. *Geoforum, 39*(6), 2039–2047. https://doi.org/10.1016/j.geoforum.2008.09.003.

Leathwood, C., & O'Connell, P. (2003). 'It's a struggle': The construction of the 'new student' in higher education. *Journal of Education Policy, 18*(6), 597–615. https://doi.org/10.1080/0268093032000145863.

Leccardi, C. (2005). Facing uncertainty: Temporality and biographies in the new century. *Young, 13*(2), 123–146. https://doi.org/10.1177/1103308805051317.

Leccardi, C. (2012). Young people's representations of the future and the acceleration of time. A generational approach. *Diskurs Kindheits-und Jugendforschung, 7*(1), 59–73.

Leccardi, C. (2014). Young people and the new semantics of the future. *SocietàMutamentoPolitica, 5*(10), 41–54. https://doi.org/10.13128/SMP-15404.

Lesjak, M., Juvan, E., Ineson, E. M., Yap, M. H., & Axelsson, E. P. (2015). Erasmus student motivation: Why and where to go? *Higher Education, 70*(5), 845–865. https://doi.org/10.1007/s10734-015-9871-0.

Longo, M. E. (2018). Youth temporalities and uncertainty: Understanding variations in young Argentinians' professional careers. *Time & Society, 27*(3), 389–414. https://doi.org/10.1177/0961463X15609828.

Mathisen, L., Carlsson, E., & Sletterød, N. A. (2017). Sami identity and preferred futures: Experiences among youth in Finnmark and Trøndelag, Norway. *Northern Review, 45*, 113–139. https://doi.org/10.22584/nr45.2017.007.

Mazzarol, T., & Soutar, G. N. (2002). "Push-pull" factors influencing international student destination choice. *International Journal of Educational Management, 16*(2), 82–90. https://doi.org/10.1108/09513540210418403.

McLeod, J. (2015). Gender identity, intergenerational dynamics, and educational aspirations: Young women's hopes for the future. In J. Wyn & H. Cahill (Eds.), *Handbook of children and youth studies* (pp. 315–327). Singapore: Springer.

McLeod, J. (2016). Memory, affective practice and teacher narratives: Researching emotion in oral histories of educational and personal change. In M. Zembylas & P. A. Schutz (Eds.), *Methodological advances in research on emotion and education* (pp. 273–284). Cham, Switzerland: Springer.

McLeod, J. (2017). Marking time, making methods: Temporality and untimely dilemmas in the sociology of youth and educational change. *British Journal of Sociology of Education, 38*(1), 13–25. https://doi.org/10.1080/01425692.2016.1254541.

Mendick, H., Allen, K., & Harvey, L. (2015). 'We can get everything we want if we try hard': Young people, celebrity, hard work. *British Journal of Educational Studies, 63*(2), 161–178. https://doi.org/10.1080/00071005.2014.1002382.

Miles, M. B., Huberman, A. M., Huberman, M. A., & Huberman, M. (1994). *Qualitative data analysis: An expanded sourcebook*. Los Angeles: Sage.

Miles, M. B., Huberman, A. M., & Saldana, J. (2014). *Qualitative data analysis: A methods sourcebook* (3rd ed.). Los Angeles: Sage.

Morales, C. L., Daccache, V., & Boman, U. (2013). *Youth in an age of uncertainty and turmoil*. Retrieved November 5, 2018, from http://www.youthpolicy.org/library/documents/youth-in-an-age-of-uncertainty-and-turmoil/.

Nikunen, M. (2017). Young people, future hopes and concerns in Finland and the European Union: Classed and gendered expectations in policy documents. *Journal of Youth Studies, 20*(6), 661–676. https://doi.org/10.1080/13676261.2016.1260693.

Nilsen, A. (1999). Where is the future? Time and space as categories in analyses of young people's images of the future. *Innovation: The European Journal of Social Science Research, 12*(2), 175–194. https://doi.org/10.1080/13511610.1999.9968596.

Nowotny, H. (1994). *Time: The modern and postmodern experience*. Cambridge: Polity Press.

Ojala, M. (2012). Hope and climate change: The importance of hope for environmental engagement among young people. *Environmental Education Research, 18*(5), 625–642. https://doi.org/10.1080/13504622.2011.637157.

Ojiaku, O. C., Nkamnebe, A. D., & Nwaizugbo, I. C. (2018). Determinants of entrepreneurial intentions among young graduates: Perspectives of push-pull-mooring model. *Journal of Global Entrepreneurship Research, 8*(1), 24. https://doi.org/10.1186/s40497-018-0109-3.

Patel, V. (2017). Parents, permission, and possibility: Young women, college, and imagined futures in Gujarat, India. *Geoforum, 80,* 39–48. https://doi.org/10.1016/j.geoforum.2017.01.008.

Peou, C., & Zinn, J. (2015). Cambodian youth managing expectations and uncertainties of the life course—A typology of biographical management. *Journal of Youth Studies, 18*(6), 726–742. https://doi.org/10.1080/13676261.2014.992328.

Pimlott-Wilson, H. (2015). Individualising the future: The emotional geographies of neoliberal governance in young people's aspirations. *Area, 49*(3), 288–295. https://doi.org/10.1111/area.12222.

Ritchie, J., Lewis, J., Nicholls, C. M., & Ormston, R. (2013). *Qualitative research practice: A guide for social science students and researchers*. Los Angeles: Sage.

Roberts, K. (2009). Opportunity structures then and now. *Journal of Education and Work, 22*(5), 355–368. https://doi.org/10.1080/13639080903453987.

Roberts, S. (2013). Youth studies, housing transitions and the 'missing middle': Time for a rethink? *Sociological Research Online, 18*(3), 11.

Roberts, S., & Evans, S. (2013). 'Aspirations' and imagined futures: The im/possibilities for Britain's young working class. In W. Atkinson, S. Roberts, & M. Savage (Eds.), *Class inequality in austerity Britain: Power, difference and suffering* (pp. 70–89). London: Palgrave Macmillan.

Robertson, S., Harris, A., & Baldassar, L. (2018). Mobile transitions: A conceptual framework for researching a generation on the move. *Journal of Youth Studies, 21*(2), 203–217. https://doi.org/10.1080/13676261.2017.1362101.

Rose, N. (1989). *Governing the soul: The shaping of the private self*. London: Routledge.

Rowlands, J., & Rawolle, S. (2013). Neoliberalism is not a theory of everything: A Bourdieuian analysis of illusio in educational research. *Critical Studies in Education, 54*(3), 260–272.

References

Sheller, M., & Urry, J. (2006). The new mobilities paradigm. *Environment and Planning A, 38*(2), 207–226. https://doi.org/10.1068/a37268.

Sheller, M., & Urry, J. (2016). Mobilizing the new mobilities paradigm. *Applied Mobilities, 1*(1), 10–25. https://doi.org/10.1080/23800127.2016.1151216.

Skelton, T., & Gough, K. V. (2013). Introduction: Young people's im/mobile urban geographies. *Urban Studies, 50*(3), 455–466. https://doi.org/10.1177/0042098012468900.

Skrbis, Z., Woodward, I., & Bean, C. (2014). Seeds of cosmopolitan future? Young people and their aspirations for future mobility. *Journal of Youth Studies, 17*(5), 614–625. https://doi.org/10.1080/13676261.2013.834314.

Smith, E. (2016). Can higher education compensate for society? Modelling the determinants of academic success at university. *British Journal of Sociology of Education, 37*(7), 970–992. https://doi.org/10.1080/01425692.2014.987728.

Smyth, J., & McInerney, P. (2013). Ordinary kids' navigating geographies of educational opportunity in the context of an Australian 'place-based intervention'. *Journal of Education Policy, 29*(3), 285–301.

Spinney, J., Aldred, R., & Brown, K. (2015). Geographies of citizenship and everyday (im)mobility. *Geoforum, 64,* 325–332. https://doi.org/10.1016/j.geoforum.2015.04.013.

Sukarieh, M., & Tannock, S. (2014). *Youth rising?: The politics of youth in the global economy.* Routledge.

Sukarieh, M., & Tannock, S. (2017). The education penalty: Schooling, learning and the diminishment of wages, working conditions and worker power. *British Journal of Sociology of Education, 38*(3), 245–264. https://doi.org/10.1080/01425692.2015.1093408.

Talburt, S., & Lesko, N. (2015). Toward a different youth studies: Youth-and-researchers as affective assemblages. In D. Woodman & A. Bennett (Eds.), *Youth cultures, transitions, and generations: Bridging the gap in youth research* (pp. 171–185). London: Springer.

Threadgold, S. (2012). 'I reckon my life will be easy, but my kids will be buggered': Ambivalence in young people's positive perceptions of individual futures and their visions of environmental collapse. *Journal of Youth Studies, 15*(1), 17–32. https://doi.org/10.1080/13676261.2011.618490.

Turner, J. (2015). Being young in the age of globalization: A look at recent literature on neoliberalism's effects on youth. *Social Justice, 41*(4), 8–22.

United Nations [UN]. (2014). *Definition of Youth.* Retrieved August 21, 2018, from http://www.un.org/esa/socdev/documents/youth/fact-sheets/youth-definition.pdf.

Walsh, L., & Black, R. (2018a). Off the radar democracy: young people's alternate acts of citizenship in Australia. In S. Pickard & J. Bessant (Eds.), *Youth politics in crisis: New forms of political participation in the austerity era* (pp. 217–232). Basingstoke: Palgrave Macmillan.

Walsh, L., & Black, R. (2018b). *Rethinking youth citizenship after the age of entitlement.* London: Bloomsbury.

Wetherell, M. (2012). *Affect and emotion: A new social science understanding.* London: Sage.

Wood, B. E. (2017). Youth studies, citizenship and transitions: Towards a new research agenda. *Journal of Youth Studies, 20*(9), 1176–1190. https://doi.org/10.1080/13676261.2017.1316363.

Wood, B. E., & Black, R. (2018). Spatial, relational and affective understandings of citizenship and belonging for young people today: Towards a new conceptual framework. In C. Halse (Ed.), *Interrogating belonging for young people in schools* (pp. 165–185). Basingstoke: Palgrave Macmillan.

Woodman, D. (2011). Young people and the future: Multiple temporal orientations shaped in interaction with significant others. *Young, 19*(2), 111–128. https://doi.org/10.1177/110330881001900201.

Woodman, D. (2013). Researching 'ordinary' young people in a changing world: The sociology of generations and the 'missing middle' in youth research. *Sociological Research Online, 18*(1), 1–12. https://doi.org/10.5153/sro.2868.

Woodman, D., & Leccardi, C. (2015). Generations, transitions, and culture as practice: A temporal approach to youth studies. In D. Woodman & A. Bennett (Eds.), *Youth cultures, transitions, and generations: Bridging the gap in youth research* (pp. 56–68). London: Palgrave Macmillan.

Woodman, D., & Wyn, J. (2014). *Youth and generation: Rethinking change and inequality in the lives of young people.* London: Sage.

Wyn, J. (2015). Thinking about childhood and youth. In J. Wyn & H. Cahill (Eds.), *Handbook of children and youth studies* (pp. 3–20). Singapore: Springer.

Wyn, J. (2016). Educating for late modernity. In A. Furlong (Ed.), *Routledge handbook of youth and young adulthood* (pp. 91–98). New York: Routledge.

Wyn, J., Cahill, H., Woodman, D., Cuervo, H., Chesters, J., Cook, J., et al. (2017). *Gen Y on Gen Y*. Carlton: University of Melbourne.

Wyn, J., & White, R. (1997). *Rethinking youth.* London: Sage.

Wyn, J., & White, R. (2015). Complex worlds, complex identities: Complexity in youth studies. In D. Woodman & A. Bennett (Eds.), *Youth cultures, transitions, and generations: Bridging the gap in youth research* (pp. 28–41). London: Palgrave Macmillan.

Chapter 3
The Changing Promises and Prospects of Higher Education

Introduction

> I am guessing the one thing about our generation – and we have been saying that probably for the past 20-ish years – is that we get loads and loads and loads of degrees, and … it's not even sure that we are going to get a job, in the end. … It is just insane (Sophia, France).

Sophia's comment points to what many young people feel is the empty or broken promise of contemporary higher education. The 'truths of youth' which we introduced at the start of this book include the promise that higher education will lead to a secure and desirable future and improved access to life chances, including geographic, social and economic mobilities. These truths belie the changes that are sweeping higher education as a system, and the new youth realities that are emerging from them. These include the massification of higher education and the fact that a degree is no longer necessarily sufficient to grant young graduates competitive advantage in a globalised workforce. Young people (and their families) are increasingly expected to acquire significant resources in pursuit of this perceived competitive benefit. They are expected to pursue strategies to boost their employability, including work experience, internships and voluntary work. Other economic factors are also shaping the university experience, such as the 'studentification' of the youth labour market, which sees more students engaging in part-time, temporary and seasonal work.

In this chapter, we draw on our interviews with 30 young university students in France, Australia and the UK and our review of the recent international literature to consider the discourses of contemporary higher education, the promises that they communicate about young futures, and how they relate to young people's own hopes, plans and concerns in relation to their higher education and their imagined future beyond it. We also consider the shifting truths of youth that are rapidly changing the nature of the educational contract between young university students, their universities and the outcomes for which they have been led to hope. We ask whether the promises of higher education have become post-truth promises, the affective appeal of which is now only poorly supported by fact.

Higher Education for Individual Success

Higher education has long been an important policy lever to achieve a range of purposes. Traditionally, these were primarily social in nature. Universities were conceived as 'agents of personal and intellectual growth' (Tomlinson 2018, p. 713) that was in the public interest, and higher education was seen as a means of promoting knowledge that was 'a public good in and of itself' (Williams 2016, p. 619). This knowledge was to be used to: make 'a key contribution to the common good' (Altbach 2015, p. 2); promote 'an enlightened and creative modern society' (Bradley and Ingram 2013, p. 51); and foster democratic citizens who could function effectively in that society (Vingaard Johansen et al. 2017).

These ideas were formalised through earlier policy documents such as the World Declaration on Higher Education for the Twenty-First Century, which positioned higher education as 'a fundamental pillar of human rights, democracy, sustainable development and peace' (UNESCO 1998, p. 1), but they still have a great deal of currency in the imaginaries of higher education, as Boliver notes:

> Why, then, do we continue to believe in the power of higher education to transform lives, communities and societies at large? Perhaps the reason we do is because we know it could (Boliver 2017, p. 424).

There is an ongoing project that constructs the young university student as an actor who can—and should—contribute to such goals. Arvanitakis and Hornsby's invocation of the 'Citizen Scholar' is a prime example of this. It is an argument for a student who is dedicated not only to the development of knowledge and skills for their personal benefit but who is also 'interested in applying their knowledge for the betterment of society' (2016, p. 1). Similar scholarly arguments position the young university student as a citizen able to promote intercultural understanding and cosmopolitanism (Caruana 2014), 'contribute to greater social justice' (McArthur 2011, p. 746) and demonstrate a 'moral sense of responsibility and obligation to others' (Clifford and Montgomery 2014, p. 2).

Despite this, recent years have seen the social possibilities of higher education largely subsumed by economic purposes. Across numerous nations, there has been a marked escalation in the attention paid by policy-makers to higher education, and in the priority given to economic goals within higher education policy (Brooks 2018; Vingaard Johansen et al. 2017). One aspect of this is the highly critiqued push across a number of nations to restructure higher education as a market-driven system (Tomlinson 2018).

In Australia, this has been accompanied by the deregulation of student fees, which forces universities to compete for student enrolments and government funding (Sellar 2013). In the UK, the costs of higher education study are being shifted from the taxpayer to the student (Bathmaker et al. 2013). In France, too, there is change in the air. The type and level of education that young people pursue, and the status of the university that they attend, has historically had a lifelong effect on their career path and social status. As a result, young people's academic choices tend to be seen as both 'decisive and irreversible' (Pickard 2014, p. 51). This has driven a growing exodus of middle-class young people to the selective and often expensive Grandes Écoles, whose smaller student numbers and greater funding per student promise stronger and more secure pathways into stable employment (Pickard 2016).

Such developments reinforce the importance of material and other resources in driving young people's orientation to their educational and economic futures, as well as their strategic efforts to secure that future. They have been accompanied by a shift in the discourses of higher education, as Tomlinson observes:

> It has become common to view the value of higher education in market-driven environments in relation to a process of commodification, or indeed reification, whereby what higher education produces is reducible to largely material and measureable market commodities. As such, higher education's value is derived from how much it can be traded or exchanged within what are essentially transactional relationships between individuals and institutions (i.e. between graduates, higher education and then employer organisations) (2018, p. 713).

There has also been a shift in the discourses that describe the university student or graduate. The depiction of students as 'learners' is giving way to their depiction as 'workers in the making' (Brooks 2017, p. 14): the contemporary university student is less the 'homo educandus' envisioned by Kant than the 'homo economicus' described by Stuart Mill and others. This economic actor may well be able to contribute to the wider public good, but the dominant discourse of higher education increasingly emphasises something else: its *private good* value—that is, something which is privately funded, consumed and utilised for personal future economic return' (Tomlinson 2018, p. 719, original emphasis).

This discourse constructs higher education as 'a consumer good purchased to ensure individual prosperity' (Bradley and Ingram 2013, p. 51). By the same token, it constructs the young student as a consumer who needs to make wise choices to further their own hopes and plans for the future (Tomlinson 2017, 2018). As Williams writes, 'students are no longer perceived to be potential contributors to the public intellectual capital of the nation, but instead as private investors seeking a financial return in the form of enhanced employability skills' (2016, p. 627). Higher education is now actively promoted by education policy as a long-term investment in the individual self and future (Budd 2017), an embodiment of the individual dream of 'getting ahead' (Grubb and Lazerson 2005). It promises the individual better employment choice and security, earnings advantages, productive social and employment networks, and resilience and agility in changing labour markets (Deloitte Access Economics 2015). It also promises them the capacity to purchase the objects, resources, services, opportunities and experiences that are associated with modern material security and success. As Brown (2003) states:

> We are told that 'the more we learn the more we earn', as better credentials are believed to lead to good jobs and higher rewards, at the same time offering an efficient and fair means of selection based on individual achievement. Credentials are the currency of opportunity (p. 142).

To Give Us the Best Prospects

These discursive promises mean that young people increasingly enter higher education with raised labour market aspirations and expectations about its personal benefits (Souto-Otero 2010). There is also evidence that these promises resonate with their families. A number of our interviewees have chosen to pursue higher education because of their parents' expectations and incitements, as some explain:

> ... I was pretty much growing up with [my parents] always telling me how crucial it is to have a university degree: 'if you want to have a successful career, if you want to achieve anything in your life, you have to go to university after school' (Irina, Australia).
>
> I was always kind of set into higher education. My teachers were kind of pushing me to it, because I had good grades. My parents were encouraging me as well. And so it had never really been questioned – a question to me – that I would do anything else, really (Lyr, France).
>
> Basically, my parents always told me to have the highest education level I could get (Paloma, France).

For some of these young people, the family culture means that university is seen as a normative pathway, one that they would naturally pursue after completing school:

> ... education was always important in my family. I was always encouraged to pursue higher education - a minimum, at least, an undergraduate degree (Lyr, France).
>
> [My parents] are very much of the same mind, in terms of the importance of a professional qualification and, you know, reaching your full potential, academically. I mean, being a tradie [tradesperson] or something would not have been accept[able] because, you know, my sister and I are fairly academic and bright, so that would be seen as a bad option (Alice, Australia).

There is nothing new about these aspirations or expectations. As we will argue in the next chapter, however, they need to be understood in the context of wider changes, including the economic pressures that young university students (and their families) face in the pursuit of their academic goals. They also need to be understood in the context of the changing nature of young women's workforce participation and aspirations. Cynthia's dreams of educational achievement and success are something that her parents have encouraged her and her sister to pursue, but they are also a way for her to meet a wider set of social expectations and hopes about young women's successful futures:

> ... it is just kind of expected of every girl to do it, especially with this whole rise of the whole feminism and all that: women can, too, have careers and be successful, similar to men. ... For me, also, I guess my parents both went to university and they hold education as really important, an important value. So it was expected for me, too, and my sister as well, to go to university, even just to get a degree. Because my mother [says], from her own experience, you at least need to have a degree in anything. But you won't even get hired nowadays if you have just finished Year 12 and gone out to the workforce (Cynthia, Australia).

Cynthia's chosen trajectory reflects the 'quiet revolution' of women's participation in education that began during the latter 20th century (Goldin and Mitchell 2017, p. 180). She wants to do more than gain academic success: she also wants to pursue a leadership role in her chosen field of education. Her partner is very encouraging of these goals: 'you have got to be pushing your career'. While Cynthia explains that she is 'not sort of aiming to do something like really big and become famous in my field or anything of that sort', she would like to 'become a principal of a school or something, maybe when my children are a bit older and all that'. For Allysa, too, who has moved to Australia from Indonesia to seek a teaching qualification, family culture and parental expectations are a strong factor in her decision to pursue higher education. Her acceptance by an Australian university has only amplified those expectations:

> My parents are teachers, so they really want me to be [an] educator. They don't care whether I can earn a good deal of money after I graduate, or not, in Indonesia. But for me, I think they have higher expectations compared to when I study in Indonesia, because they think that after I graduate from [Australian university], they have some sort of expectation that I can be a lecturer in the future. … It motivates me: of course it motivates me. Also, it pressures me because I know once I go back to Indonesia, I cannot just simply teach, for example, elementary school or teach in an English course like I used to do, even though I might enjoy it. But I think my parents' expectation influence me a little bit. So I want to achieve more (Allysa, Australia).

For some of our other interviewees, higher education has a more explicitly economic dimension. Their degree is both a safety net for their immediate future and an investment in their long-term security. It is an essential component of their 'strategic self-management' and their attempt to 'create a meaningful life-trajectory in a complex world with a wide range of possibilities' (Mørch et al. 2018, p. 422). This emerges strongly from our pre-interview survey, which included a question about what had motivated interviewees to undertake their current course of study. Across all three cohorts, the most frequent response was: 'to develop my professional skills and improve my employability'. When asked to imagine their lives in 10 years' time and rank 10 possible hopes or plans for that future, all three cohorts ranked the following choice very highly: 'I'd have stable and secure professional employment'. A number also make it very clear that higher education is a central strategy in securing this future:

> I didn't really have the feeling I had the tools to enter the job market and I didn't really feel ready to do that. So this is one reason why I wanted to do a Master's degree, to get more knowledge. Also, I have the feeling that the student status protects you a little bit. If I would have said okay, I will start work now, I will not do a Master's degree, I would maybe [have] been jobless or looking for a job (Juliane, France).

> While it may take a few years, in the end, you are going to come out with something that's going to help you in the future (Mark, UK).

> I think being in France, and trying to work in France, I am better off with a Master's degree than without (Zaynab, France).

For some of these young people, a university qualification is in fact perceived to be the only means of gaining access to a specific desired career:

> Basically, I am doing a Master's because I don't really have a choice if I want to pursue a career that I would like to do, which is teaching (Sophia, France).

> … since high school, I just knew that I wanted to get into teaching. I had some really, really brilliant teachers, so I knew that I wanted to teach (Mel, Australia).

> ... in France, when you don't have a degree, it's really hard to get a job, especially in journalism. There was a time where you could be a journalist with no degree at all: you could start being a journalist because you had someone of your family as a journalist or because you had good writing. But nowadays, it's impossible (Juliette, France).
>
> Prior to coming to uni, I decided to take a gap year,[1] because I wasn't too set on coming to university. By then, I kind of got a bit sick of school: in particular, I was having quite early wake-ups and getting back quite late, so I was just tired I think from it all. But during my gap year, whilst I enjoyed it in some ways, I realised that if I wanted to have – I wouldn't say serious career, but certainly the career path I wanted, I realised I needed that degree behind me (George, UK).

Cultivating these educational hopes may also help these young people to achieve their imagined working futures. Jackson's (2014) study of Australian university students suggests a close bond between university participation and improved postgraduation employment outcomes, partly because university participation promotes life-long learning and confidence in the acquisition and mastery of employment-related skills and knowledge. Such equations are not always straightforward for the young people concerned, however. Speaking from the UK, Becky finds the assumption that she would go on to higher education to be a problematic one:

> I think a lot more stock now is on education. I think maybe even just one/two generations before me, it was mainly about work experience, and I remember having that exact conversation with my tutor at college about, you know: 'you are going to university, you do this, da, da, da. It's planned out for you'. ... I thought: hold on, why did you do that and that was the way to do it then, and why is now the acceptable way to do it? We follow this little level of you know, we go to college, we go to uni, *da, da, da,* and that is what we do (Becky, UK).

Becky's narrative reflects the traditional, normative assumption that schooling would be followed by higher education. At the same time, it represents a change in her own family culture, something that emerges elsewhere in our discussion as well. While some young people wish to follow the settled achievements or assumptions of their parents' generation, economic and sociological factors are pulling them into other life-courses.

The Truths and Promises of Higher Education

In the Introduction, we alluded to the 'truths of youth' which Kelly has evoked over a number of years (e.g. 2000, 2011). As we explained, we are using the phrase to reflect on the assumed truths of young people's lives as well as some of the untold truths about the effects of uncertainty on those lives. The promises of higher education that we have discussed earlier belie a number of these truths, truths that are rapidly changing the nature of the educational contract between young university students, their universities and the outcomes for which they have been led to hope.

The personal benefits promised by higher education do appear to be holding steady, where these can be accessed. In both Australia and the UK, while many

---

[1] A gap year is typically taken as a break or sabbatical between school and university.

recent graduates find it difficult to obtain full-time work and while the transition from university to work can be slow, the unemployment rate for graduates remains low and they still tend to earn significantly more over the course of their working lives than non-graduates (Bathmaker et al. 2013; Norton and Cherastidtham 2018). The case is similar in France: in 2012, around 30% of young people with no university qualifications were deemed to be in poverty, a considerably higher rate than for those with a degree (10%) (Pickard 2014).

The realisation of these promises is becoming more difficult, however, as Bessant and her colleagues observe: 'Today it is clear that the implied promise that more education would deliver jobs and the good life is in tatters' (2017, p. 2). The promises of higher education need to be understood within a complex nexus of trends and factors, ranging from changes in student demand and a growth in the supply of opportunities to participate in higher education, along with credential inflation and wider macro-shifts in the global labour market. For example, the promise that higher education will lead to secure work is challenged by the global massification of higher education at a time when job futures are becoming increasingly insecure for all but high socioeconomic groups. This massification is the result of a series of deliberate policies that have sought to widen higher education participation. It means that across numerous nations, higher education is undergoing a transformation from an elite to a mass system.

Let's consider the scale of this growth. The global gross enrolment ratio in tertiary education has been steadily rising over the last five decades (World Bank 2017), and there is every sign that this trend will continue (Marginson 2016). At the national level, too, university enrolments are passing historic records. In Australia, the annual number of enrolled domestic students grew by 144% from 420,000 in 1989 to just over one million in 2014: this is in comparison to only 40% of growth in the overall Australian population over that period. In 2013, more than a third of Australians aged 25 to 34 held a bachelor degree or higher qualification (Marginson 2013). This massification has also seen a growing proportion of 'non-traditional' students entering higher education, including students from age, cultural or socioeconomic groups that have traditionally been under-represented within the sector (Alves and Korhonen 2016). This is the result of deliberate policies, particularly in the UK and Australia, to build social capital, equity and mobility by improving individual employability, earnings and job security through higher education (Williams 2016; Gale and Parker 2013). Together with the greater mobility of qualified workers across countries, this is greatly intensifying competition for skilled employment (Roberts and Li 2017; Vina 2016). As Marginson notes, greater participation in higher education 'increases the pool of graduates but does not increase the number of high value social outcomes that graduates can reach' (2016, p. 414). The result of this 'graduate glut' (Koh 2018) is a 'global war' for—and amongst—the most talented graduates (Brown and Tannock 2009).

This competition is a real issue for the young people we interviewed. In Australia, Tyler is pursuing a postgraduate psychology degree after failing to gain employment in his undergraduate area of marketing. This is how he explains his decision to return to study having re-focused his career plans:

> In terms of getting into the business industry and things like that, it was a flooded labour market. ... There would be one job available and there would be 2,000 applicants for the job, for example. ... it was also during the GFC, that stage that I was coming out of my undergraduate. Obviously, a lot of businesses had kind of slowed down their recruitment and stuff like that, which made it a difficult stage in terms of getting a job in that industry (Tyler, Australia).

In the UK, Becky has made a similar choice, returning to university to retrain in forensic psychology after working as a teacher. She is currently engaged in a Bachelor degree but hopes to progress to a Master's degree and then a Ph.D. This qualification escalation is a central aspect of Becky's dream to secure a good life for herself and her family:

> I am very competitive, myself. If I start something, and I get my Master's, I think, 'well, I can do a Master's - I can probably do a PhD'. Also, I am really interested in my subject. It drives me and the more that I learn about it, the more that I realise that's - I won't say 'employed', because I want to get a point where I don't need an employer. I kind of want to be self-sufficient in that way. And I think with that, a PhD is your own research, your own ideas: you are carving your own way into a market. That's what like the idea of. The aim of my life is to get to a point where I don't really need anybody to validate me for what I am doing. That's my whole ethos - financially, work ethic, everything. I just want to be able to go, 'no, we are all good here' (Becky, UK).

Tyler and Becky's choices to attempt further qualifications may be important personal and affective decisions—exercises in hope—but there are other dimensions at play here. Credential inflation is another outcome of the growth in higher education participation, one that has real implications for young people across numerous nations. As Brown and his colleagues observe, 'the economic value of educational qualifications depends on maintaining their scarcity within the labour market' (2016, p. 192): as this scarcity diminishes, so do the better outcomes that it promises. The pressure to keep accumulating qualifications is one that is felt by our interviewees across all three nations, including Becky herself:

> I think for my daughter's generation, education is paramount. I mean, now, it is competitive as well, because everybody is getting degrees. So then you have to get a Master's degree just to have what used to be the category of a degree, and then the PhD because then everyone will be having Master's degrees - you know what I mean, it is that one upmanship. It is quite scary, really: it is a lot of money (Becky, UK).

> ... in Russia, everyone feels like, 'I have to do it as quick as possible'. So after high school, immediately go to university. After Bachelor's degree, immediately get Master's degree: that's how it's done. That's also what happened to me. ... It's still considered if you don't get higher education, you are almost a failure (Irina, Australia).

> ... people have more diplomas, so you need more to get the same positions and everything (Lyr, France).

There are also personal costs or investments involved in the decision to continue studying at a higher level. When we ask Becky whether coming back to university has been a challenge in any way, she replies:

> Mmm, in every way. Financially, obviously, going down from two salary household, fairly decent salaries as well, to one, and a child on top of that, it was really quite a struggle in the

first year. ... She was three months old when I went back to university. So I had a newborn, a degree, my other half was working away as well - it was all a bit up in the air. But I think now, a year and a half later, two years later, it's definitely paid off. Can see the light at the end of the tunnel, finally [laughs] (Becky, UK).

We began this chapter by noting that not only young people but their families are increasingly expected to invest significant resources in the pursuit of higher education and the competitive benefit it promises. For Becky and also for Abi, whose account we consider shortly, realising the imagined future has concrete implications for their lives as family members. This means that the educational contract is not simply between young university students and their universities, but extends to their families as well, with implications which we will consider at length in this chapter.

Higher Education and Mobility

This pressure to keep accumulating qualifications comes from the need to secure positional benefits that are becoming increasingly difficult to access. One reason for this is the increasingly competitive graduate labour market which we have mentioned and which we will discuss at greater length in Chap. 5. The onus is squarely on the graduate to make the choices which will secure their success within this market (Budd 2017), but this individualised choice-making begins well before graduation. As Bathmaker and her colleagues have observed, 'getting a degree is no longer enough, and students are urged to mobilise different forms of "capital" during their undergraduate study to enhance their future social and economic positioning' (2013, p. 724). Particularly in Australia and the UK, where government funding changes have seen a vast increase in the private cost of higher education, the student is expected to regard their degree as an investment. They are expected 'to be prepared to accumulate significant debt in order to acquire it' and to 'shop around', comparing institutions and courses to secure the 'best possible education' (Brooks 2018, p. 501).

This is nothing particularly new. Higher education has long been implicit in the reproduction of social capital. It has long been promoted as a means by which young people can secure long-term positional advantage over those who do not participate in the qualifications game. In the UK, for example, middle-class students remain better able to access higher education. They also remain better placed to mobilise various forms of capital to improve their access to the internships and work experience that have become essential in translating degrees into concrete economic access and success (Leathwood and O'Connell 2003): we discuss this further in the next section of this chapter. For at least one of our interviewees, Irina from Russia, a university qualification is synonymous with this kind of social capital and mobility:

... when [my parents] were my age, you know, it was still the Soviet Union and this ideology was different there. People, like, the government was trying to tell people, 'it is not important to have higher education. You can still work without it'. ... But then the Soviet Union was over and people suddenly saw that life was different: everything changed in the country. So, yep, my parents, they always wanted me to get higher education, to be able to get to another level of – I don't know – another level of society (Irina, Australia).

While unequal outcomes for university graduates is nothing new, then, what is new is the vulnerability for so many young graduates to the cumulative effects of rising global inequality, chronic youth unemployment, underemployment and precarity of employment. Souto-Otero warns that the losers in the struggle for competitive educational advantage will be what he calls the 'dissatisfied lumpenintelligentsia' (2010, p. 404). If the university has previously been, as he suggests, 'a vending machine of opportunity tickets in the form of qualifications', it now looks likely to become primarily 'a reproductive organ of society' (2010, p. 404), one that perpetuates social and economic division. This uncertainty, and the individualising pressure it exerts on young people to ensure their own security, is a source of anxiety for some of our young interviewees:

> I am doing a degree but I don't really know where it's taking me, because we don't really talk about it at the university. They don't really tell us where the degrees are going to take us, what are we going to do with it. So maybe there's that. I don't really feel like my degree is going to be worth it, and I won't be able to jump onto something else or to do something - or have job prospects (Grace, France).
>
> I know that after my Master's degree, it will be my responsibility to train myself in professional formation or to try to have a job, but more with my qualities than my degrees, I think (Ines, France).

In the face of escalating global uncertainty, higher education also promises young graduates an important form of symbolic competitive capital (Bradley and Ingram 2013): the capacity to take their place amongst the 'globalisers' rather than the 'globalised' (Gacel-Ávila 2005, p. 121). It promises that graduates—especially high-achieving graduates—will be able to take their place as mobile, adaptive actors with broad career prospects and a global geographic, economic and cultural field in which to make their mark (Ball 2010; Power et al. 2013). Such young people are also exempt from the kind of punitive policy strategies that discourage young people's early labour market entry without higher qualifications and that reduce the welfare support available to young people not in work or study (Furlong 2014).

For many of our interviewees, this desire for the best possible education and educational outcomes is a key factor in their choice of university, as these two explain:

> The decision to study here [at a prestigious university] was to ensure higher education quality. … for a Master's degree, I have noticed there are hundreds and hundreds of them in the country. They are cheap, everywhere, so it's like, 'I need to try and find a university that is more renowned'. So that's why I decided to study here (Zaynab, France).
>
> It took quite a while to choose which university. It was a very considered decision, even to the level where I phoned up the university to find out more about the course at this one. It was based on quite a few factors. I really like the town here and it just seemed like a really friendly university, really, and the course appealed, as well. And it was quite a well-regarded education course (Alice, UK).

In a number of instances, this strategy to maximise their educational success has also driven our interviewees' geographic mobility. Abi has relocated from Indonesia in order to take up a place at an Australian university. Like Becky in the UK, his choice conveys the degree of commitment and hope which both he and his family have invested in his higher education and the future that it promises. He is not alone in making this decision to be mobile in pursuit of promised competitive advantage. In France, Juliane has moved from Germany in order to pursue her studies. In the UK, Isabella has moved from Italy. In Australia, a third of our cohort has relocated from another country to attend their chosen university. Rose has come from India, Allysa and Abi have come from Indonesia, Jack and Lila have come from China, and Irina has a scholarship provided by the Russian government on the condition that she returns to Russia after she graduates, to work in her field of study for three years.

For these young people, the nexus between higher education and mobility works in two ways: their choice of university both compels their mobility and offers them greater choice to be mobile once they graduate. Their decision to seek transnational routes in pursuit of higher education also shows how the globalisation of higher education manifests itself in individual young lives. Higher education promises graduates the capacity to take their place as mobile global citizens: for those of our interviewees who have moved countries in order to take up a place at their preferred university, this process has already begun. They are already travelling on what Max in Chap. 2 called 'globalisation's conveyor belt' (Adler et al. 2017). For these young people, the internationalisation and globalisation of higher education is not merely a political concept: it has real and far-reaching practical and affective implications, which we unpack later in this book.

Not Working but Learning: The Rise and Rise of 'Homo Economicus'

The perceived quality of university study has another dimension that has recently emerged as a driver of student attitudes to the value of their qualification: the exposure to work opportunities during study. University students' investment in the future increasingly extends to strategies such as internships, voluntary work and work experience to improve their market edge: that is, their employability and attractiveness within a competitive graduate labour market (Bathmaker et al. 2013; Binder et al. 2016; Holdsworth 2017; Oinonen 2018). The drivers for this investment are clear: a 2016 UK survey of over 2,000 young people aged 16–25 found that the chief barrier to their employment was lack of experience (63%) followed by a competitive labour market (51%) and a lack of suitable employment opportunities (29%). Universities were seen to be in part responsible for not providing sufficient work experience: half of the students in the survey said that they had not been offered any work experience and just under half (48%) reported that 'their university wasn't helpful in connecting them to employers' (Reed in Partnership 2015, p. 4). Students who work while studying perceive themselves as being advantaged by this: they are also assessed as more successful and employable by post-graduation employers (Creed et al. 2015; Evans et al. 2014; Roberts and Li 2017). This is especially the case if their employment is related to their field of study (Geel and Backes-Gellner 2012).

One issue with this trend is that it exacerbates unequal outcomes amongst young graduates. Citing a study that found an estimated 58% of 18–29 year olds participate in unpaid work for the experience (Oliver et al. 2016), Torii and O'Connell suggest that a large proportion engage in such work 'just to get a foot in the door, which makes it harder for those who cannot afford to work for free' (2017, p. 2). Another issue is that working while studying may have detrimental outcomes for the young people concerned. It is accepted that students compete for work experience for little or no pay and under constrained working conditions because they are deemed to be outside the formal workforce: they are 'not working but learning' (Sukarieh and Tannock 2017, p. 249). As we will discuss at greater length in this chapter, the personal costs of this indeterminate status are high: studies in the UK (Allen 2016; Antonucci 2016; Roberts and Li 2017) and in Australia (Munro 2011a, b) show that students seek career-related credentials even to the detriment of their health, relationships, academic outcomes or social lives. This may mean that young people are partly complicit in their own exploitation, as they strive to achieve their employability advantage and to curate their preferred future employed selves. The accounts of some of our interviewees suggest that they see little choice in the matter, however.

In Australia, Allysa is volunteering as a student ambassador while working part-time as an English support facilitator 'to boost my employability because it's going to add to my experience.' She has also 'been attending a lot of workshops for employability'. Also in Australia, Jessica is preparing for her career success by trying to gain as much work experience as she can before she is 'pushed out to the real world'. As she explains, 'I have been teaching since I was 14. I have been teaching sailing to kids aged six to about 15 or so, and then some adults, too'.

As we mentioned earlier, Isabella has moved from Italy to the UK in order to pursue her studies. She has undertaken an internship at the United Nations in order to promote her dream of working in an embassy or a consulate. This was an experience which she describes as 'one of the best experiences of my life', but it was also 'really, really, really competitive'. Still in the UK, George has also deliberately undertaken an internship to improve his prospects. He has his eye out 'looking for good opportunities… I think that's where the internship helped me'. He is now considering taking a Master's degree:

> … because I think that will help me as well. … And then just trying to keep an eye out on what job I might eventually take. There's so many different opportunities: I think it is just going to be [competitive] going up against probably two to three hundred people that are probably going apply (George, UK).

When we ask Ellie from the same university what she might be thinking about doing in order to secure her imagined working future, she explains:

> I am definitely considering something over the summer break. I think now is the time that I need to start putting things into place because the end of third year, in dissertation hand-in, is sitting around the corner. I know it's about a year in advance but that's going to come around so quickly. I don't want to get to that point and have not put things into place already (Ellie, UK).

For our postgraduate students of journalism in France, an internship is an essential stage in their employability. Securing an internship is a highly competitive process, however, one that they have to pursue without assistance from the university. As we will elaborate later in this chapter, they have to rely instead on their own social networks, as Zaynab explains:

> Yeah, the first big hurdle will be if I choose not to go into research and choose the professional branch of my Master's degree. I will have to look for an internship and I feel like your connections matter a lot and I don't have a lot of those in [my city]. So that is one big hurdle (Zaynab, France).

Even after the efforts required to secure an internship, there is no assurance that it will result in employment. Juliette explains:

> … it's even hard to get internships, and you have an internship, you don't know if you are going to work for a publication you have the internship in. So it's really hard. [My university education] is helping me in the way that I have a foot in the door, if I can say I have a foot in what it's like to be a journalist (Juliette, France).

Alice from Australia is reading a book about how to build her much-desired music career:

> … and it talks about [how] you are probably going to need a part-time job [during study] because you are earning crap-all money. But you have got to choose that job really carefully, and you want a job that's not going to take your mind/energy too much. You need something you can just 'do the job, be done with it, get out and go and do your thing', not a job that will be really long hours or really draining (Alice, Australia).

The challenge for Alice is to find the right balance of working while studying. This brings us to another dimension of the young university student as 'homo economicus': the fact that increasing numbers of students must work to survive. The expansion of these circumstances coincides with the rise of the student labour market or 'studentification' of the youth labour market (Sukarieh and Tannock 2014). As tertiary enrolments increase, so too are students engaging in part-time, temporary and seasonal jobs for essential financial support while studying. This phenomenon emerged initially in the US, but has become a widespread experience for young people in many countries including the UK (Purcell 2010), Australia (Cameron 2013) and Europe (Orr et al. 2011).

The increasing costs of higher education and changes in student funding systems in many countries make work particularly necessary for those students with fewer personal financial resources. Studies in the UK (Antonucci 2018; Evans et al. 2014; Kirby 2016), in Australia (Coates 2011; Landstedt et al. 2017; Munro 2011a, b), and in Europe (Sanchez-Gelabert et al. 2017) reveal that financial necessity is a primary driver of young people's part-time work while studying. In France, where undergraduate degree fees are capped by the government and postgraduate fees are low by comparison to other countries, only around 40% of young people work while studying (Hauschildt et al. 2015; Power et al. 2013). Still, meeting the high costs of living (particularly in large French cities) remains a strong motivation for their engagement in part-time work, particularly for working-class students (Beffy et al.

2010; Body et al. 2014). Maintaining a desired standard of living against rising living costs is also a motivation to work while studying (Robotham 2013).

There is no doubt that for some young people, the increasing costs of higher education are having a negative impact on their attainment of higher education qualifications. According to one European study (Mourshed et al. 2017), 19% of young people in France and 18% in the UK do not enrol in post-secondary education, including higher education, because they have to work. The figures are even higher for those young people who embark on study but do not complete it because of the claims made on their time by work: 35% in France and 22% in the UK. In the UK, 14% have not enrolled in post-secondary education because they do not think that it would pay itself back. Of the rest, 69% have taken out a loan to cover their university tuition fees, 40% rely on themselves or their family, and 6% rely on a scholarship. By contrast, where tuition is free (Sweden) or almost free (France), or where financial support is available in the form of grants, a much lower proportion of young people (fewer than 6%) cite finances as a reason not to enrol. These figures are salient to the proportion of young people completing tertiary education: 63% in the UK compared to 42% in France.

This does not mean that young university students in France do not need financial support, though. The same study found that 71% fund their education by themselves or through their families, compared to only 24% who receive a state-backed loan or have their costs otherwise covered by a higher education provider, an employer or through a scholarship. There are inherent inequities in this, a situation about which one of our French interviewees feels strongly:

> … it tends to be very classist, I feel. For instance … I work to be able to live here in [my city], to follow classes and to do everything – well, pay everything that I need to do my studies. But that also means I have less time to study. So, in a way, someone who is better off, or who has parents who can pay the rent, who actually has parents living here, is in a better situation (Lyr, France).

What Matters Is Who I Know

We have already described the growing trend for young university students to engage in part-time work, voluntary work, work experience and internships as a means of securing their employability and competitiveness in a tough graduate labour market. For many, social capital and social networks are essential in obtaining these opportunities, and positioning them for graduate employment. As Butler and Muir observe, 'young people's education pathways in late modernity are strongly dependent on their ability to draw on the range of resources available' (2017, p. 316). Tomlinson's model of graduate capital (2017) is particularly useful in unpacking what these resources might comprise. It identifies a range of capitals on which young university students may draw to navigate the uncertain environments of the current era. These include cultural capital, which arises from the opportunities created through the credentials that higher education enables. They include human capital, which is required where credentials are seen to provide positional advantages in accessing work in a globally competitive labour market where individual employability is measured against the employability of others. They include psychological capital, a form of capital based on the psychological resources that would enable graduates to adapt and respond proactively to inevitable career challenges, such as the feelings of self-efficacy that are intrinsic to their capacity to navigate challenging labour market conditions. They include identity capital, which concerns the way that individuals curate their identities and sense of vocation. They also include social capital: that is, the networks and human relationships that can help young people to position themselves competitively in relation to tight labour markets.

One of our interview questions asked interviewees to rank the following in terms of their importance for their imagined future working lives: 'what you know', 'who you know' and 'what you can do with what you know'. While each of these areas of knowledge was felt to be important, a number of our interviewees feel that who they know (or might know in future) is a powerful factor in ensuring the realisation of their career hopes and plans. For Allysa, having professional contacts and networks is essential: it is, quite simply, the only way of ensuring that she can stay abreast of the employment opportunities available in her field once she has completed her Master's degree in Education:

> ... in Indonesia or maybe in my university, there's no actual advertisement for the job, a job opening for that. So as long as I have networks, I will get the advertisement first and I will apply for it first [laughs] (Allysa, Australia).

For Lyr in France, having the right social connections has already been helpful. For financial reasons, he needs to work while studying but has secured a particularly lucrative and ongoing job in the university library. This was only possible because his godfather had connections: as he explains, 'you don't really get a position in the library unless you know someone inside it, which I did'. Lyr started work in the library in 2011 and has moved from one attractive role to the next:

> Now I am actually, funnily enough, in the department led by the first person who greeted me in 2011, because she remembered me and she was like: 'I want you' [laughs]. And, yeah, it's going very well.

Lyr goes on to testify to the influence of contacts and networks in creating work and career opportunities:

> Who you come in contact with definitely determines what you are going to do, what you are going to know as well and how you use what you are going to know. ... The only reason I have been able to use my knowledge is because of people I met, who are able to teach me how to use it, that I drew inspiration from. So it is the most important thing. Also, they can push you or open doors for you (Lyr, France).

His philosophy of social connections is one that is also shared by Isabella and Becky in the UK and by Mel in Australia:

> I am of the view that anyone can be anyone - can become anyone. But if you know the right people, it will be easier and sometimes the only way to get where you want to go (Isabella, UK).

> So we have family friends who have done a Bachelor of Science for three/four years and [when] they come out, they can't get a job. ... I guess you have to be very, very good or you need to have connections (Mel, Australia).
>
> ... who you know ... crikey, that is 90 per cent of the battle, most of the time (Becky, UK).

The facilitating potential of social networks and contacts is something that Tyler and Grace also acknowledge. For them, though, it is symbolic of a deeper and more systemic inequality, a reflection of the concrete and practical value of social capital in competitive times:

> ... maybe I am particularly cynical, but my sense is: regardless of what industry you are in, if you have got two people on equal footing in terms of knowledge and skill and things like that, the person that knows the right people are going to be more successful. Sometimes even the person that has lower skill/knowledge, if they know the right people, can still succeed. And that is partially, you know, who you are born - like, what family you are born into, where you are born into (Tyler, Australia).
>
> ... I think in the world we are living right now – um, what's the word – nepotism is really important. Like, if you know someone, you can pretty much do anything. ... You need to have friends in high places. If you do that, you can pretty much achieve anything you want (Grace, France).

Conclusion

In their book about the politics of youth in an uncertain global economy, Sukarieh and Tannock (2014) refer to Thomas Friedman's widely cited quote:

> When I was growing up, my parents used to say to me: "Finish your dinner – people in China are starving." I, by contrast, find myself wanting to say to my daughters: "Finish your homework – people in China and India are starving for your job" (Friedman 2004).

As we were writing this conclusion, the Grattan Institute released the latest in their biennial report series on Australian higher education (Norton and Cherastidtham 2018). Coincidentally, this year's report focuses on graduate employment and earnings. It explains that while employment rates for new graduates have improved in recent years, 'the labour market is still tough for younger graduates' (p. 3), with 'many more people ... chasing the jobs that graduates aspire to hold' (p. 77). Recent Australian graduates are earning less than their previous counterparts, and these effects are strongly age-related. As the report explains:

> Many early-career graduates entered the job market during the GFC, when it was difficult to find full-time work. This affected young people more than older people. The effects are likely to be long-lasting (p. 81).

Earlier in this chapter, we cited Tomlinson's argument that 'higher education's value is derived from how much it can be traded or exchanged within what are essentially transactional relationships between individuals and institutions (i.e. between graduates, higher education and then employer organisations)' (2018, p. 713). That a university qualification is a private consumer good and a lever for individual benefit has become an accepted truth within the discourses of higher education. What has been called 'a cultural juggernaut' continues to urge young people into higher education despite evidence that its financial benefits are no longer holding up (Bolton 2018). The equation between higher education and a better future is firmly in place, then, but the promises inherent in this may be what we have earlier called post-truth promises. Higher education, both as a system and an idea, produce what Sellar and Zipin have called 'Educational incitements to optimism about better life prospects through intensified self-investment' (2018, p. 2). They promote an individualised image of the young university student as an actor who is primarily—even solely—responsible for the formulation of their own hopeful imagined future and for its realisation.

What these incitements conceal is the fact that many young people develop their hopes and embark on whatever strategies and sacrifices are needed to realise those hopes in concert with significant others—partners and parents, in particular. In Chap. 2, we noted that individual responsibility has become the assumed youth response to most life challenges, including the challenges of securing a well-regarded degree and the positional goods that this promises. In this chapter, we have begun to contest this individualisation of the young university student. We have highlighted the increasing reliance of young university students on social networks and capital. We have also suggested that the contemporary educational contract is not merely one that operates between young university students and their universities, but one that extends to their families as well. We have touched on the role that family culture and parental expectations play in the decision of some of our interviewees to pursue higher education, as well as in directing their specific higher education choices and career hopes. We have alluded to the role that their families play in their decisions to relocate, as well as in the other investments they have made in their higher education.

This is a theme to which we will return in the next chapter, when we critically investigate young people's current and imagined future lives as family members and how these relate both to the promises of higher education and to the factors and forces of uncertainty that give context to those promises. We will suggest, amongst other things, that young people's hope for the future is not an individualised but a shared resource, one that may be fostered and supported by their partners and family. After that, in Chap. 5, we will discuss the individualisation of the contemporary labour market and its implications for the realisation of these promises and hopes.

References

Adler, P., Lindell, J., Marsh, A., Gattas, S., Turner, Z., Brooks, P., et al. (2017, February 21). 'We need leadership—quickly': First-year students on the biggest issue facing Australia. *The Guardian*. Retrieved February 23, 2017, from https://www.theguardian.com/australia-news/2017/feb/21/we-need-leadership-quickly-first-year-students-on-the-biggest-issue-facing-australia.

Allen, K. (2016). Top girls navigating austere times: Interrogating youth transitions since the 'crisis'. *Journal of Youth Studies, 19*(6), 805–820. https://doi.org/10.1080/13676261.2015.1112885.

Altbach, P. G. (2015). Knowledge and education as international commodities: The collapse of the common good. *International Higher Education, 28,* 2–5.

Alves, M. G., & Korhonen, V. (2016). Transitions and trajectories from higher education to work and back: A comparison between Finnish and Portuguese graduates. *European Educational Research Journal, 15*(6), 676–695. https://doi.org/10.1177/1474904116661200.

Antonucci, L. (2016). *Student lives in crisis: Deepening inequality in times of austerity.* Bristol: Policy Press.

Antonucci, L. (2018). Not all experiences of precarious work lead to precarity: The case study of young people at university and their welfare mixes. *Journal of Youth Studies, 21*(7), 888–904. https://doi.org/10.1080/13676261.2017.1421749.

Arvanitakis, J., & Hornsby, D. J. (2016). Introduction. In J. Arvanitakis & D. J. Hornsby (Eds.), *Universities, the citizen scholar and the future of higher education* (pp. 1–6). Basingstoke: Springer.

Ball, S. J. (2010). Is there a global middle class? The beginnings of a cosmopolitan sociology of education: A review. *Journal of Comparative Education, 69*(1), 137–161.

Bathmaker, A.-M., Ingram, N., & Waller, R. (2013). Higher education, social class and the mobilisation of capitals: recognising and playing the game. *British Journal of Sociology of Education, 34*(5–6), 723–743. https://doi.org/10.1080/01425692.2013.816041.

Beffy, M., Fougère, D., & Maurel, A. (2010). The effect of part-time work on post-secondary educational attainment: New evidence from French data. *IZA discussion paper no. 5069.* Bonn: IZA.

Bessant, J., Farthing, R., & Watts, R. (2017). *The precarious generation: A political economy of young people.* Abingdon: Routledge.

Binder, A. J., Davis, D. B., & Bloom, N. (2016). Career funnelling: How elite students learn to define and desire "prestigious" jobs. *Sociology of Education, 89*(1), 20–39. https://doi.org/10.1177/0038040715610883.

Body, K. M.-D., Bonnal, L., & Giret, J.-F. (2014). Does student employment really impact academic achievement? The case of France. *Applied Economics, 46*(25), 3061–3073. https://doi.org/10.1080/00036846.2014.920483.

Boliver, V. (2017). Misplaced optimism: How higher education reproduces rather than reduces social inequality. *British Journal of Sociology of Education, 38*(3), 423–432. https://doi.org/10.1080/01425692.2017.1281648.

Bolton, R. (2018, September 12). Uni degrees lose some of their allure as the premium for being a graduate falls. *Australian Financial Review.* Retrieved October 4, 2018, from https://www.afr.com/news/policy/education/university-degrees-lose-some-of-their-allure-as-the-premium-for-being-a-graduate-starts-to-fall-20180912-h15an7.

Bradley, H., & Ingram, N. (2013). Banking on the future: Choices, aspirations and economic hardship in working-class student experience. In W. Atkinson, S. Roberts, & M. Savage (Eds.), *Class inequality in austerity Britain: Power, difference and suffering* (pp. 51–69). Basingstoke: Palgrave Macmillan.

Brooks, R. (2017). The construction of higher education students in English policy documents. *British Journal of Sociology of Education, 39*(6), 745–761. https://doi.org/10.1080/01425692.2017.1406339.

Brooks, R. (2018). Understanding the higher education student in Europe: A comparative analysis. *Compare: A Journal of Comparative and International Education, 48*(4), 500–517. https://doi.org/10.1080/03057925.2017.1318047.

Brown, P. (2003). The opportunity trap: Education and employment in a global economy. *European Educational Research Journal, 2*(1), 141–179. https://doi.org/10.2304/eerj.2003.2.1.4.

Brown, P., Power, S., Tholen, G., & Allouch, A. (2016). Credentials, talent and cultural capital: A comparative study of educational elites in England and France. *British Journal of Sociology of Education, 37*(2), 191–211. https://doi.org/10.1080/01425692.2014.920247.

Brown, P., & Tannock, S. (2009). Education, meritocracy and the global war for talent. *Journal of Education Policy, 24*(4), 377–392. https://doi.org/10.1080/02680930802669938.

References

Budd, R. (2017). Undergraduate orientations towards higher education in Germany and England: Problematizing the notion of 'student as customer'. *Higher Education, 73*(1), 23–37. https://doi.org/10.1007/s10734-015-9977-4.

Butler, R., & Muir, K. (2017). Young people's education biographies: Family relationships, social capital and belonging. *Journal of Youth Studies, 20*(3), 316–331. https://doi.org/10.1080/13676261.2016.1217318.

Cameron, C. (2013). The vulnerable worker? A labor law challenge for WIL and work experience. *Asia-Pacific Journal of Cooperative Education, 14*(3), 135–146.

Caruana, V. (2014). Re-thinking global citizenship in higher education: From cosmopolitanism and international mobility to cosmopolitanisation, resilience and resilient thinking. *Higher Education Quarterly, 68*(1), 85–104. https://doi.org/10.1111/hequ.12030.

Clifford, V., & Montgomery, C. (2014). Challenging conceptions of western higher education and promoting graduates as global citizens. *Higher Education Quarterly, 68*(1), 28–45. https://doi.org/10.1111/hequ.12029.

Coates, H. (2011). Working on a dream: Educational returns from off-campus paid work. *AUSSE research briefing no. 8*. Melbourne: ACER.

Creed, P. A., French, J., & Hood, M. (2015). Working while studying at university: The relationship between work benefits and demands and engagement and well-being. *Journal of Vocational Behavior, 86*, 48–57. https://doi.org/10.1016/j.jvb.2014.11.002.

Deloitte Access Economics. (2015). *The importance of universities to Australia's prosperity*. Canberra: Universities Australia.

Evans, C., Gbadamosi, G., & Richardson, M. (2014). Flexibility, compromise and opportunity: Students' perceptions of balancing part-time work with a full-time business degree. *International Journal of Management Education, 12*(2), 80–90. https://doi.org/10.1016/j.ijme.2014.02.001.

Friedman, T. I. (2004, June 24). Doing our homework. *The New York Times*. Retrieved May 5, 2018, from https://www.nytimes.com/2004/06/24/opinion/doing-our-homework.html.

Furlong, A. (2014). Foreword. In L. Antonucci, M. Hamilton, & S. Roberts (Eds.), *Young people and social policy in Europe: Dealing with risk, inequality and precarity in times of crisis* (pp. x–xi). London: Palgrave Macmillan UK.

Gacel-Ávila, J. (2005). The internationalisation of higher education: A paradigm for global citizenry. *Journal of Studies in International Education, 9*(2), 121–136. https://doi.org/10.1177/1028315304263795.

Gale, T., & Parker, S. (2013). *Widening participation in Australian higher education: Report submitted to the Higher Education Funding Council for England (HEFCE) and the Office for Fair Access (OFFA), England*. Lancashire: Edge Hill University.

Geel, R., & Backes-Gellner, U. (2012). Earning while learning: When and how student employment is beneficial. *Labour, 26*(3), 313–340. https://doi.org/10.1111/j.1467-9914.2012.00548.x.

Goldin, C., & Mitchell, J. (2017). The new life cycle of women's employment: Disappearing humps, sagging middles, expanding tops. *Journal of Economic Perspectives, 31*(1), 161–182. https://doi.org/10.1257/jep.31.1.161.

Grubb, W. N., & Lazerson, M. (2005). Vocationalism in higher education: The triumph of the education gospel. *The Journal of Higher Education, 76*(1), 1–25. https://doi.org/10.1080/00221546.2005.11772273.

Hauschildt, K., Gwosc, C., Netz, N., & Mishra, S. (2015). *Social and economic conditions of student life in Europe. Synopsis of indicators: Eurostudent V 2012–2015*. Hannover: Eurostudent.

Holdsworth, C. (2017). The cult of experience: Standing out from the crowd in an era of austerity. *Area, 49*(3), 296–302. https://doi.org/10.1111/area.12201.

Jackson, D. (2014). Factors influencing job attainment in recent Bachelor graduates: Evidence from Australia. *Higher Education, 68*(1), 135–153. https://doi.org/10.1007/s10734-013-9696-7.

Kelly, P. (2000). Youth as an artefact of expertise: Problematizing the practice of youth studies in an age of uncertainty. *Journal of Youth Studies, 3*(3), 301–315. https://doi.org/10.1080/713684381.

Kelly, P. (2011). Breath and the truths of youth at risk: allegory and the social scientific imagination. *Journal of Youth Studies, 14*(4), 431–447. https://doi.org/10.1080/13676261.2010.543668.

Kirby, P. (2016). *Degrees of debt: Funding and finance for undergraduates in Anglophone countries.* London: The Sutton Trust.

Koh, A. (2018). Youth mobilities in elite schools: Elite circuit, reflexive youth biographies and their mobility blips. *Applied Mobilities, 3*(2), 184–197. https://doi.org/10.1080/23800127.2017.1360548.

Landstedt, E., Coffey, J., Wyn, J., Cuervo, H., & Woodman, D. (2017). The complex relationship between mental health and social conditions in the lives of young Australians mixing work and study. *Young, 25*(4), 339–358. https://doi.org/10.1177/1103308816649486.

Leathwood, C., & O'Connell, P. (2003). 'It's a struggle': The construction of the 'new student' in higher education. *Journal of Education Policy, 18*(6), 597–615. https://doi.org/10.1080/0268093032000145863.

Marginson, S. (2013). Introduction. In S. Marginson (Ed.), *Tertiary education policy in Australia* (pp. 7–10). Melbourne: University of Melbourne.

Marginson, S. (2016). The worldwide trend to high participation higher education: Dynamics of social stratification in inclusive systems. *Higher Education, 72*(4), 413–434. https://doi.org/10.1007/s10734-016-0016-x.

McArthur, J. (2011). Reconsidering the social and economic purposes of higher education. *Higher Education Research and Development, 30*(6), 737–749. https://doi.org/10.1080/07294360.2010.539596.

Mørch, S., Pultz, S., & Stroebaek, P. (2018). Strategic self-management: The new youth challenge. *Journal of Youth Studies, 21*(4), 422–438. https://doi.org/10.1080/13676261.2017.1385747.

Mourshed, M., Patel, J. & Suder, K. (2017). *Education to employment: Getting Europe's youth into work.* McKinsey Center for Government. Retrieved June 2, 2018, from http://egdcfoundation.org/work/assets/McKinsey-Education-to-Employment-Europe.pdf.

Munro, L. (2011a). 'Go boldly, dream large!' The challenges confronting non-traditional students at university. *Australian Journal of Education, 55*(2), 115–131. https://doi.org/10.1177/000494411105500203.

Munro, L. (2011b). 'It's a lot of hard work': The experiences of student-workers in university term-time employment. *Australian Bulletin of Labour, 37*(1), 33–50.

Norton, A., & Cherastidtham, I. (2018). *Mapping Australian higher education 2018*. Retrieved September 15, 2018, from https://grattan.edu.au/report/mapping-australian-higher-education-2018/.

Oinonen, E. (2018). Under pressure to become—From a student to entrepreneurial self. *Journal of Youth Studies, 21*(10), 1344–1360. https://doi.org/10.1080/13676261.2018.1468022.

Oliver, D., McDonald, P., Stewart, A., & Hewitt, A. (2016). *Unpaid work experience in Australia: Prevalence, nature and impact.* Retrieved November 15, 2017, from https://docs.employment.gov.au/system/files/doc/other/unpaid_work_experience_report_-_december_2016.pdf.

Orr, D., Gwosc, C., & Netz, N. (2011). *Social and economic conditions of student life in Europe.* Bielefeld: Bertelsmann Verlag.

Pickard, S. (2014). French youth policy in an age of austerity: plus ça change? *International Journal of Adolescence and Youth, 19*(sup1), 48–61. https://doi.org/10.1080/02673843.2013.863732.

Pickard, S. (2016). Higher education in France: Social stratification and social reproduction. In J. E. Côté & A. Furlong (Eds.), *Routledge handbook of the sociology of higher education* (pp. 223–233). London & New York: Routledge.

Power, S., Brown, P., Allouch, A., & Tholen, G. (2013). Self, career and nationhood: The contrasting aspirations of British and French elite graduates. *The British Journal of Sociology, 64*(4), 578–596. https://doi.org/10.1111/1468-4446.12048.

Purcell, K. (2010). *Flexible employment, student labour and the changing structure of the UK labour market in university cities.* Sao Paulo, Brazil: Centro de Estudos da Metrópole.

Reed in Partnership. (2015). *Young people and employment. Our UK Survey*. Retrieved July 3, 2018, from http://www.reedinpartnership.co.uk/latest-news/youth-report-2015.

References

Roberts, S., & Li, Z. (2017). Capital limits: Social class, motivations for term-time job searching and the consequences of joblessness among UK university students. *Journal of Youth Studies, 20*(6), 732–749. https://doi.org/10.1080/13676261.2016.1260697.

Robotham, D. (2013). Students' perspectives on term-time employment: An exploratory qualitative study. *Journal of Further and Higher Education, 37*(3), 431–442. https://doi.org/10.1080/0309877X.2012.666892.

Sanchez-Gelabert, A., Figueroa, M., & Elias, M. (2017). Working whilst studying in higher education: The impact of the economic crisis on academic and labour market success. *European Journal of Education, 52,* 232–245. https://doi.org/10.1111/ejed.12212.

Sellar, S. (2013). Equity, markets and the politics of aspiration in Australian higher education. *Discourse: Studies in the Cultural Politics of Education, 34*(2), 245–258. https://doi.org/10.1080/01596306.2013.770250.

Sellar, S., & Zipin, L. (2018). Conjuring optimism in dark times: Education, affect and human capital. *Educational Philosophy and Theory,* 1–15. https://doi.org/10.1080/00131857.2018.1485566.

Souto-Otero, M. (2010). Education, meritocracy and redistribution. *Journal of Education Policy, 25*(3), 397–413. https://doi.org/10.1080/02680930903576396.

Sukarieh, M., & Tannock, S. (2014). *Youth rising? The politics of youth in the global economy.* New York: Routledge.

Sukarieh, M., & Tannock, S. (2017). The education penalty: Schooling, learning and the diminishment of wages, working conditions and worker power. *British Journal of Sociology of Education, 38*(3), 245–264. https://doi.org/10.1080/01425692.2015.1093408.

Tomlinson, M. (2017). Student perceptions of themselves as 'consumers' of higher education. *British Journal of Sociology of Education, 38*(4), 450–467.

Tomlinson, M. (2018). Conceptions of the value of higher education in a measured market. *Higher Education, 75*(4), 711–727. https://doi.org/10.1007/s10734-017-0165-6.

Torii, K., & O'Connell, M. (2017). *Preparing young people for the future of work.* Mitchell Institute Policy Paper No. 01/2017. Melbourne: Mitchell Institute.

United Nations Educational, Scientific, and Cultural Organization [UNESCO]. (1998). *World declaration on higher education for the twenty-first century: Vision and action.* Paris: UNESCO.

Vina, G. (2016, April 26). Young UK graduates struggle to find skilled work. *Financial Times.* Retrieved September 13, 2017, from https://www.ft.com/content/480d0ad6-0ba9-11e6-b0f1-61f222853ff3.

Vingaard Johansen, U., Knudsen, F. B., Engelbrecht Kristoffersen, C., Stellfeld Rasmussen, J., Saaby Steffen, E., & Sund, K. J. (2017). Political discourse on higher education in Denmark: From enlightened citizen to homo economicus. *Studies in Higher Education, 42*(2), 264–277. https://doi.org/10.1080/03075079.2015.1045477.

Williams, J. (2016). A critical exploration of changing definitions of public good in relation to higher education. *Studies in Higher Education, 41*(4), 619–630. https://doi.org/10.1080/03075079.2014.942270.

World Bank. (2017). Gross enrolment ratio, tertiary, both sexes (%). Retrieved February 9, 2018, from https://data.worldbank.org/indicator/SE.TER.ENRR.

Chapter 4
Imagining the Family in Post-truth Times

Introduction

> I know it's kind of expected for me, coming from my school, to be: 'oh, I want to be really career-driven and really excel in my career and that', but I don't know, you feel a bit embarrassed to kind of say, 'well, my whole purpose in life, what I want to do most, is to be a mother; to have kids and stuff' …. But definitely my biggest goal in life is to have a family and raise children (Cynthia, Australia).

We began this book with an observation by Bauman which captures the liquid uncertainty of the contemporary era. Bauman has also argued that in these uncertain times, 'Safe ports for trust are few and far between, and most of the time trust floats unanchored vainly seeking storm-protected havens' (2000, p. 139). The family as a unit is as subject to the forces of uncertainty as any other social structure, but for young university students it (and other intimate relationships) may also act as a safe haven as well as a central reference point for their hopes and plans for the imagined future, as Cynthia suggests above. For some young people, these relationships are key forms of social capital, affective and practical resources for managing the uncertainties of life, and 'the most important components for a good life' (Oinonen 2018, p. 2).

It is already some years since Wyn and her colleagues mounted an argument for the reinsertion of the family into youth studies, observing that 'although family is almost universally acknowledged to be important in young people's lives, families in youth research are … seldom the focus of analysis' (Wyn et al. 2012, pp. 3–4). As they also argued, 'the fragmentation and decline of institutional structures and older certainties that has occurred during the period of late modernity actually heightens the significance of family for young people' (2012, p. 4). Understanding young people's current and imagined futures as family members brings an important dimension to their experiences of uncertainty and their responses to it. It highlights both the change and the continuity that characterises young people's lives in uncertain times. It sheds light on the ways in which family may act as a push or pull factor in young people's educational and other choices. It also sheds light on the ways in which they may navigate the uncertain labour markets which we will describe in the next chapter.

Early in Chap. 2, we noted that higher education discourses construct young university students as resilient, aspirational subjects able to secure their own successful biographies in the face of uncertainty. These discourses also tend to depict the young university student as an isolated actor, an 'independent, autonomous learner—confident, and unencumbered by self-doubt … and abstracted from the context of his or her private life' (Brooks 2015, p. 507), yet the realities for most young university students are very different to this. Young people's life choices, imaginings and movements 'cannot be seen independently of their relationships to significant others as daughters, sons, siblings, mothers and partners' (Langevang 2008, p. 2046). Their roles as family members are important factors in their experience of higher education as well as in the construction of their imagined future and their hopes and plans for that future. In this chapter, we draw on our interviews with 30 young university students in France, the UK and Australia and on our review of the recent international literature to critically investigate young people's current and imagined future lives as family members in greater depth, and how these relate to other factors and forces such as the studentification of higher education which we discussed in Chap. 3.

Reinserting the Family into Higher Education

Before we consider these, we need to clarify our definition of the family and consider what being a family member may mean for young people in uncertain times. Previously in this book, we described the contemporary plasticity and prolongation of youth as a category and an experience. We argued in concert with many other youth studies scholars that youth as a state has become prolonged into an extended present (Nowotny 1994), or what Honwana characterises as 'waithood' (2014, p. 19).

Across the Global North, many young people are postponing the formation of committed partnerships, marriage and/or family (Cook 2016; Forsberg and Timonen 2018), but these changes in family roles are not limited to the Global North. What Wyn and her colleagues have described as 'the changing nature of relationships between young people and their families (including patterns of interdependence and multi-directional flows of support)' (2012, p. 7) is also captured in studies such as Punch's (2015) examination of rural Bolivian young people moving back and forth between home and migrant destinations, which highlights the ways in which these young lives are 'negotiated both within and across generations as well as across time and space' (p. 263). In other areas of the Global South too, such as Ghana, navigating the accepted markers of adulthood such as financial independence, marriage and parenthood 'is a complicated and convoluted journey involving the careful management of social relationships' (Langevang 2008, p. 2039).

For many young people, there has also been an unbundling or decoupling of marriage, parenthood and household formation (Gray et al. 2017; Valentine 2003). This uncoupling was described by Beck-Gernsheim twenty years ago, when she argued that the 'post-familial family' had replaced traditional family relationships and reliances (1998). She argued that whereas the preindustrial family had been primarily a community of need, 'a relationship centred on work and economics' (p. 57), the contemporary 'logic of individually designed lives' (p. 58) is morphing the family into an 'elective relationship, an association of individual persons, who each bring to it their own interests, experiences and plans, and who are each subjected to different controls, risks and constraints' (p. 67). This hyper-individualised portrayal risks understating the ties of obligation and interdependence that characterise many families, but it does capture the fluidity and negotiation that is part of contemporary family life, especially where young people's mobility for education or employment are concerned.

Our conceptualisation of young people as family members includes these fluid, complex and multidirectional relationships of the contemporary family. It also encapsulates any definition of family which our interviewees may choose to adopt. This may include their role as children of parents or carers, as parents or carers of children or other significant people, or as current or prospective partners in any form of romantic relationship, whether cohabiting or not (Berger 2017; Hakim 2018).

In Chap. 3, we considered the accounts of some of our interviewees whose decision to pursue higher education was expected and encouraged by their parents, or else was met with their parents' keen approval. The family is a crucial influence in shaping young people's orientation towards the future (Furlong 2016b; Woodman 2011). It also plays a key role in shaping their education pathways. A recent global study of 8,481 parents in 15 countries and territories found that almost all parents (95% of those involved in the study) would consider a university education for their child (HSBC 2017). 91% of parents across the study would also consider postgraduate education for their child. The same figures were found in Australia, with slightly fewer in France (89%) and the UK (88%).

At a time when established structures and institutions of social support are weakening, the family also represents an increasingly significant resource for many young people (Wyn et al. 2012). In significant part, this resource is financial in nature. As we touched on earlier, the cost of post-secondary education has become the biggest barrier to young people's enrolment and completion. In France, for example, a quarter of the young people involved in one study did not complete their post-secondary education because they 'could not afford the fees'. Similar figures emerged from the UK, where 24% did not complete their post-secondary education for financial reasons (Mourshed et al. 2017). In such instances, the role of the family may include funding or subsidising their child's higher education: the study of 8,481 parents we mention above found that 85% were helping to fund their child's higher education, while 82% were prepared to make personal sacrifices for their child to succeed educationally (HSBC 2017).

The family also plays other roles in supporting young people's higher education hopes and plans. Wyn and her colleagues argue that in the face of generalised uncertainty, 'family support, resources and contact, which have arguably always been important, are now more important than ever' (2012, p. 4). Furlong goes further to suggest that in these uncertain times, many parents and their children have 'signed a new pact of solidarity' (2016a, p. 2). This has seen a greatly intensified and protracted degree of financial and other practical support given to young people, reflecting the prolongation of their education and economic dependence.

Once again, this is not necessarily a new phenomenon across all nations. In France, for example, the state benefit systems actually presume that the family will be the first and primary source of support for young people. The effect of this is that 'young people are obliged to remain in a position of family dependence before becoming financially independent adults' (Pickard 2014, p. 51). This is known as 'familialisation', a traditional process whereby those young people in higher education are supported through their families rather than the state (Williamson 2016, p. 221). Similar traditions of youth dependence on the family persist in other nations. In Portugal, it is traditional for young people to remain dependent on their families for financial and other support well into adulthood (Cairns et al. 2014). In southern Italy, increasing numbers of young people are continuing the cultural tradition of staying at home with their parents. In these cases, the family provides a form of 'temporal continuity', something that ameliorates the uncertainty and instability that characterises their lives (Leccardi 2005, p. 141).

For many young people, the family also represents responsibility. In Brazil, for example, while youth is a time of economic dependency on parents or relatives, it can also be a time marked by serious economic responsibility towards supporting those parents or relatives, especially where working-class young people are the only income earners in the family (Wildermuth and Dalsgaard 2006). In the UK, numerous university students—especially those from working-class or low socioeconomic backgrounds—may be juggling study with managing childcare responsibilities (Leathwood and O'Connell 2003). This was apparent in our interviews, as we explore below.

Dreaming of Home

At a time when financial independence is so much less accessible for many young people, many find themselves in a state of protracted dependence on their family. This may be particularly felt by young people in cultural contexts where residential independence has been an important historic milestone signifying adulthood (Stone et al. 2014). In the UK, for example, where years of austerity and precarity have seen a reduction in the availability of social housing at the same time as dramatic increases in house prices and rents, independent living has become both much less attractive and much less realistic for many young people (Williamson 2016). Increasing numbers are compelled to work while studying. Some extend their stay in the family home while others find themselves compelled to return to the 'safety net' of that home at key milestones or crises such as when they complete or cease full-time education, become unemployed, or break up with a partner with whom they were living: returning home then becomes a reversal of the transition to independent adulthood (Stone et al. 2014). Across the EU, 48% of young people between 18 and 29 years are living with their parent/s, an increase from 44% a decade ago: especially for growing numbers of young people living in extended families with their parent/s and their own children, the ability to move out of the family home has declined over that time (Eurofound 2014). In Ireland, an estimated third of young people between 18 and 34 are still living with their parent/s (Forsberg and Timonen 2018). In Australia, 27% of young people live with their parent/s, with 21% expecting to continue doing so until they are at least 30 years of age (Hunt 2017).

Up until the GFC of 2007–2008, it might be supposed that many young people had hoped—or assumed—that their experience of adulthood might be similar to that of their parents. The long-standing, longitudinal Australian Life Patterns study certainly shows that at least some young people's hopes for the future are based on the life experiences of their parents' generation: 'establishing home, family, predictable work, and the opportunity to construct meaningful relationships' (Wyn et al. 2017, p. 15). When questioned more closely, however, these young people express anxiety and a sense of being under pressure to achieve these indicators of independence and security. In Chap. 2, we suggested that push and pull factors can shed light on the familial factors and forces that may underpin young people's movements in pursuit of higher education and the future it promises. Some of the tensions experienced by young people arise from push factors such as the desire to follow what may be the settled achievements of their parents' generation, but economic and sociological pull factors are also dragging young people into other life-courses, obliging them 'to imagine life in other terms' (Howie and Campbell 2016, p. 2).

In some cases, these terms are profoundly shaped by new or recreated inequalities to which young people are particularly subject (Woodman and Wyn 2014). A recent UK survey of 2,194 16–25 year olds found that one in four (26%) believed they would have a worse standard of living than their parents or guardians, a theme to which we return in our Conclusion to this book (The Prince's Trust 2018). In Australia, where home ownership has long been a key marker or 'cultural gold standard' (Robertson 2014) of adulthood, Australian house prices are now amongst the least affordable in the world (ABC 2014), with direct consequences for young people. This is how one young person portrays their situation:

> For most people our age, participation in the job-marriage-mortgage-kids pathway is a virtual impossibility. We live with our parents or in sharehouses. Our jobs are often crappy, if we're lucky enough to have one rather than being on the dole or having our work exploited for nothing by dodgy internship merchants. Home ownership will happen not when we've worked hard and saved a deposit, but when our parents' generation, who make up 25% of the population but control over half our total wealth, retire or die (Robertson 2014).

For many such young people, the disappearing feasibility of home ownership has been a source of anger, one which flared up following what has become known as the 'smashed avo' controversy. In 2016, Australian demographer Bernard Salt penned an article in a leading broadsheet which began by spoofing the fashions of 'hipster cafes' but ended with the following homily:

> I have seen young people order smashed avocado with crumbled feta on five-grain toasted bread at [AUD]$22 a pop and more. I can afford to eat this for lunch because I am middle-aged and have raised my family. But how can young people afford to eat like this? Shouldn't

they be economising by eating at home? How often are they eating out? Twenty-two dollars several times a week could go towards a deposit on a house (Salt 2016).

The publication of this article was met with a flood of furious responses about its assumptions and constructions of youth, including calculations about the true nature of home affordability for most young people. These are just two of the many tweets that followed in its wake:

> @BernardSalt is right of course, just give up [AUD]$22 a week and you'll have a deposit on a median priced house in Sydney in 175 years (Ryan 2016).
>
> My generation loves brunch because it's two hours of distraction from the fact we'll never own real estate (Pritchard 2017).

As Ryan notes, the uproar was so great that a major home lender launched a new home loan marketing campaign with the catchphrase 'Have your smashed avo and eat it too'. Other responses included the creation of an online Avocado Toast House Deposit Calculator (Datasuarusrex 2017). The term 'smashed avo' has now become a meme in Australia that captures the despair of a generation of young people being buffeted by 'economic headwinds' that have seen the cost of housing in major cities increase by up to 20% a year (Tovey 2017). This in turn has led to a dependence on parents to either provide financial support to access housing or

> the reluctant compromise [of a] "cubby house syndrome", with underutilised spaces such as garages or rumpus rooms repurposed "to give young people some semblance of independence, even when they can't afford to fly the nest completely" (Claes, cited in Hunt 2017).

For some of our interviewees, home ownership is a key component of the imagined future. When we asked Juliette and Rose to describe their imagined personal lives in 10 years' time, a home—and the financial stability that this is implies—emerged as an important aspect for both:

> Um, it would be having a family, having a house, being close to my family in the south. It would be having a salary every month that's enough to support at least my children because my husband would have a job, I guess [laughs]. So, yes, that's basically it (Juliette, France).
>
> … one of the things that's most important to me is to have my own home because, like, I am a very home sort of person. If I have a secure place to live and I don't have to worry that much about paying my rent and mortgage, I will be the happiest [laughs] (Rose, Australia).

For both Tom and Allysa as well, owning a home is an important component of the imagined future: especially in Allysa's case, it is symbolic of the family life which she hopes will be part of that future. As for so many other young people, though, the cost of achieving this home is also a real concern:

> I would love to own a home - one day. I don't know how soon, how far, with like how expensive housing prices are. I would love – that's the dream to own my own home, not rent somewhere. It's my place: I can hang up pictures and I can make a mess. I don't have to worry about having a landlord come along and charge me 500 quid or whatever it is to fix it (Tom, UK).
>
> … it's probably going to be difficult for me to buy my new house but I am on my way … Maybe in the future, in 10 years, I am going to … have my own family. It's really important to have a house, our own house (Allysa, Australia).

Tyler and his wife already own their home but have a mortgage, like so many other Australians. In his imagined future, little will have changed in this regard in 10 years' time, a circumstance that represents both security and economic constraint:

> Realistically in the current housing market and economy and things like that, I don't see much movement … I pretty much will be in the same home, paying off the same mortgage. I don't really see a substantial ability for social mobility, I guess. I probably believe that I am probably middle-class and will be for the rest of my life (Tyler, Australia).

The costs associated with home ownership are less of a concern for Mel. Like some of her French counterparts, her parents have been able to support her while she accrues the funds she will need to buy her own home:

> I'm not the kind of person that really spends a lot of money and, like, my parents are happy for me to live at home until, like, I have that stability financially to move out. So I think buying a house should - like, there's no pressure for me to rent or move out immediately. So I think I have that time to slowly accumulate money and be in a good place before I purchase (Mel, Australia).

For Mel, this reliance on her parents is a comfortable prospect, but not all of our interviewees are content to keep accepting the financial support of their parents while they work towards home ownership or other personal goals. For Juliane, for example, the prolonged dependency which we discuss earlier is a source of some concern. She feels a sense of personal pressure to demonstrate the financial independence which is traditionally synonymous with adulthood:

> … I know that I would always have my family's back, so they would never leave me alone. … But I feel like I want to be independent. Even though I know they have the money and they are happy to support me, I think at some point it's over. My dad made his own money at 15. 10 years later, I'm not making - I am 25 - I'm not making my own money. We are in different times, but still, yep (Juliane, France).

Leaving Home to Learn

While it is clearly important to some, home ownership is not a goal to which all of our interviewees aspire. For Finlay in the UK, it is 'not a given'. He is concerned about the cost of buying a home, but it is not his first priority, either: 'there would be other things that we would—well, I would like to focus on'. For a number of our interviewees, these other things include travel and the freedom to be mobile. For Ninon, for example, owning a home may restrict her hopes to travel more widely after her studies. When we ask what her imagined home situation would be in 10 years' time, she replies:

> I think I will be renting, definitely, because if you own a house, that means that you actually stay put: you stay at one place. So not in 10 years. Also, it is very expensive and you have to work a bit before you can buy a house. So I think I will be renting (Ninon, France).

For Zaynab, too, her hopes of flexible mobility take priority over the geographic stability represented by home ownership: 'I would see myself not buying a house in 10 years, for example, and moving around'. Similarly for Isabella, the prospect of owning a home is less attractive than her dream of working in an embassy or a consulate. She began by studying political science and is now studying law with an emphasis on international relations, all of which is designed to help her realise her 'big dream, big aim'. This dream presumes a high degree of mobility, although having a 'base' from which she could come and go remains important:

> Well, if my plan goes, as I expect, I won't have to have a place because you live in the embassy, so you have got all expenses paid. But, yes, I would like - I will certainly have, like, a base, so a place where I would always go back to. And that would probably be my home in Florence. But if the travelling part adds to my life, I will probably be renting places and just have my base in Florence, where I go back to (Isabella, UK).

As we have discussed in Chap. 3, it is one of the promises of higher education that successful graduates will have access to greater social, economic and geographic mobility. It is also increasingly presumed that young people will be geographically mobile - often globally so - to take up higher education opportunities, even when this means the loss of familiar places and relationships (Marginson 2014; Pedersen and Gram 2018; Sellar and Gale 2011). In 2017, an estimated 4.6 million students moved countries for this reason, more than double the estimated figure of 2.1 million in 2001 (HSBC 2017). In Australia in the same year, the number of international students hit a record high of more than half a million: 43% of these were enrolled in higher education (Doyle 2017). These 'international sojourners' have to navigate cultural unfamiliarity as well as all the practical challenges of relocation (Tran 2013, p. 124). The vast majority also have to pay for their own education, or else their families do (Altbach and Knight 2007).

Later in this book, we will explore young people's geographic mobility in pursuit of their hopes and plans. What we would like to consider here is the way in which their mobility in pursuit of higher education is tied up with other circumstances that stem from and affect their role as family members. As we have noted earlier in the book, a number of our interviewees have relocated in order to study. In Australia, Rose has come from India, Allysa and Abi have come from Indonesia, Jack and Lila have come from China and Irina has come from Russia. A number of this cohort are receiving financial support from their families, as Lila explains:

> My mum hopes that my work doesn't affect my studies so she really supports - wishes me spend all my time to study. And then if you have extra, like, interest or time, you can do a part-time job as an interest, but not for economics reason (Lila, Australia).

In France, Juliane has relocated from Germany in order to study. Like Tom below, university for Juliane represents both geographical and social mobility. Her parents' capacity and willingness to financially support her studies reflect their hopes for her future, one that represents greater economic and other opportunity than they have had themselves:

> My dad did the lowest school education; my mum did the one just above. And my dad grew up without parents, never having money, just paying his mum rent at the age of 15. So they

really had a hard way to get where they are now. Now they are in the position to support us in our education, me going abroad and everything (Juliane, France).

Juliane's statement highlights the hope that is invested in many young people's trajectories into and from higher education, but it also points to something more: the way in which this hope may be inherited or passed down to the young university student by their parents or other family members. Like so many aspects of young people's lives, hope is typically constructed as an individualised resource, the fulfilment of which depends on the young person alone. What emerges from Juliane's account and a number of the following accounts is the degree to which hope may be shared and supported by the family. For Rose, for example, her parents' encouragement is integral to her decision to take up higher education studies in Australia. Her embarkation on these studies, with the international mobility which this entails, is an investment in a shared hope, a shared decision: 'for me, I am so intertwined with my parents and how we have, like, lived, that for me it is impossible to imagine that I would do something all by myself. It is not an option'.

Sharing and Supporting Hope Beyond Money and Shelter

For many young people, the family remains instrumental in creating key opportunity structures including access to higher education (Roberts 2009). It remains a significant source of provision and support in relation to their educational and other life goals: some young people's educational pathways may in fact depend on their family's ability to provide material resources (Butler and Muir 2017; Cuervo and Wyn 2014; Wyn et al. 2012). This is certainly the case for some of our interviewees, but parents and carers also provide important forms of support that go beyond financial resources. We observed in Chap. 3 that a number of our interviewees have chosen to pursue higher education largely because of the encouragement of their parents. Juliette's observation highlights the affective importance of this kind of family support in the pursuit of her career hopes and plans:

> Yes, [my parents] are helping me. We are not at all a rich family. So they are having difficulties helping me. But they are supporting me financially and mentally and they want me to succeed. They know I like it. I have proven to them through different experiences that I was maybe able to try and succeed in doing something in journalism. So they are behind me, yes - financially and morally, mentally (Juliette, France).

For Lila, too, the emotional support of her mother, in particular, is an essential affective resource:

> My mum doesn't, like other traditional Chinese parents, push their kids to study every day, in order to pass different kind of test and then send them to play different instrument and do extra tutorial after-school. But my parent always support my own decision, whatever is relevant to study or, like, do sport or something like that. My mum supports me (Lila, Australia).

Ninon tells a similar story. She has relocated from her family home elsewhere in France in order to study, something that her parents strongly encouraged her to do. Like Lila and a number of our other interviewees, her mother in particular has encouraged her to pursue her education and life dreams:

> ... my mum [has] always been very worried about our studies. She's always been very supportive - not just in studies, but in general, always pushing us to do things, to try things. ... She's always - she thinks: the more you do, the best it will be for you (Ninon, France).

Jessica's mother has been a similar influence and source of support in her pursuit of her imagined future. Where her father wanted her to become a pilot, 'which was never going to happen [laughs]', her mother has 'always just allowed me to do whatever I want'. She goes on to describe a familiar theme across many of our interviews—the desire of parents to see their child achieve the most that they can through their university education:

> As long as I am happy with what I am doing and I am successful at doing that, she's okay with whatever career path I choose. So as long as I don't go teach and do a half-hearted job and become like a mediocre teacher, sort of: she wants me to be the best that I can be, pretty much (Jessica, Australia).

For Lyr, too, parental support serves as an important push factor in the pursuit of his career hopes. His parents have supported his choice to take up postgraduate studies in a university quite far from the family home on the west coast of France. His first Master's degree in Japanese studies has now been followed by a second Master's degree in education, and he hopes to move on to PhD studies after this. His decision to pursue these educational goals stems from his own interests and abilities, but his mother has also been a strong influence. His studies, and the future they may enable, is also an investment in her hopes and dreams:

> I talk a lot with my parents, my mother specifically, about my studies. ... They have copies of my works. For my Japanese Master's degree, they went to the oral final thing and so they listened to me talking about 'porn' for about half an hour [laughs], which was fine. So they know precisely what I am doing. ... And with my mother, specifically ... she wanted to do a lot of things with her life, studies or arts or anything. She wasn't really allowed to by her parents. ... In a way, I feel like she's living the life she didn't have through me. ... well, I am doing it for myself, obviously, but I am happy that I do it for her as well, that she can kind of fulfil what she didn't have, through me. It is also something that pushes me (Lyr, France).

In Australia, Alice's parents have been a key influence in her decision to undertake a different professional trajectory than she might otherwise have done. She is training to be a Maths teacher even though her heart belongs to her music and her songwriting. She attributes her decision to study teaching to the strength of her parents' influence and, perhaps, her unwillingness to disappoint them:

> ... my parents are unbelievably influential and I listen to them way more than maybe I should, and I'm a good girl ... and I could kind of see their point. I'm like: yeah, fair enough. Even if I do music, I am still going to need that part-time job. Maybe teaching is not so bad: maybe the hours are cushy, maybe it's long holidays. I am okay at it, anyway. I like Maths, so maybe - maybe I will just do it (Alice, Australia).

In this way, Alice's parents are acting as a kind of pull factor in her higher education decisions: they are pulling her towards their own version of the imagined future. Like Lyr, she faces the challenge of navigating the complex contemporary labour market while carrying or trying to fulfil the hopes and aspirations of her parents. This does not seem to feel like a burden for either her or Lyr, but for some of the other young people we interviewed, the influence of parent/s and other family members on their higher education choices and plans has been more equivocal. For Tom in the UK, who grew up in a working-class area, the decision to pursue a higher degree sets him somewhat outside the family tradition, as he explains: 'higher education is not really running deep in our family. My mum went to university but apart from that, no-one else has really done it before'. His mother has encouraged his hopes to become a university lecturer—'we will try and help you the best we can: do whatever you want'—but his father is more dubious:

> ... [he] never really gave me a shot of going to university. Not a bad dad in the slightest. He just didn't see it in me as an academic-type. He was always like: 'oh, Tom will end up ... being a technician', or something like him.

Perhaps because of this, Tom has an almost militant determination to fulfil his career hopes, unencumbered by the challenges we have described earlier in this book:

> I have never seen anything that can hold me back ... people have told me I can't do a lot of things and you just end up doing it. People say, 'you will never go to Africa' – [I] got to Africa. Most people don't do that in life. I got told I would never get First on any of my essays last year - I got First in at least three of them. I don't believe people can tell you what you can't do in life. You can do anything you set your mind to, really (Tom, UK).

Forming Families of Their Own

The importance of parents and carers in shaping and supporting young university students' education hopes and plans raises the question of how these hopes and plans relate to the prospect or experience of forming their own families. While one UK study has found that 66% of young people born after 1995 are optimistic about being able to form a family of their own (NCB 2014), for others, such as the young Finnish people interviewed by Gordon and Lahelma, the prospect of a future family is a source of uncertainty and concern: 'Do they want children, who with and when?' (2002, p. 11). The young women in that study have particular concerns about assuming the responsibilities associated with children: many want to postpone motherhood for as long as possible, in order to have time to travel and build a career. This is a concern shared by some of our own interviewees as well. For Morgane, for example, combining family formation with her imagined career in journalism already feels like a juggling act, even before either circumstance has eventuated:

> I think there are two directions ... I am struggling to ... stay in the middle, like, to have values, to keep them, to give them to next generations, but at the same time to be flexible in my mind, to consider many different life perspectives – to not just stay on one idea, like to

have a family, children, husband, that's all. That is my prospect. It is part of what I want to do but at the same time I want to have a career, have a job … to be free (Morgane, France).

Echoing the 'quiet revolution' of women's participation in education for career-building in the latter 20th century described earlier in the book (Goldin and Mitchell 2017), Ines acknowledges that there may be push and pull tensions between family formation, pursuing a career and satisfying other life goals, but she is more optimistic than Morgane about the possibility of doing all of those things:

I have many friends at my age who don't want to marry, who don't want to have children. … I think it's very fashionable today to be just independent woman … because sometimes we think marriage or children is going back to the old times and being a housewife. But I think you can mix the two. You can be an independent woman: you can have responsibilities, a good wage, and have a husband or family (Ines, France).

Forsberg and Timonen's study of young Irish people's imagined future families found that for some, romantic love as an idea is less important than economic outcomes such as work. As one of these young people explains, 'romantic relationships are not highly valued above work life goals. … The concept of love is seen as an inefficient use of time' (2018, p. 774). Certainly for Zaynab, Kim and Paloma, pursuing their desired career currently takes priority over the prospect of a partner and/or children. Children, in particular, represent a possible distraction or deflection from their ability to achieve their career goals:

I don't think I have that priority of finding a partner and having a family. I have been so, sort of, interested in languages for so long: I just want to make sure I have a job that can sort of fit that passion, those requirements. So I would say I would be fine single, I think… but I don't know. No goals for that - no precise goals for that (Zaynab, France).

When I was small, I wanted to have kids. I was like: 'yeah, when I am 25, I will get married. At 27, my first child'. Now I am almost 26 and a half, even more than 26 and a half, and, like, yeah [laughs], it didn't work out like that; which is not that bad. But I don't know, because kids would be a lot of responsibility - a lot of time, a lot of nerves [laughs]. I don't know (Kim, France).

… I don't really see myself with a big family, like husband/wife, children et cetera, et cetera … As I see myself now, living alone in 10 years would be nice, with a nice job and that sort of thing. I am really career oriented, so – [laughs] (Paloma, France).

In the UK, George expresses much the same view. While he clearly sees a partner and children in his long-term imagined future, career is the priority at present, and the two do not appear to be compatible:

I just don't really know how things are going to shape up. I very much would like to have a partner, like to have kids one day. I was speaking with a girl that I nearly got with a couple of months ago and I think we kind of both realised we are very career-driven. So at the moment, at least, I feel like I am prepared to make those sacrifices within my personal life, if it pays off in my career. Equally, at the moment, I don't really feel a rush. If you said to me, 'you are going to be 50 and you are going to be alone', then I would be more concerned, versus 32 and alone (George, UK).

For Alice too, in Australia, the great priority is to further her music career, 'which is a slow and painful process'. Her imagined future includes 'performing full-time, touring or something, releasing music'. It leaves little room for 'partners and houses and cars and mortgages and kids'. For some of our other interviewees, though, an intimate relationship and family is a key priority. Some, such as Becky and Abi, already have a child, while others are either in a stable intimate relationship or comfortable about the prospect of such a relationship and family formation. Juliette imagines having at least two children:

> I would like to be married in 10 years. I think that would be possible [laughs]. Because I am in a relationship, so it's highly prob. Um, kids? Yes, I would be 34, so yes, I would say one kid and a second on its way [laughs], maybe (Juliette, France).

Juliane, too, imagines forming a family, but also has a strong sense of where she would like to raise her children. In this way, geography emerges as a pull factor in forming her imagined future as a family member:

> I would be living in - close to a city that I like, preferably Berlin, but not right in the city, because I don't think it is a good place to raise children right in the city. I would have children: maybe one and then a second one is coming, sometime (Juliane, France).

For Lyr, too, who describes his career aims in detail and who is doing a great deal to bring those aims to fruition, the 'main hope' remains 'to have someone romantically'. He goes on to explain this:

> I guess it might be surprising because I seem to be pursuing a career in teaching and everything, but, to me, I feel like even if I had a successful teaching life, recognised by my peers and everything - it would be great, and obviously blessed with all that - but I still feel like something would be missing. I would be failing in a way, if I didn't really happen to be happy, romantically speaking (Lyr, France).

This hope of a future relationship is also a push factor in Lyr's intended eventual mobility away from France. In the Introduction, we refer to the technological developments and changes in young people's use of media and social media that are shaping their worlds. Lyr's future mobility may be driven by his desire to form a relationship, one that has only been possible through technological mediation:

> ... because I am a gay man, I meet a lot of people online and I was met people romantically online, one of which I am currently interested in [laughs], and who happens to be an American. Hopefully, in 10 years, I will be with him in America. But you never know.

For others still, family expectations play a strong part in the way in which they envisage their future relationships. Rose is expected to return to India after her studies in Australia, and to get married there. As she explains, 'the culture I come from, you have to get married ... So it's really not in my hands'. Her imagined future is subject to the interwoven pull factors of family, culture and geography. At the same time, completing her Master of Counselling and realising her dream of working in her own private practice remains a firm priority. This emerges when we ask her whether she might marry someone in Australia instead, and stay in the country:

> ... I am really not the sort of person who would want to uproot my whole life for just one decision. Something that I have worked for so much, something that I have wanted so badly, and to just take all that away and to just go back, just because you are married - no. But if

you find someone who is supportive of your dream, then I don't mind. As long as I am doing what I want to do, it doesn't matter if it is here or there. But just to move back for marriage, that's something I won't do (Rose, Australia).

Comments such as this recall our suggestion at the start of this chapter that intimate relationships and family may still represent an important resource for managing the uncertainties of life, a safe haven amidst flux and fluidity. For Rose, though, this safe haven must provide recognition and support for her hopes and plans: it must help her to realise her educational goals and the imagined future she has worked so hard to achieve.

Parenting and Higher Education

As we have seen, the imagined future for some of our interviewees includes the hope of having children. For university students who are already parents of dependent children, higher education may have other affective meanings. Earlier in this chapter, we observed that some of our interviewees are carrying their parents' hopes as well as their own. For students who are also parents, higher education can represent a similar transmission of hope to the next generation. As Brooks (2015) notes, undertaking a degree can be seen as one way of being a positive role model for one's children. This is certainly a consideration for at least one of our interviewees. For Abi, the degree he hopes to obtain is also a legacy, something that will benefit his daughter:

> ...I have a daughter, I need to educate her ... maybe the knowledge/experience from learning at this university, can help me not only to empower me to get better career in the future, but, also, how to educate my daughter at the same time (Abi, Australia).

For the parents of young children, higher education may also be a means of securing the future for those children. For Becky, the degree she hopes to obtain is the key to realising her and her partner's dreams of leaving the UK with their young daughter for what they hope will be a better life in Australia:

> My original plan was to go into educational psychology. I had a little girl, and while I was on maternity, I realised I was never going to earn enough money teaching, doing what I was doing, and there wasn't enough time in the day to do it altogether. So I decided that - we want to travel, we want to move country as a family, so in order to give us the best prospects, in being able to get somewhere, I would have the highest level of education that I could possibly get. And the easiest way to do that is to go back to university.

This plan comes at a cost, however. While the future may look better than it may have done had Becky not returned to study, the decision to do so has had an immediate impact on her family life. She describes the need to balance this family life with her academic plans:

> This is the time that you settle, you buy your home, you home-make, and I am out there getting another degree and then starting a Master's and not being at moment with my daughter. She's in nursery four days a week, which is what has to happen (Becky, UK).

Becky's comments recall Brooks' interviews with student-parents in two UK universities. In this case, the emotion that they most commonly express is that of guilt. She cites one young woman, Emily, who describes her feelings of being torn between her responsibilities as a parent and child carer and the responsibilities that arise from her studies:

> At home she sometimes says 'Oh mummy, are you doing your work?' And I say, 'Yes I'm doing my work.' She's like, 'And then can we go to the park?' And I'm just like, 'OK'. It makes me feel quite guilty really a lot of the time, because I've got to do, you know spend so much time on the work and I feel like it's not fair on her (Brooks 2015, p. 510).

Brooks' work also highlights the contradictory discourses and expectations that can confront young university students who are parents. By contrast to Scandinavian nations, which tend to accept that parents may also be workers or students, education policy in Anglophone countries such as the UK and Australia promotes 'a normative parent, who is expected to be closely involved in his or her child's education, facilitate and support homework, monitor progress, "police" schools, and actively intervene with teachers when necessary' (Brooks 2015, p. 511). This normative parenting role is in direct conflict with the normative role of the higher education student that we described in Chap. 2: the 'aspirational, enterprising young person who has a prudential eye to the future' (Kelly 2017, p. 62). This conflict is not simply conceptual: it is one that is affectively experienced by the student-parent, especially by the student-mother. As Brooks notes:

> Given the negative impact such feelings of guilt are likely to have on students (in terms of their wellbeing if not their academic progress), and the likelihood that they will deter some women from entering higher education entirely, it is important that the public nature of such feelings – and their clear links to socially constructed national norms – is made visible' (2015, p. 517).

Conclusion

Earlier in this book, we suggested that higher education, both as a system and an idea, promotes an individualised image of the young university student as an actor who is primarily—even solely—responsible for the formulation of their own hopeful imagined future and for its realisation. The truth is that the contemporary educational contract operates not only between young university students and their universities, but extends to their families as well: many young people develop their hopes in concert with significant others such as partners, parents and even children.

In this chapter, we have considered how the entrepreneurial strategies required for educational and employment success may depend on and affect important family relationships. We have also noted that those family relationships are intrinsic to the kinds of strategies and sacrifices that young university students may make to realise their hopes. If anything, the family is playing a more central role in the hopes, plans and strategies that are invested in higher education. Just as paid work is becoming more essential for greater numbers of young university students, so too there has been an increase in the importance of family support for those students (Antonucci 2016; Brooks 2018). This has real affective as well as practical implications. It can see an increased 'mental weight' being carried by young university students, as mounting student debts and competitive educational and labour markets take their toll in feelings of pressure to succeed, anxiety and even guilt (Antonucci 2016, p. 82). As we have seen from Becky's account, this anxiety and guilt may also be felt by students who are parents themselves.

Whatever the nature of their family situation, family bonds and family hopes can be essential influences in young people's imagined and actual trajectories through and beyond higher education. At a time when youth is being increasingly protracted and prolonged, the role of the family for young university students is arguably becoming more significant rather than diminishing. This is one of the less well-rehearsed truths of contemporary youth, but one that underpins and gives context to the hopes and strategies that many young people pursue for the future.

References

Altbach, P. G., & Knight, J. (2007). The internationalization of higher education: Motivations and realities. *Journal of Studies in International Education, 11*(3–4), 290–305. https://doi.org/10.1177/1028315307303542.

Antonucci, L. (2016). *Student lives in crisis: Deepening inequality in times of austerity*. Bristol: Policy Press.

ABC (Australian Broadcasting Corporation) (2014, Sept 14). Australia has third highest house price-to-income ratio in the world: IMF. *ABC News*. Retrieved November 1, 2018, from https://www.abc.net.au/news/2014-06-12/australia-has-third-highest-house-price-to-income-ratio/5517452.

Bauman, Z. (2000). *Liquid modernity*. Cambridge: Polity Press.

Beck-Gernsheim, E. (1998). On the way to a post-familial family: From a community of need to elective affinities. *Theory, Culture & Society, 15*(3–4), 53–70. https://doi.org/10.1177/0263276498015003004.

Berger, B. (2017). *The family in the modern age: More than a lifestyle choice*. New York: Routledge.

Brooks, R. (2015). Social and spatial disparities in emotional responses to education: Feelings of 'guilt' among student-parents. *British Educational Research Journal, 41*(3), 505–519. https://doi.org/10.1002/berj.3154.

Brooks, R. (2018). Understanding the higher education student in Europe: A comparative analysis. *Compare: A Journal of Comparative and International Education, 48*(4), 500–517. https://doi.org/10.1080/03057925.2017.1318047.

Butler, R., & Muir, K. (2017). Young people's education biographies: Family relationships, social capital and belonging. *Journal of Youth Studies, 20*(3), 316–331. https://doi.org/10.1080/13676261.2016.1217318.

Cairns, D., Growiec, K., & de Almeida Alves, N. (2014). Another 'missing middle'? The marginalised majority of tertiary-educated youth in Portugal during the economic crisis. *Journal of Youth Studies, 17*(8), 1046–1060. https://doi.org/10.1080/13676261.2013.878789.

Cook, J. (2016). Young people's strategies for coping with parallel imaginings of the future. *Time & Society, 25*(3), 700–717. https://doi.org/10.1177/0961463x15609829.

Cuervo, H., & Wyn, J. (2014). Reflections on the use of spatial and relational metaphors in youth studies. *Journal of Youth Studies, 17*(7), 901–915. https://doi.org/10.1080/13676261.2013.878796.

References

Datasuarusrex. (2017). *Avocado Toast House Deposit Calculator*. Retrieved February 3, 2018, from https://datasaurus-rex.com/gallery/avocado-toast-house-deposit-calculator.

Doyle, J. (2017, Feb 22). International students studying in Australia reach record number, Education Department figures show. *ABC News*. Retrieved January 11, 2019, from http://www.abc.net.au/news/2017-02-22/record-number-of-international-students-in-australia-in-2016/8291284.

Eurofound. (2014). *Social situation of young people in Europe*. Luxembourg: Publications Office of the European Union.

Forsberg, H., & Timonen, V. (2018). The future of the family as envisioned by young adults in Ireland. *Journal of Youth Studies, 21*(6), 765–779. https://doi.org/10.1080/13676261.2017.1420761.

Furlong, A. (2016a). Foreword. In C. Leccardi & E. Ruspini (Eds.), *A new youth? Young people, generations and family life* (pp. xv–xix). London & New York: Routledge.

Furlong, A. (2016b). The changing landscape of youth and young adulthood. In A. Furlong (Ed.), *Routledge handbook of youth and young adulthood* (2nd ed., pp. 3–11). London: Routledge.

Goldin, C., & Mitchell, J. (2017). The new life cycle of women's employment: Disappearing humps, sagging middles, expanding tops. *Journal of Economic Perspectives, 31*(1), 161–182. https://doi.org/10.1257/jep.31.1.161.

Gordon, T., & Lahelma, E. (2002). Becoming an adult: Possibilities and limitations-dreams and fears. *Young, 10*(2), 2–18.

Gray, J., Geraghty, R., & Ralph, D. (2017). *Family rhythms: The changing textures of family life in Ireland*. Oxford: Oxford University Press.

Hakim, C. (2018). *Models of the family in modern societies: Ideals and realities*. Oxon and New York: Routledge.

Honwana, A. (2014). Waithood: Youth transitions and social change. In D. Foeken, T. Dietz, L. Haan & L. Johnson (Eds.), *Development and equity: An interdisciplinary exploration by ten scholars from Africa, Asia and Latin America*. (pp. 28–40). Brill Online.

Howie, L., & Campbell, P. (2016). Guerrilla selfhood: Imagining young people's entrepreneurial futures. *Journal of Youth Studies, 19*(7), 906–920. https://doi.org/10.1080/13676261.2015.1123236.

HSBC (2017). *The value of education: Higher and higher. Global Report*. London: HSBC.

Hunt, E. (2017, May 8). Australia's housing affordability crisis creating 'dependent generation' – study. *The Guardian*. Retrieved November 1, 2018, from https://www.theguardian.com/australia-news/2017/may/08/australias-housing-affordability-crisis-creating-dependent-generation-study.

Kelly, P. (2017). Growing up after the GFC: Responsibilisation and mortgaged futures. *Discourse: Studies in the Cultural Politics of Education, 38*(1), 57–69. https://doi.org/10.1080/01596306.2015.1104852.

Langevang, T. (2008). 'We are managing!' Uncertain paths to respectable adulthoods in Accra Ghana. *Geoforum, 39*(6), 2039–2047. https://doi.org/10.1016/j.geoforum.2008.09.003.

Leathwood, C., & O'Connell, P. (2003). 'It's a struggle': The construction of the 'new student' in higher education. *Journal of Education Policy, 18*(6), 597–615. https://doi.org/10.1080/0268093032000145863.

Leccardi, C. (2005). Facing uncertainty: Temporality and biographies in the new century. *Young, 13*(2), 123–146. https://doi.org/10.1177/1103308805051317.

Marginson, S. (2014). Foreword. In B. Streitwieser (Ed.), *Internationalisation of higher education and global mobility* (pp. 7–10). Oxford: Symposium Books Ltd.

Mourshed, M., Patel, J. & Suder, K. (2017). *Education to employment: Getting Europe's youth into work*. McKinsey Center for Government. Retrieved June 2, 2018, from http://egdcfoundation.org/work/assets/McKinsey-Education-to-Employment-Europe.pdf.

National Children's Bureau [NCB]. (2014). *Who is generation next?*. London: National Children's Bureau.

Nowotny, H. (1994). *Time: The modern and postmodern experience*. Cambridge: Polity Press.

Oinonen, E. (2018). Under pressure to become – from a student to entrepreneurial self. *Journal of Youth Studies, 21*(10), 1344–1360. https://doi.org/10.1080/13676261.2018.1468022.

Pedersen, H. D., & Gram, M. (2018). 'The brainy ones are leaving': The subtlety of (un) cool places through the eyes of rural youth. *Journal of Youth Studies, 21*(5), 620–635. https://doi.org/10.1080/13676261.2017.1406071.

Pickard, S. (2014). French youth policy in an age of austerity: Plus ça change? *International Journal of Adolescence and Youth, 19*(sup1), 48–61. https://doi.org/10.1080/02673843.2013.863732.

Pritchard, T. (2017). 17 tweets about smashed avo and houses that'll make you laugh or cry, either one. Retrieved October 13, 2017, from https://www.buzzfeed.com/tahliapritchard/i-dont-even-like-avo-wheres-my-damn-house?utm_term=.jlOdmBQr6#.ehyWvPBAM.

Punch, S. (2015). Youth transitions and migration: Negotiated and constrained interdependencies within and across generations. *Journal of Youth Studies, 18*(2), 262–276. https://doi.org/10.1080/13676261.2014.944118.

Roberts, K. (2009). Opportunity structures then and now. *Journal of Education and Work, 22*(5), 355–368. https://doi.org/10.1080/13639080903453987.

Robertson, E. (2014, Oct 17). Generation Y didn't go crazy in a vacuum. How can we enjoy life when our future is so uncertain? *The Guardian*. Retrieved November 15, 2017, from https://www.theguardian.com/commentisfree/2014/oct/17/generation-y-didnt-go-crazy-in-a-vacuum-how-can-we-enjoy-life-when-our-future-is-so-uncertain.

Ryan, B. (2016, Oct 18). Millennials react to Bernard Salt's attack on smashed avo. *The Australian*. Retrieved November 15, 2017, from https://www.theaustralian.com.au/life/columnists/bernard-salt/millenials-react-to-bernard-salts-attack-on-smashed-avo/news-story/a0e8473f9e80663d7569364930aa0321.

Salt, B. (2016, Oct 16). Moralisers, we need you! *The Australian*. Retrieved November 15, 2017, from http://www.theaustralian.com.au/life/weekend-australian-magazine/moralisers-we-need-you/news-story/6bdb24f77572be68330bd306c14ee8a3#itm=tauslnewslaus_authors_index|1|authors_storyBlock_headline|Moralisers%2C_we_need_you!|index|author&itmt=1476580893995.

Sellar, S., & Gale, T. (2011). Mobility, aspiration, voice: A new structure of feeling for student equity in higher education. *Critical Studies in Education, 52*(2), 115–134. https://doi.org/10.1080/17508487.2011.572826.

Stone, J., Berrington, A., & Falkingham, J. (2014). Gender, turning points, and boomerangs: Returning home in young adulthood in Great Britain. *Demography, 51*(1), 257–276. https://doi.org/10.1007/s13524-013-0247-8.

The Prince's Trust (2018). *The Prince's Trust Macquarie Youth Index 2018*. Retrieved September 22, 2018, from https://www.princes-trust.org.uk/about-the-trust/news-views/macquarie-youth-index-2018-annual-report.

Tovey, J. (2017, May 18). Why the smashed avo meme refuses to die. *Sydney Morning Herald*. Retrieved November 15, 2017, from http://www.smh.com.au/comment/why-the-smashed-avo-meme-refuses-to-die-20170518-gw7m6i.html.

Tran, L. (2013). Transformative learning and international students negotiating higher education. In S. Sovic & M. Blythman (Eds.), *International students negotiating higher education: Critical perspectives* (pp. 124–141). London and New York: Routledge.

Valentine, G. (2003). Boundary crossings: Transitions from childhood to adulthood. *Children's Geographies, 1*(1), 37–52.

Wildermuth, N., & Dalsgaard, A. L. (2006). Imagined futures, present lives youth, media and modernity in the changing economy of northeast Brazil. *Young, 14*(1), 9–31. https://doi.org/10.1177/1103308806059811.

Williamson, H. (2016). Complex knowledge, coherent policy? Understanding and responding to young people's needs in times of austerity and crisis. *Italian Journal of Sociology of Education, 8*(2), 213–224. https://doi.org/10.14658/pupj-ijse-2016-2-10.

Woodman, D. (2011). Young people and the future: Multiple temporal orientations shaped in interaction with significant others. *Young, 19*(2), 111–128. https://doi.org/10.1177/110330881001900201.

References

Woodman, D., & Wyn, J. (2014). *Youth and generation: Rethinking change and inequality in the lives of young people*. London: Sage.

Wyn, J., Cahill, H., Woodman, D., Cuervo, H., Chesters, J., Cook, J., et al. (2017). *Gen Y on Gen Y*. Melbourne: University of Melbourne.

Wyn, J., Lantz, S., & Harris, A. (2012). Beyond the 'transitions' metaphor: Family relations and young people in late modernity. *Journal of Sociology, 48*(1), 3–22. https://doi.org/10.1177/1440783311408971.

Chapter 5
Planning for Uncertainty: The Workforce Ahead

Introduction

> I think [the future for young people] is not too bright … for the moment, not all people but middle-aged people from the baby-boom, for example, are really assertive and privileged and they think they have everything owed to them. And young people just have to eat… eat shit and to work, to work, to work, to work. We have to have two jobs; we have to wait a lot for us to buy a house; and even paid enough… middle-aged people are always telling us 'oh, you should work more'. Yeah, well, if I already have two jobs, I can't (Paloma, France).

As the 21st century progresses, more people than ever have higher education qualifications. These qualifications are widely seen to be important tools for young people navigating complex global labour markets. They are also promoted as tools that may help them navigate a future which, as we note earlier, is often conceived as 'a space crowded with risks and contingencies' (Cook 2016, p. 700) Higher education and other post-school qualifications are predictors of labour market participation as well as social outcomes such as self-reported health, community engagement and interpersonal trust (AIHW 2015; OECD 2014a, b), but labour market conditions and young people's attitudes towards them appear to be changing in light of the uncertainty which we have described earlier. As one study has argued:

> Youth is a crucial time of life when young people start realizing their aspirations, assuming their economic independence and finding their place in society. The global jobs crisis has exacerbated the vulnerability of young people in terms of: (i) higher unemployment, (ii) lower quality jobs for those who find work, (iii) greater labour market inequalities among different groups of young people, (iv) longer and more insecure school to-work transitions, and (v) increased detachment from the labour market (Elder and Kring 2016, p. iii).

Higher education, its promises in relation to work, and the value of qualifications are also changing. Following Brooks' (2018) work, this book draws on our review of the recent international literature and our interviews with 30 young university students in France, the UK and Australia to consider the current and imagined future lives of young university students as family members, workers and political actors. This chapter continues our close analysis of these roles by looking at what might lie ahead in the labour market for our interviewees and, more broadly, for other young university students. In it, we reflect on how young people construct their own hopes and plans for their imagined futures as workers within the contemporary worlds of work. We also explore the impact of other factors and developments such as the massification of higher education, the impact of economic downturns, technology, and the emergence of the gig economy. These combined trends provide the context for the new concept of homo promptus that we develop in the following chapter.

The Changing Value of Higher Education Qualifications

As we have discussed in detail in Chap. 3, the acquisition of higher qualifications has been steadily rising over the past decades across OECD nations (OECD 2015a). By OECD standards, the levels of higher education attainment across the three main countries discussed in this book are comparatively high. In 2016, Australia, France and the UK were ranked in the top 15 OECD countries for higher education attainment by 25–34 year olds: 49.3%, 44% and 52% of this age group respectively were tertiary qualified (OECD 2016).

This growth has largely been the product of policy. Widening access, raising standards and further investment in education have been promoted as strategies to deliver opportunity, prosperity and justice to both individuals and whole nations (Woodman and Wyn 2015). The importance attached to post-school educational credentials also reflects a tightening bond between education, work and reward within educational policy and discourses: better credentials are promised to lead to greater post-graduation employment and career advantage. They also offer employers an efficient means of selection for employment, based on individual achievement.

In Chap. 3, we also argued that the locus of responsibility rests on individuals both to invest in higher levels of education to match the growing demands of a competitive and uncertain skilled labour market, and to secure desirable work within that labour market (Cuervo et al. 2013; Robertson and Dale 2015; Thomson 2013). Particularly in individualised and flexible labour markets such as Australia and the UK, higher education is constructed as an investment in work credentials, a necessary response to employers' preferences for talent and competence: a significant motivation for undertaking university study is to ameliorate the risk of being uncompetitive in the labour market. As Kelly notes, education 'is an enterprise in which an investment in education and training and work increasingly looks like a mortgaging of an uncertain future' (2017, p. 57). Student identities as consumers, clients and investors are formed and influenced within this context (Antonucci 2016; Brooks 2018; Sukarieh and Tannock 2017). As one study suggests:

> Without significant postsecondary education, today's youth face a future of downward mobility, social marginalization and even exclusion. With a multitude of potential paths and the high risks of becoming marginalized in society without adequate education and occupational training, a successful transition to adulthood depends on how much a youth invests in postsecondary education after graduating from high school (Heckhausen et al. 2013, p. 1385).

The case is somewhat different in France where, as we found earlier, young people's academic choices can be constrained or even predetermined by the state allocation system (Pickard 2016). In France, the relationship between education and the labour market is still predominantly influenced by meritocratic *Concours Général* examination outcomes. French student identities are largely formed within the context of this meritocracy and by civil service aspirations: the language of investment that frames university students as workers-in-the-making is rarely drawn upon (Antonucci 2016; Brooks 2018; Brown et al. 2016). Despite such differences between countries, some common themes emerge.

Strategies for an Imagined Career

Virtually all of our interviewees across France, Australia and the UK are working towards an imagined career, as opposed to a more ephemeral job. When we asked her whether she anticipates having a career or a job in 10 years' time, Grace says that she will 'definitely' have a career

> because I feel a job sounds like something that you have to do because you need to have a salary. You need to have a wage to just live. But a career is something that you choose to do, something that you are very passionate about, that you like (Grace, France).

In Australia, Jessica is also seeking 'a career over a job'. As she explains, 'a job is short-term. It is a very short outlook, whereas career is long-term, it's for life'. In France, Ines, too, draws a clear contrast between a career and a job. She is hoping for 'a career with responsibilities because I really admire women with responsibilities and that's what I want to become later'. While she is working towards this career, she is happy 'to start with a job, maybe, and evolve with time and gain responsibility with time'.

Analyses of investment rates of return on higher education qualifications amongst OECD countries (2017), in the US (Oreopoulos and Petronijevic 2013), Australia (Corliss et al. 2013; Daly et al. 2015; Dockery and Miller 2012) and the UK (Green and Zhu 2010) all show generally positive benefits in the wage-earning potential and career trajectories of graduates compared to those without the same qualifications. For our interviewees, though, the link between higher education and career is more than about earning a better salary. Abi wants to be a teacher not because of the money, but because he wants to see his students succeed. For Mel, too, pursuing her desired career is about more than income. She uses the language of investment that is so commonly promoted by the discourses of higher education, but she does so in a way that is more affectively nuanced:

> You don't do it for the pay … whatever I end up doing, I want to do it because there's a personal investment and because it's more than just 'oh, 9 to 5, I leave the school and then it is out of my mind'. Like, I want it to be something that I can genuinely invest myself into and I can genuinely see some kind of impact happening (Mel, Australia).

Like Abi, Lila speaks of having a 'lifetime commitment' to teaching, but it is clear that paid work is only one aspect of what matters to her in the long term:

> I [would] prefer to take part-time teaching and half of the time I can spend on my own, like, interests. My own interests from two years ago until now and probably still keep going is health and nutrition. It is really interesting, like, diet and healthy food, like paleo food and stuff. Willing to help others to improve their health and not [eating] too many processed food. I also want to … do my own research and write books and recipes and things like that, like, related to my teaching job because it is helping others (Lila, Australia).

A desire for this kind of career satisfaction, including the satisfaction of 'helping others', is shared by some of our other interviewees as well. We asked Jessica what it was about her dream career (teaching the International Baccalaureate in Hong Kong, where she grew up) that was most important to her:

> I think mostly just being able to say that, at the end of the day, when I get home, 'yes, I'm tired, yes, I may be not wanting to see the kids anymore that day, but I am loving the job still' … but then also, at the same time, [be] able to continue to expand my specialisation which is business, to be able to expand that and then apply that back to the students in real-world perspectives (Jessica, Australia).

Part of the attraction of career as an idea is the flexibility and adaptability with which our interviewees associate it. In Australia, for example, Rose's dreams of setting up a private counselling practice are partly motivated by the prospect of 'working according to my hours and my preferences and my client groups'. Some are also keenly aware of the need for this flexibility and adaptability in the light of a complex and changing labour market. In France, Sophia has wanted to be a teacher since her early teenage years. This is how she describes the future as she has imagined it since then:

> Just yes, I am going to … get my baccalauréat and get my Bachelor, Master's, CAPES [teacher training], boom! That's it! At age 23, I am a teacher. Everything is good. I can do whatever I want. I still get paid holidays, lots of holidays during the year. I can do whatever I want, I can travel and all of that.

This imagined pathway is now changing under the influence of her partner and exposure to other career possibilities, as she explains:

> … I went to Berlin last year. I encountered so many different people with different backgrounds. … now, I have had this idea, maybe, of being a promoter for festivals because that's what my partner does. And I helped him for a festival and I did a good job. Also, I really liked it [realising]: 'oh, okay, there's something else out there'. I know, like in my core, that I need to be a teacher at some point, but maybe now I am realising that I can also do that for a couple of years and then maybe I could try and do something else, to see what else there is out there for me. Maybe about writing, maybe about music, or organisation of events (Sophia, France).

Also in France, Ninon believes that she 'will have a career with different jobs'. She sees this as intrinsic to her chosen field of journalism: 'people change a lot, and you don't keep the same job your entire life, where you actually change your field of expertise, maybe or the country you work in'. This is not a source of anxiety for

Ninon: it is an accepted aspect of her preferred professional work. Still in France, Juliette is similarly 'open to everything'. She is also aware of the forces beyond her control—including labour market forces—that may require her to be flexible about her career hopes and plans. As part of her efforts to strategically manage an unknowable future, she is already preparing herself for the prospect of having to seek other options if her hopes and plans cannot be fulfilled:

> I don't think it's sad to have the same career our whole lives … but I also know it's very hard. I don't want to be broken if it doesn't work or it doesn't work anymore at a certain point. That's why I thought about those other options that would please me as well (Juliette, France).

These young people understand their careers as projects that are not linear but that may change with circumstances and experience. They also understand this change to be a function of external factors as much as of personal choice. In Australia, Tyler retains a strong intention to work in his chosen field of psychology. At the same time, he is sharply aware of the labour market circumstances that may affect his future employment in that field:

> … culturally at the moment, there is a very strong focus on mental health and things like that, which, you know, in terms of my career prospect is unfortunately a positive thing. The more focus on mental health, obviously, the more psychologists are going to be in demand and things like that. Whereas … particularly in the US, you see a lot of right wing extreme kind of culture that probably don't believe in a lot of that – that is probably a bit of a generalisation, but … if that were to become more mainstream, then I would certainly see a lower demand in my skill-set. You know, sometimes I joke that we are at 'peak psychology' (Tyler, Australia).

As Tyler's account suggests, young people's career hopes, plans and strategies are subject to wider forces that may shape their working lives during and following university study. Here are four examples of those forces or trends.

Work and the Massification of Higher Education

Firstly, as we discussed in Chap. 3, the promise of returns on young people's investment in higher education is increasingly challenged by the recent massification of the sector. The number of universities continues to grow and with them the number of graduates, but this does not necessarily increase the 'high value social outcomes that graduates can reach' (Marginson 2016, p. 414). As Holmes suggests:

> Given that higher education institutions do not themselves control the labour market (and neither does any other agency, in a market-based economy and free society), they cannot guarantee employment outcomes. What they can do, it is argued, is take steps to promote the *likelihood* that their graduates will gain what may be deemed as appropriate employment (2013, pp. 540–541, original emphasis).

Concerns that the expansion of education will lead to a surplus of graduates are not new. Over 40 years ago in the US, Freeman (1976) argued that an excessive supply of university graduates would lead to a lasting underutilisation of graduates' skills. More recently, the OECD (2015b) has questioned the capacity of global labour markets to keep rewarding higher levels of education with higher earnings and better chances of employment, and to absorb the projected 45% of people in OECD countries likely to have higher education qualifications by 2030. The crowding of skilled labour markets has already been noted in both Australia (Karmel and Carroll 2016) and the UK (Tholen 2017a; Tomlinson 2012).

As the number of tertiary qualified individuals rises globally, the value of higher educational credentials as a strategy for gaining secure and meaningful employment is also eroding (Côté 2014; Mavromaras et al. 2013; Vuolo et al. 2016). Two effects arise from this, both with implications for young people. 'Credentialism' (Karmel 2015; Mavromaras and McGuinness 2007) involves 'an increase over time in the education standards for specific jobs and which is not necessary for the effective achievement of tasks across positions in the labour market' (Dockery and Miller 2012, p. 7). 'Credential inflation' (Collins 1979) occurs where labour market entry requirements are raised as increasing numbers of higher educated young people complete for limited roles and greater earning power. These two processes have become part of the lexicon that describes higher education's relationship to the contemporary workforce.

Some graduate qualifications do appear to have greater value in relation to workforce mobility, as we have shown earlier, but recent studies suggest a decline in the availability of graduate jobs overall (e.g. Karmel and Carroll 2016). Some European and UK-based studies show an emerging 'hourglass' (Goos and Manning 2007) shape to graduate labour markets, with increases in the proportion of top-end and low-end jobs coming at the expense of jobs in the middle-skill range (Holmes and Mayhew 2015; Tholen 2017a, b; Tholen et al. 2016). There are also examples of a mismatch of certain qualifications with available work (notwithstanding other influences such as gender and socioeconomic status). This is most visible in the higher returns for those graduating from the medical sciences compared to those who study the humanities.

What becomes apparent is that there is an emerging generation of over-educated graduates who face the risk of both unemployment and underemployment in their fields of study, despite their qualifications and despite the strategies they have undertaken to avoid such outcomes (Green and Henseke 2016; ILO 2013a, b). Many qualified individuals are accepting work in occupations that do not use the skills, knowledge and abilities developed through their higher education study. In their US study, Fogg and Harrington (2011) describe a graduate 'mal-employment' (p. 54), where the mismatch between qualifications and available work has resulted in skill underutilisation, lower employment status, poor job quality, limited choices and wages penalties. This trend is also evident in Australia (Karmel 2015; Karmel and Carroll 2016; Mavromaras et al. 2013), Europe (Aina and Pastore 2012; Antonucci 2018; Holmes and Mayhew 2015) and the UK (BIS 2015; Formby 2017; ONS 2017).

A different picture emerges in France, with its more co-ordinated occupational labour market—not unlike those found in Holland and Germany—that tends towards a stronger coupling of education qualifications to specific jobs and careers (Mary 2012; Power et al. 2013; Tomlinson 2017). French graduates appear to experience a lesser risk of mismatch compared to graduates in Australia or the UK, although this trend is on the rise elsewhere: a recent study of 17 OECD countries found an over-education of graduates relative to the educational requirements of available work in most developed countries, with around half of all employees showing some form of educational mismatch (Mateos-Romero and del Mar Salina-Jiménez 2018).

Compounding these changes are wider demographic factors. In continental Europe, the proportion of the population seeking work is rising, with a corresponding rise in competition for work. This includes older cohorts who are either returning to or staying longer in the labour market and who have greater experience to offer employers than young people entering the market for the first time. In both France and the UK, the proportion of people in the labour market who are aged over 50 has already grown during this millennium, with a 14 percentage-point increase for people aged 55–59 between 2005 and 2013 (Mourshed et al. 2017).

To add complexity and uncertainty to this mix, the labour market value of higher education credentials is also tied to which particular university graduates have attended. While this has long been the case, the recent differentiation of individual universities has become a powerful mediator of student opportunity and success, with the economic benefits of a degree varying markedly depending on the prestige of the university that awards it (Britton et al. 2016). Some of our interviewees are well aware of this. Particularly amongst the Australian cohort, the chief motivation for their choice of university is its national or global reputation: in the survey which preceded our interviews with them, 10 out of the 11 students ranked this as the most important reason for enrolling. For Abi, for example, there are other personal and cultural reasons for his selection of this university, but its global ranking remains the primary one:

> Ah, the first is about the … university ranking … and, also, teachers, the qualifications of the teachers and … whether the research of the university can support for my future careers. Maybe one more thing, the environments. I try to find the university that can accommodate not only the academic stuff but, also, my religion stuff. Like, in [Australian university], why I chose them is because [it] provides rooms for praying and some organisations that can help me to be, feel like I am in my home (Abi, Australia).

In the UK, George notes that 'there's definitely a concern that the reputation of the university could hold us back'. This forms part of a greater hierarchy that extends to class and socioeconomic standing, one that continues to have an effect on the career prospects of young people whom he knows:

> I had a friend that had applied for an internship at Barclays [bank] a few weeks ago and he goes into the interview and [they say]: 'you are coming from a disadvantaged, coming from [my city] - why should we give you the internship?' So he had to pivot to his other skills… In the end, he went through a really extensive process. He had to get extra letters of recommendations and stuff like that. He got the internship in the end, not that it was that enjoyable [laughs].

George also sees 'social standing' as a factor in his own employability: 'you know, not being a David Cameron type, where you know everyone in the political world, to an extent could be a barrier'. At the same time, he believes that this equation between class and career opportunity has shifted slightly, in ways that have been of direct benefit to him:

> But I think equally there has been a shift, however small, over the last century, that ... more and more people are coming from all types of background. Whether that is for show or deliberate, I don't know, but I think there's at least an opportunity now that I don't think I would have had a century ago (George, UK).

The Impact of Economic Downturns

A second trend arises from economic recession. The negative impact of the GFC of 2007–2008 has further challenged the idea that higher qualifications lead to better jobs. In the UK, the austerity measures and stagnating or falling wages that followed the GFC have affected young people more than any other group. More young adults are in poverty than before the GFC. Young people in their 20s have seen a 12.5% reduction in median real-term pay, with many trapped in temporary, low-paid work. In 2014, for example, 34% of UK persons employed under the zero-hours contract arrangements, in which the employer does not guarantee any hours of work, were aged 16–24 (Allen 2016). While such contracts are promoted as mutually beneficial arrangements that offer flexibility to both employer and employee, they are also associated with greater volatility and job insecurity. For young workers at the vulnerable end of the labour market, they represent uncertain pathways to further and more stable work. This is one of the reasons for the fact, which we will discuss in the Conclusion, that 'young people growing up in the years of austerity face a future in which their prospects of social mobility, perhaps for the first time for decades, are significantly worse than they were for their parents' (McDowell 2017, p. 311).

Like their counterparts in the UK, young people in France were especially affected by the GFC and its economic downturn. While youth unemployment in France has never fallen below 15% during the past 30 years and has regularly been higher than 20% (Pickard 2014), the post-GFC era has seen higher degrees of poverty amongst young people. At the end of 2012, the poverty rate among 16–25 year olds was more 22%, more than double that of older age groups (Pickard 2014). During the GFC, employment rates of overall populations in the France and the UK fell significantly, although demand for work began to increase in 2011 (Mourshed et al. 2017). The nature, stability and quality of the jobs available are, at the time of writing, still to be determined.

Australia avoided the worst effects of the GFC, although young people felt its impact disproportionately in relation to employment, unemployment and underemployment, a condition in which part-time workers are available to do more work but are unable to get it (Walsh 2016). Youth unemployment and underemployment have both remained high since that time. The unemployment rate of Australians aged 15–24 increased from 9.4% in 2007 to 12.7% in 2016 (ABS 2016). In 2007, before the GFC, 34% of young people aged 15–24 who were not studying had full-time work, compared to 25% in 2016 (ABS 2016). The rate of full-time employment for

Bachelor degree graduates was 85% in 2007, but lowered to 71% in 2016 (QILT 2016; Torii and O'Connell 2017).

Back in Europe, many young people have part-time employment but seek full-time work, a trend that has been increasing over time. In 2008, 9.7% of young people aged 15–24 were in part-time employment but desired full-time employment. This figure rose to 10.8% in 2012. In the UK, this figure increased from 5.3 to 11.5% during the same period (Mourshed et al. 2017). Such recent trends, again, need to be located in a longer-term view. Furlong summarises their global implications in the following way:

> In many countries policy is framed by assumptions of linear, unbroken, transitions [from school to work], by traditional notions of independence and with confidence that most employment is relatively stable and provides an acceptable standard of living. Such assumptions are challenged in the post-recession economy where many of those fortunate enough to have jobs work under conditions of uncertainty and are unable to work sufficient hours to secure a decent living. Inequality is rising and new divisions are opening up as social policy is framed in ways that marginalise those most affected by contemporary conditions, many of whom are young (2014, p. xi).

Technology, Digital Skills and the Automation of Labour

A third trend that is reshaping young people's current and future workforce participation is technology. As one 2016 study suggests:

> Young people in education or entering the workforce … face the most turbulent, rapidly evolving labor market seen by any generation. The global economy is approaching a Fourth Industrial Revolution, driven by increasing automation of the labor market – enabled by rapid innovations in robotics, Artificial Intelligence and smart technologies (Infosys, p. 5).

It has been argued that 60% of Australian students are being trained in areas that will be radically affected by technology and that 70% of young people currently entering the labour market will be affected by automation. Technology is also driving increased demands for digital literacy, with an estimation that over half the workforce will need the skills to 'use, configure and or build digital systems in the next 2–3 years' (FYA 2015). According to another report, two-fifths of jobs in the eastern Australian state of New South Wales 'are at high risk of being lost to computerisation and low- to middle-skilled workers across the state are expected to bear the brunt of pain brought by artificial intelligence, cloud computing, the Internet of Things and big data' (Dumas 2016). The impact of technology on labour markets is global in nature but not fully understood.

At least one of our interviewees is already aware of this development in his field of study. Tyler's Ph.D. research examines how aspects of his area of work can be automated, which in turn may have implications for his own and other people's work prospects:

> … you look at automation – in any industry at the moment, there are some arguing that it is essentially going to lead to another Great Depression, and I certainly sometimes think

that's a possibility. But then, on the other hand, there are many others that argue it's actually going to create new jobs and things like that. ... you know, you read research on artificial intelligence being more accurate than GPs [General Medical Practitioners] in diagnosing medical issues and things like that. But, realistically, we are at the point where GPs are being replaced. ... I think most people's jobs are up for redundancy. So that would be a huge societal issue. You know, there's only really two options: that you end up with a huge underclass, disenfranchised underclass, or something's done, whether that's reduction of the normal working week or something like that, to even it out or something like that. But, yeah, that is certainly something that sits in the back of my mind, is about automation and things like that. Probably less of a risk in the next few years for my job, but certainly long-term I can see it happening (Tyler, Australia).

Mel is also cognisant of the changes to the labour market that may come with automation. Her response takes us back to the themes of flexibility and adaptability that emerged from some of our interviewees' earlier accounts. She is not anxious about the prospect of automation and labour market redundancy, but it is certainly on her radar as a possible driver of her own career change in the future:

I think that the world and the economy right now is evolving a lot ... I saw somewhere which is like in 10/20 years, or in 50 years or whatever, there will be so many new jobs that we have never considered, because of the way technology is evolving or because of Internet, because of how the global market is evolving. ... So I can say I want to teach now, but how do I know that in 10–20 years' time robots come in and taken over my job or whatever? I don't know. So I'm going to see what happens and see what works for me and what works for the economy, and where's there's a demand (Mel, Australia).

The Emergence of the Gig Economy

For many young people, having a career decreasingly resembles what it did for generations moving from school to work during the previous century. As we saw earlier, the idea of a career remains desirable for many of our interviewees, but for other young people, it may seem less attainable. A survey of 5,029 Australians aged 18–29 found that 67% were concerned about their ability to secure career-related work (Co-Op BDO 2015). A majority (56%) believed that job prospects in their field were not very strong. While most (69%) were happy to have multiple careers, nearly the same number—like our interviewees—wanted 'a career, not just a job.' Another report suggests that a young person who is 15 today is likely to experience a 'portfolio career', potentially having 17 different jobs over five careers in their lifetime (FYA 2017, p. 6). Rose's plans to build a private practice and Morgane's envisagement of a series of positions, which we describe above, exhibit some qualities of this flexible portfolio career.

These changes also require a changed approach to student and graduate behaviours and orientations to work. As Kelly (2016, p. 2) has observed, 'cultural, technological and economic transformations ... have changed the nature and meanings of work and the sorts of behaviours and dispositions imagined as being necessary for ongoing participation in paid labour'. University students are required to think and behave in entrepreneurial ways, to gain and master the skills, attitudes, experiences and credentials necessary to engage in the business of life (Kelly 2017; Oinonen 2018; Peters 2001). In short, they are required to curate the 'self as enterprise' (McNay 2009).

The fourth trend that is affecting young people's labour market participation during and beyond their university study relies on and encourages this curation. The emergence of the 'peer-to-peer (P2P)' or gig economy reflects the latest phase of the individualisation of the labour market. In this economy, companies are reducing their staff and replacing many other roles with the 'freelancer or portfolio worker community' (Hajkowicz et al. 2016, p. 36). Though freelancing has not yet become prevalent in Australia, it has become common in other countries such as the UK. Working in this way demands an 'entrepreneurial self' (Kelly 2017). While being entrepreneurial is a potentially valuable disposition, risk and responsibility is transferred to individual workers working in P2P job markets. This is captured by Howie and Campbell's (2017) depiction of the emergence of a 'guerrilla self' (p. 91), one that embodies individual responsibility and investment, but also survival and resilience in uncertain contemporary landscapes.

US anthropologist Ilana Gershon (2017) suggests that where labour has conventionally involved a transaction of the employee's time and effort for money, it is no longer sufficient for a young person to identify as an employee seeking to get hired: an attractive 'personal brand' is required. Gershon's study of employers and jobseekers in the San Francisco Bay area found that young people were marketing themselves as a business working within and across other businesses. In Australia, people working in sectors such as cleaning and hospitality, both big employers of young people, are increasingly asked to register themselves as individual business and provide business numbers accordingly: that is, to provide their services *and themselves* as a business. In doing so, labour protections can be bypassed. It has been pointed out, for example, that if Deliveroo delivery riders in Australia do not receive an order within an hour, they will earn less than the delivery courier award rate (AUD$18.31 per hour of work), with 'no superannuation, no annual leave, no penalty rates and no insurance if they have an accident on their bike' (McVeigh and McCormack 2016). In short, the securities and entitlements traditionally attached to work are eroding, and young university students and graduates are not immune to this erosion.

Keeping Faith in the Opportunity Bargain

A number of studies have argued that young people reaching adulthood in the 21st century experience anxiety during their transitions to work because of an emergent generational narcissism. It has been suggested that some young people have grown accustomed to an easier lifestyle and feel entitled to things that they believe they deserve; that they have 'excessive expectations' of interesting employment, high career achievement and pecuniary and extrinsic benefits; and that they are, at the same time, less willing to work hard or compromise their values and beliefs for the sake of work (Kuron et al. 2015, p. 1003: see also Chow et al. 2017; Krahn and Galambos 2014; Smith et al. 2017). But other research suggests something more nuanced. Snowden and Lewis (2015) argue that university students receive mixed messages about their employment potential and post-qualification outcomes and that their overestimation of their likely starting graduate salaries and earnings may be the result of these messages.

While the four labour market trends we described earlier are by no means confined to young people, young people do face additional challenges at a critically formative period of their lives. Our interviewees face a changing and sometimes hostile labour market. They are keenly aware of this, yet not all are concerned. Some still believe firmly in the opportunity bargain of higher education which we discussed in the Introduction: that if one puts in the hard work, one can move up in the world. As we will see in the next chapter, not all of our interviewees share this view, but it does emerges strongly from Becky's discussion. Despite her many concerns about the future, which we consider in various other sections of this book, she maintains a relatively high degree of confidence that higher education will provide a 'gateway' to the future she wants, although she also acknowledges that this future depends in part on the vagaries of chance:

> I think there's a definite respect for people who go through higher education. Don't get me wrong, I think it's been diluted over the years because there are now a vast quantity of degrees in various different subjects that aren't level to each other, they are not equal. You know, a degree in psychology, let's just say, is not equal to a football studies degree—or in my view, it is not because what you can do with it is very, very different. But the work, I suppose, is still there.
>
> Education is a gateway for it. There's lots of different ways to skin a cat. You can either work really, really hard in a career and hope that you get to management and experience and whatever else, or you can go to university and get that knowledge that you would acquire in, say, 10 years within three, four/five, and then get to that point and, also, have a piece of paper to prove that you have that knowledge.
>
> ... I use this analogy to my other half [Becky's partner]: it's like going into gaol on Monopoly, and then waiting the three goes to see if you roll a six or just paying your $50 and getting out (Becky, UK).

Becky's relative confidence that higher education will provide a 'gateway' to the future echoes the findings of a survey of 1,000 16–25 year olds in Australia, Brazil, China, France, Germany, India, South Africa, the UK and the US, which concluded that some young people, at least, are optimistic even in the face of an uncertain employment future. Two thirds of the young people surveyed felt positive about their own job prospects, even while a similar number recognized that the global labour market would continue to be complex and competitive. Interestingly, young people in emerging countries indicated a higher degree confidence in their readiness for the future. For example, where 60% of respondents in India agreed that they had the skills needed for 'a positive career', only 25% of young respondents in France felt this way (Infosys 2016, p. 3).

Conclusion

David Graeber's recent treatise on what he calls 'bullshit jobs' describes the unprecedented expansion of work which is seen to be purposeless at best or harmful at worst by the people who perform them. In Graeber's terms, a bullshit job is 'one that could be erased from the Earth and no one would be worse off' (Purves 2018). By his definition, these jobs exist mostly within the administrative sector and financial industries, but they also include the multiple roles which provide support for these industries as well as the countless ancillary industries that have sprung up to provide services for the 'cash rich, time poor' workers who populate them. For vast numbers of young people, though, a so-called bullshit job may be preferable to the labour market uncertainty which many feel awaits them.

The testimonies of our interviewees present a wide range of views about working life after study. When asked to speculate as to where they will be 10 years after the time of the interview, the answers vary. Most are looking for careers rather than paid jobs, although they define those careers in more flexible and adaptive terms than the traditional notion of career suggests. Nearly all are hoping for labour market security, while envisaging that the workforce of the future will be highly competitive and possibly transformed by technology and geopolitical shifts such as Brexit. Some are optimistic but nearly all acknowledge the spectre of uncertainty in their imagined working futures.

While our discussion has also identified some potentially troubling trends in graduate pathways to work, this needs to be tempered by certain key data. We have already touched on the financial advantage that still accompanies higher qualifications to some degree. Young people with post-school qualifications also remain more likely to start their careers in stable, satisfactory employment than those without such qualifications. Globally, where those with only primary school qualifications take 22.2 months on average to get into work (based on data from 2012 to 16), secondary graduates take 14.3 months, and higher education graduates take 8.5 months (ILO 2017). It is likely, therefore, that most of the university students we spoke to will go on to some form of relatively secure work, although the stakes for other young people are much higher. Employment conditions in established economies such as Australia generally improve after the age of 25 (Stanwick et al. 2013), but it would appear that for many young people throughout the world, options to secure stable full-time work are increasingly out of reach.

This has particular implications for young people who are already economically or socially marginalised. In one Australian study of young people with extensive experience of homelessness, incarceration and addiction, those young people identified paid employment as the 'first and most important stage in the sequencing of their futures' (Bryant and Ellard 2015, p. 491), yet the labour market trends we have described suggest that this stage may be hard to achieve. Arguably what most young people have in common is change and the acceleration of change in the worlds of work (or at the very least a perception that this is the case). Returning to Leccardi's observation in Chap. 2 (2014), young people find themselves having to define themselves and their life choices within this context of accelerated change. In response, many are curating or fostering an emergent form of youth selfhood that we have called homo promptus. We will describe this form of selfhood in the coming chapter.

References

Aina, C., & Pastore, F. (2012). Delayed graduation and overeducation: A test of the human capital model versus screening hypothesis. *IZA discussion paper no. 6413*, March 2012. Bonn: IZA.

Allen, K. (2016). Top girls navigating austere times: Interrogating youth transitions since the 'crisis'. *Journal of Youth Studies, 19*(6), 805–820. https://doi.org/10.1080/13676261.2015.1112885.

Antonucci, L. (2016). *Student lives in crisis: Deepening inequality in times of austerity*. Bristol, UK: Policy Press.

Antonucci, L. (2018). Not all experiences of precarious work lead to precarity: The case study of young people at university and their welfare mixes. *Journal of Youth Studies, 21*(7), 888–904. https://doi.org/10.1080/13676261.2017.1421749.

Australian Bureau of Statistics [ABS]. (2016, December). *6202.0—Labour Force, Australia*. Retrieved November 15, 2017, from http://www.abs.gov.au/AUSSTATS/abs@.nsf/DetailsPage/6202.0Dec%202016?OpenDocument.

Australian Institute of Health and Welfare [AIHW]. (2015). *Australia's welfare 2015*. Canberra: Australian Institute of Health and Welfare. Retrieved November 15, 2017, from http://www.aihw.gov.au/publication-detail/?id=60129552015.

Britton, J., Dearden, L., Shephard, N., & Vignoles, A. (2016). *How English domiciled graduate earnings vary with gender, institution attended, subject and socio-economic background* (No. W16/06). IFS Working Papers.

Brooks, R. (2018). Understanding the higher education student in Europe: A comparative analysis. *Compare: A Journal of Comparative and International Education, 48*(4), 500–517. https://doi.org/10.1080/03057925.2017.1318047.

Brown, P., Power, S., Tholen, G., & Allouch, A. (2016). Credentials, talent and cultural capital: A comparative study of educational elites in England and France. *British Journal of Sociology of Education, 37*(2), 191–211.

Bryant, Joanne, & Ellard, Jeanne. (2015). Hope as a form of agency in the future thinking of disenfranchised young people. *Journal of Youth Studies, 18*(4), 485–499.

Chow, A., Glamabos, N. L., & Krahn, H. J. (2017). Work values during the transition to adulthood and mid-life satisfaction: Cascading effects across 25 years. *International Journal of Behavioral Development, 41*(1), 105–114. https://doi.org/10.1177/0165025415608518.

Collins, R. (1979). *The credential society: An historical sociology of education and stratification*. New York: Academic Press.

Cook, J. (2016). Young people's strategies for coping with parallel imaginings of the future. *Time & Society, 25*(3), 700–717. https://doi.org/10.1177/0961463X15609829.

Co-Op BDO. (2015). *2015 Future leaders index*. Retrieved June 19, 2018, from http://www.bdo.com.au/getattachment/Insights/Publications/Future-Leaders-Index/Future-Leaders-Index-Part-3/FLI_PAPER-3_Infographics_Final.pdf.aspx.

Corliss, M., Lewis, P., & Daly, A. (2013). The rate of return to higher education over the business cycle. *Australian Journal of Labour Economics, 16*, 219–236.

Côté, J. E. (2014). Towards a new political economy of youth. *Journal of Youth Studies, 17*(4), 527–543. https://doi.org/10.1080/13676261.2013.836592.

Cuervo, H., Crofts, J., & Wyn, J. (2013). *Generational insights into new labour market landscapes for youth. Research Report 42*. Youth Research Centre. Melbourne: University of Melbourne.

References

Daly, A., Lewis, P., Corliss, M., & Heaslip, T. (2015). The private rate of return to a university degree in Australia. *Australian Journal of Education, 59*(1), 97–112. https://doi.org/10.1177/000-4944114565117.

Department for Business, Innovation, and Skills [BIS]. (2015). *Fulfilling our potential: Teaching excellence, social mobility and student choice*. London: Department for Business, Innovation, and Skills.

Dockery, A. M., & Miller, P. W. (2012). Over-education, under-education and credentialism in the Australian labour market. *NCVER monograph series 10/2012*. Adelaide, Australia: NCVER.

Dumas, D. (2016, January 9). Man v Machine: Half of NSW jobs at risk of computerisation. *The Sydney Morning Herald*. Retrieved March 5, 2018, from https://www.smh.com.au/national/nsw/man-vs-machine-half-of-nsw-jobs-at-risk-of-computerisation-20160107-gm18t1.html.

Elder, S., & Kring, S. (2016). *Young and female—A double strike? Gender analysis of school-to-work transition surveys in 32 developing economies*. Geneva: International Labour Office.

Fogg, N. P., & Harrington, P. E. (2011). Rising mal-employment and the great recession: The growing disconnection between recent college graduates and the college labor market. *Continuing Higher Education Review, 75*, 51–65.

Formby, A. P. (2017). 'Got a degree…all of a sudden I'm in a Jobcentre': The role of 'stigma' in 'precarious' graduate transitions. *Journal of Poverty and Social Justice, 25*(3), 249–262. https://doi.org/10.1332/175982717X14877669275128.

Freeman, R. (1976). *The overeducated American*. Cambridge: Academic Press.

Furlong, A. (2014). Foreword. In L. Antonucci, M. Hamilton, & S. Roberts (Eds.), *Young people and social policy in Europe: Dealing with risk, inequality and precarity in times of crisis* (pp. x–xi). London, UK: Palgrave Macmillan.

Gershon, I. (2017). *Down and out in the new economy: How people find (or don't find) work today*. Chicago: University of Chicago Press.

Goos, M., & Manning, A. (2007). Lousy and lovely jobs: The rising polarization of work in Britain. *Review of Economics and Statistics, 89*(1), 118–133.

Green, F., & Henseke, G. (2016). Should governments of OECD countries worry about graduate underemployment? *Oxford Review of Economic Policy, 32*(4), 514–537. https://doi.org/10.1093/oxrep/grw024.

Green, F., & Zhu, Y. (2010). Overqualification, job dissatisfaction, and increasing dispersion in the returns to graduate education. *Oxford Economic Papers, 62*(4), 740–763. https://doi.org/10.1093/oep/gpq002.

Hajkowicz, S. A., Reeson, A., Rudd, L., Bratanova, A., Hodgers, L., Mason, C., et al. (2016). *Tomorrow's digitally enabled workforce: Megatrends and scenarios for jobs and employment in Australia over the coming twenty years*. Brisbane: CSIRO.

Heckhausen, J., Chang, E. S., Greenberger, E., & Chen, C. (2013). Striving for educational and career goals during the transition after high school: What is beneficial? *Journal of Youth Adolescence, 42*, 1385–1398. https://doi.org/10.1007/s10964-012-9812-5.

Holmes, L. (2013). Competing perspectives on graduate employability: Possession, position or process? *Studies in Higher Education, 38*(4), 538–554. https://doi.org/10.1080/03075079.2011.587140.

Holmes, C., & Mayhew, K. (2015). *Over-qualification and skills mismatch in the graduate labour market: Policy report*. London: CIPD.

Howie, L., & Campbell, P. (2017). *Crisis and terror in the age of anxiety*. London: Palgrave Macmillan.

Infosys. (2016). *Amplifying human potential: Education and skills for the fourth industrial revolution*. Retrieved May 25, 2017, from http://www.experienceinfosys.com/humanpotential.

International Labour Organisation [ILO]. (2013a). *Global employment trends 2013: Recovering from a second jobs dip*. Geneva: International Labour Organisation. Retrieved November 15, 2017, from http://www.ilo.org/wcmsp5/groups/public/-dgreports/-dcomm/-publ/documents/publication/wcms_202326.pdf.

International Labour Organisation [ILO]. (2013b). *Mobilizing support for the call for action on the youth employment crisis*. Geneva: International Labour Organisation. Retrieved November 15, 2017, from http://www.ilo.org/pardev/donors/WCMS_205743/lang-en/index.htm.

International Labour Organisation [ILO]. (2017). *Global employment trends for youth 2017: Paths to a better working future*. Geneva: International Labour Organisation. Retrieved February 3, 2018, from https://www.ilo.org/global/publications/books/global-employment-trends/WCMS_598669/lang-en/index.htm.

Karmel, T. (2015). Skills deepening or credentialism? Education qualifications and occupational outcomes, 1996–2011. *Australian Journal of Labour Economics, 18*(1), 29–51.

Karmel, T., & Carroll, D. (2016). Has the graduate job market been swamped? *NILS Working Paper Series No. 228/2016*. Adelaide: Flinders University, National Institute of Labour Studies.

Kelly, P. (2016). *The self as enterprise: Foucault and the spirit of 21st century capitalism*. Surrey: Gower.

Kelly, P. (2017). Growing up after the GFC: Responsibilisation and mortgaged futures. *Discourse: Studies in the Cultural Politics of Education, 38*(1), 57–69. https://doi.org/10.1080/01596306.2015.1104852.

Krahn, H. J., & Galambos, N. L. (2014). Work values and beliefs of 'Generation X' and 'Generation Y'. *Journal of Youth Studies, 17*(1), 92–112. https://doi.org/10.1080/13676261.2013.815701.

Kuron, L. K. J., Lyons, S. T., Schweitzer, L., & Ng, E. S. W. (2015). Millennials' work values: Differences across the school to work transition. *Personnel Review, 44*(6), 991–1009. https://doi.org/10.1108/PR-01-2014-0024.

Leccardi, C. (2014). Young people and the new semantics of the future. *SocietàMutamentoPolitica, 5*(10), 41–54. https://doi.org/10.13128/SMP-15404.

Marginson, S. (2016). The worldwide trend to high participation higher education: Dynamics of social stratification in inclusive systems. *Higher Education, 72*(4), 413–434. https://doi.org/10.1007/s10734-016-0016-x.

Mary, A. (2012). *The illusion of the prolongation of youth: Transition to adulthood among Finnish and French female university students*. Tampere, Finland: Tampere University Press.

Mateos-Romero, L., & del Mar Salina-Jiménez, M. (2018). Labor mismatches: Effects on wages and on job satisfaction in 17 OECD countries. *Social Indicators Research*, 1–23. https://doi.org/10.1007/s11205-017-1830-y.

Mavromaras, K., Mahuteau, S., Sloane, P., & Wei, Z. (2013). The effect of overskilling dynamics on wages. *Education Economics, 21*(3), 281–303. https://doi.org/10.1080/09645292.2013.797382.

Mavromaras, K., & McGuiness, S. (2007). Education and skill mismatches in the labour market: Editors' introduction. *The Australian Economic Review, 40*(3), 279–285.

McDowell, L. (2017). Youth, children and families in austere times: Change, politics and a new gender contract. *Area, 49*(3), 311–316.

McNay, L. (2009). Self as enterprise: Dilemmas of control and resistance in Foucault's The Birth of Biopolitics. *Theory, Culture & Society, 26*(6), 55–77. https://doi.org/10.1177/0263276409347697.

McVeigh, S. and McCormack, A. (2016, April 1). Deliveroo and Foodora: Getting paid but not on the payroll. *Triple J Hack Australian Broadcasting Corporation*. Retrieved July 9, 2018, from http://www.abc.net.au/triplej/programs/hack/deliveroo-foodora-courier-riders/7292816.

Mourshed, M., Patel, J. & Suder, K. (2017). *Education to employment: Getting Europe's youth into work*. McKinsey Center for Government. Retrieved June 2, 2018, from http://egdcfoundation.org/work/assets/McKinsey-Education-to-Employment-Europe.pdf.

Office for National Statistics [ONS]. (2017). *Graduates in the UK labour market: 2017*. London: Office for National Statistics. Retrieved February 3, 2018, from https://www.ons.gov.uk/releases/graduatesintheuklabourmarket2017.

Oinonen, E. (2018). Under pressure to become—From a student to entrepreneurial self. *Journal of Youth Studies, 21*(10), 1344–1360. https://doi.org/10.1080/13676261.2018.1468022.

References

Oreopoulos, P., & Petronijevic, U. (2013). *Making college worth it: A review of research on the returns to higher education.* Working paper 19053, National Bureau of Economic Research working paper series. Cambridge: National Bureau of Economic Research.

Organisation for Economic Development [OECD]. (2014a). *Society at a glance 2014.* Paris: Organisation for Economic Co-operation and Development. Retrieved February 3, 2018, from http://www.oecd.org/social/societyataglance.htm.

Organisation for Economic Development [OECD]. (2014b). *Skills beyond school.* Paris: Organisation for Economic Co-operation and Development. Retrieved February 3, 2018, from http://www.oecd.org/edu/innovation-education/skillsbeyondschool.htm.

Organisation for Economic Development [OECD]. (2015a). *Education at a glance 2015: OECD indicators.* Paris: Organisation for Economic Co-operation and Development. Retrieved February 3, 2018, from http://www.oecd.org/education/education-at-a-glance-2015.htm.

Organisation for Economic Development [OECD]. (2015b). *How is the global talent pool changing (2013 2030)?.* Paris: Organisation for Economic Co-operation and Development. Retrieved February 3, 2018, from http://www.oecd-ilibrary.org/education/how-is-the-global-talent-pool-changing-2013-2030_5js33lf9jk41-en.

Organisation for Economic Development [OECD]. (2016). *Population with tertiary education.* Paris: Organisation for Economic Co-operation and Development. Retrieved February 3, 2018, from https://data.oecd.org/eduatt/population-with-tertiary-education.htm.

Organisation for Economic Development [OECD]. (2017). *Education at a glance 2017: OECD indicators.* Paris: Organisation for Economic Co-operation and Development. Retrieved February 3, 2018, from http://www.oecd.org/education/education-at-a-glance-19991487.htm.

Peters, M. (2001). Education, enterprise culture and the entrepreneurial self: A Foucauldian perspective. *Journal of Educational Enquiry, 2*(2), 58–71.

Pickard, S. (2014). French youth policy in an age of austerity: Plus ça change? *International Journal of Adolescence and Youth, 19*(sup1), 48–61. https://doi.org/10.1080/02673843.2013.863732.

Pickard, S. (2016). Higher education in France: Social stratification and social reproduction. In J. E. Côté & A. Furlong (Eds.), *Routledge handbook of the sociology of higher education* (pp. 223–233). London & New York: Routledge.

Power, S., Brown, P., Allouch, A., & Tholen, G. (2013). Self, career and nationhood: The contrasting aspirations of British and French elite graduates. *The British Journal of Sociology, 64*(4), 578–596. https://doi.org/10.1111/1468-4446.12048.

Purves, M. (2018, May 15). David Graeber's new book 'Bullshit Jobs: A Theory' calls time on your career. *Financial Review.* Retrieved June 3, 2018, from http://www.afr.com/leadership/careers/david-graebers-new-book-bullshit-jobs-a-theory-calls-time-on-your-career-20180515-h1041n.

The Foundation for Young Australians [FYA]. (2015). *New work order (excerpt).* Melbourne: The Foundation for Young Australians (FYA). Retrieved April 9, 2016, from www.fya.org.au/wp-content/uploads/2015/08/The-New-Work-Order-infographic-1-overview1.png.

The Foundation for Young Australians [FYA]. (2017). *The new work smarts: Thriving in the new work order.* https://www.fya.org.au/wp-content/uploads/2017/07/FYA_TheNewWorkSmarts_July2017.pdf.

Quality Indicators for Learning and Teaching [QILT]. (2016). *2016 Graduate outcomes survey national report.* Retrieved February 3, 2018, from https://www.qilt.edu.au/docs/default-source/gos-reports/2016/gos-national-report.pdf?sfvrsn=423de23c_10.

Robertson, S., & Dale, R. (2015). Towards a 'critical cultural political economy' account of the globalising of education. *Globalisation, Societies and Education, 13*(1), 149–170. https://doi.org/10.1080/1467724.2014.967502.

Smith, A., Bodell, L. P., Holm-Denoma, J., Joiner, T., Gordon, K., Perez, M., et al. (2017). "I don't want to grow up, I'm a [Gen X, Y, Me] kid": Increasing maturity fears across the decades. *International Journal of Behavioral Development, 41*(6), 655–662. https://doi.org/10.1177/0165025416654302.

Snowden, C., & Lewis, S. (2015). Mixed messages: Public communication about higher education and non-traditional students in Australia. *Higher Education, 70,* 585–599. https://doi.org/10.1007/s10734-014-9858-2.

Stanwick, J., Lu, T., Karmel, T., & Wibrow, B. (2013). *How young people are faring 2013.* Melbourne: The Foundation for Young Australians.

Sukarieh, M., & Tannock, S. (2017). The education penalty: Schooling, learning and the diminishment of wages, working conditions and worker power. *British Journal of Sociology of Education, 38*(3), 245–264. https://doi.org/10.1080/01425692.2015.1093408.

Tholen, G. (2017a). *Graduate work: Skills, credentials, careers, and labour markets.* London: Oxford University Press.

Tholen, G. (2017b). The changing opportunities of professionalization for graduate occupations. *Comparative Sociology, 16,* 613–633. https://doi.org/10.1163/15691330-12341438.

Tholen, G., Relly, S. J., Warhurst, C., & Commander, J. (2016). Higher education, graduate skills and the skills of graduates: The case of graduates as residential sales estate agents. *British Educational Research Journal, 42*(3), 508–523. https://doi.org/10.1002/berj.3222.

Thomson, P. (2013). Romancing the market: Narrativising equity in globalising times. *Discourse: Studies in the Cultural Politics of Education, 34*(2), 170–184. https://doi.org/10.1080/01596306.2013.770245.

Tomlinson, M. (2012). Graduate employability: A review of conceptual and empirical themes. *Higher Education Policy, 25,* 407–431. https://doi.org/10.1057/hep.2011.26.

Tomlinson, M. (2017). Forms of graduate capital and their relationship to graduate employability. *Education+Training, 59*(4), 338–352. https://doi.org/10.1108/et-05-2016-0090.

Torii, K., & O'Connell, M. (2017). *Preparing young people for the future of work.* Mitchell Institute Policy Paper No. 01/2017. Melbourne: Mitchell Institute.

Vuolo, M., Mortimer, J. T., & Staff, J. (2016). The value of educational degrees in turbulent economic times: Evidence from the Youth Development Study. *Social Science Research, 57,* 233–252. https://doi.org/10.1016/j.ssresearch.2015.12.014.

Walsh, L. (2016). *Educating generation next: Young people, teachers and schooling in transition.* Basingstoke: Palgrave Macmillan.

Woodman, D., & Wyn, J. (2015). *Youth and generation: Rethinking change and inequality in the lives of young people.* London: Sage.

Chapter 6
Reacting to the Future: The University Student as Homo Promptus

Introduction

> I think competition is good, if you let it be good. If you think of everything as a competition, you need to win it, you are going to eventually end up winning some things. … Some people are going to get dragged down; some people are going to get up; but you need to move. If everyone fights and the target is raised, then everything gets even better, which is just better for society in the long-run (Tom, UK).

As we have shown already, young people face a working world characterised by uncertainty and change. Global competition, labour market flux, the massification of higher education and the reduction of work opportunities due to technological developments are just a few factors contributing both directly and indirectly to this uncertainty and change. Within this context, higher education is increasingly framed by individualised economic goals as a long-term investment in the self. University students are understood less as learners and more as 'workers in the making' (Brooks 2017, p. 14): individual consumers and agents responsible not only for their choices within an uncertain education and labour market but for the resultant outcomes, and for managing the economic and emotional costs of those outcomes.

We have previously noted Budd's suggestion that the contemporary young university student is less 'homo educandus' than 'homo economicus' (2017). This characterisation captures much of what we have just described, but we believe that what now appears to be emerging from the current era of uncertainty is something more—a new youth subjectivity and selfhood which we have called *homo promptus*. Cicero first coined this phrase to describe someone prepared and ready to do whatever is needed. We use it to describe the individualised and entrepreneurial self that is produced and expected by contemporary education and labour market forces and discourses, and actively cultivated by the young university student in response to these forces and discourses.

In Chap. 2, we mentioned Peou and Zinn's typology, which suggests that young people approach the future either in 'entrepreneurial' mode, seeing it as something to be planned and enacted proactively, or in 'situational' mode, seeing it as something that is 'mainly unknowable' (Peou and Zinn 2015, pp. 734–736). In this chapter, we draw on our interviews with 30 young university students in France, Australia and the UK to suggest that homo promptus combines these two modes with five dispositions or behaviours, which we will discuss shortly. We argue that the key driving impetus for these dispositions and behaviours is the uncertainty that attends young people's current and imagined future working lives, although the uncertainty of their personal lives also plays a role. As we will show in the next chapter, they are also prompted and rendered necessary in order to realise young people's imagined futures as political actors.

Homo Promptus Is Entrepreneurial and Strategic

The first disposition of homo promptus is to be entrepreneurial, in the sense that we have discussed in the previous chapter. As we saw in that chapter and in Chap. 3, the nature and meanings of work and the behaviours and dispositions perceived to be necessary for employment require an entrepreneurial approach to the gaining of skills, qualifications and networks. The studentification of youth labour markets has also seen increasing competition for work experience and the increased take-up of activities such as traineeships, internships, and work placements—often on little or no pay—to make young people appear more employable. In response, as we noted in the previous chapter, some young people are cultivating themselves as businesses with a brand, or, at the very least, are cultivating a set of skills and experiences that add to their perceived employability. This is a common strategy amongst our interviewees across all three countries, a means of distinguishing themselves from other possible competition. As Juliette in France explains: 'I am a really proactive person; so I would go and try and do everything [to prepare for] work. But there are other people who would not'.

Homo promptus also embraces uncertainty and contingency. Homo promptus is constantly 'on the move' and seeking to position themselves competitively. At the start of the chapter, we share Tom's observation that 'competition is good'. This reflects many young people's response to uncertainty: they become what Leccardi calls a 'hyper-activist individual', one with 'the desire and the determination not to be overwhelmed by events, to keep uncertainty at bay, to gain mastery over one's own time' (2014, p. 49). This characterisation certainly captures Tom's philosophy, one which he believes is of primary importance to other young people as well:

> ... I think that is a really good message for young people. Especially being from an area of high deprivation and low-income stuff, there's a lot of people who just think they are stuck here, there's nothing they can do. It's like: you are not stuck here. You can – it's going to be hard ... if it was easy, everyone would do it. But you have got to put your mind to it (Tom, UK).

Like Tom, most of our interviewees are already taking entrepreneurial steps to realise their imagined working futures. Allysa reflects the spirit of homo promptus when she says:

everything is precarious ... I just pick everything that I think is going to be beneficial for me at this moment, despite of everything that I am going to do in the future, and hope that one day what I am doing right now is going to contribute to that (Allysa, Australia).

Becky's pursuit of higher education qualifications is to 'get a point where I don't need an employer. I kind of want to be self-sufficient in that way' (Becky, UK). Like Rose, Becky sees herself carving out an individual, independent niche of self-employment that will protect her from the vagaries of the labour market. Allysa has similar hopes. She wants to return to Indonesia to be a lecturer and perhaps even 'head of department at the institution that I used to work'. Once she graduates, she will first try to gain employment at that university 'and start building up my career from the bottom'. Despite the clarity of her goals, she understands the imperative to keep her plans flexible:

> ... I am also trying to convince myself that I should not fix on one plan. So that's my long-term plan and that's good if I can achieve it, but I don't want to be too hard on myself. Maybe while I am reaching to that point, I can be flexible. ... It's good if it is related to education, but I am going to be open to other possibilities because it's going to be difficult for me if I just focus on that thing (Allysa, Australia).

In France, Juliette is ready to do whatever is needed to get by financially:

> If there was a big, economic situation, or political, yeah, I would change my job. It could happen. I think about this. ... I would not hesitate to work in a supermarket or something to have money. I have done it already, so I am ready do it again if it's needed (Juliette, France).

Still in France, similar themes emerge from our discussion with Kim. Kim is being strategic by 'looking at the internships that I have to do in the studies. So I try to pick the right ones, the ones that will help me get to the point where I want to be.' But she also acknowledges that this kind of planning has a fatalistic dimension 'because I have heard stories from other journalists that, for example, in TV/radio, everything can go very quick. So I think it will be a bit of hard work but a little bit of luck, too'. She uses a French verb to describe this particular aspect of homo promptus and to capture how many young people seek to manage risk and opportunity:

> ... in French, you have this word 'se débrouiller', like to make it work out, even though you are lost. Like you go to a foreign country. You don't know anyone, you don't know anything about the place. But, anyhow, you get through everything, like difficult situations (Kim, France).

It is a widely held view that as pathways to work become extended, more uncertain and less linear, young people need '21st century' or 'soft skills'. Having reportedly analysed more than 20 billion hours of work undertaken by 12 million young Australians, a 2017 report by the Foundation for Young Australians argues that such portable skills and capabilities are vital to succeed in the increasingly automated and globalised workplace (FYA 2017). Homo promptus also requires what another study calls 'a liquid skills mindset' (Infosys 2016, p. 25): that is, the flexible and adaptive mindset that enables them to respond to the fluid demands of their job or sector, to acquire new skills as they go, or to move to a new career path. This mindset also extends to the wider project of crafting what Bauman has characterised as a liquid life (2000), as Juliane explains:

> I think that nowadays, people are living more and more in their own bubbles. Something like society thinks, or norms/values, have maybe been more important in the past. So in the past: 'you should go to school and then do an apprenticeship or do studies and then work and then happy family' – oh, no, sorry – 'meet your partner, marry, have your family, buy a house, da, da, da, da, da'. A lot of that sounds like a nightmare to young people, nowadays. ... So people study longer. ... They are freelancing a little bit here and they are doing their art project a little bit there and they are working part-time here but then they go travelling again, or they live from their whatever vlog - things that were not possible in the past (Juliane, France).

Homo Promptus Plans for the Future While Living Life in the Short-Term

The adaptability that homo promptus is expected to embody involves being able to form plans for the future and then change those plans as circumstances change. This requires young people to develop what Leccardi has characterised as 'the capacity to maintain a direction or a trajectory notwithstanding the impossibility of anticipating the final destination' (2014, p. 48). This theme of *adaptive planning* emerges from many of our interviewees' statements, even where they are talking about other issues. When Abi in Australia describes the complexities of his present life and his hopes for the future, he explains: 'I make [an] everyday plan and I make [a] plan for some years ahead'. He gives the example of supporting her wife's study in Jakarta: this requires financial support which must be planned for. In the UK, George describes the imperative for adaptive planning even in the face of unknowable and unmanageable circumstances:

> You have to plan out, like, trying to save some money for yourself, like, be prepared for anything that comes unexpected, and sometimes you can't plan for stuff like that and that becomes a big issue, itself (George, UK).

But planning remains a challenge for many young people, especially for those who are preoccupied with work, unemployed or employed on temporary contracts. Woodman has noted that 'the contemporary world does not facilitate planning, but this does not mean that young people no longer care about the future or actively try to shape it, but that they shape it in new ways, primarily by keeping options open' (2011, p. 125). For some of our interviewees, however, the inability to plan locks them into a constant short-termism that creates pressure and anxiety. Becky describes her experience before taking up her first career in teaching and returning to study:

> When I first started working years ago, I worked in a holiday park. ... I would work morning until lunchtime, I would have two hours off at lunch. I was back in again at four o'clock in the afternoon, all the way through till two o'clock the next morning, six days a week, with one day off. ... that one day a week, you want to sleep anyway. But then you have got those two hours a day, you have to do shopping, you have to get your haircut - you know, those are

Introduction

the things that you need to do within two hours. I always felt on a constant edge, constant stress: 'oh, I have got to be somewhere in this time. Oh, I have got to do this' (Becky, UK).

For Jessica in Australia, her working life before starting university absorbed most of her energy:

> ... after high school ... I worked in a bar for a lot of the time and did two jobs. I was taught during the day and worked at a bar during the night, for about a good three/four months. At that time, I wasn't really thinking about what I was doing next. It was more the fact that I am going to go and do both jobs, going to earn money: that way I can go and do what I want on the weekends.

Although she lived with her parents at this time, her working hours were such that Jessica rarely saw them:

> ... I would wake up, I would go to work. From work, I would go to my next job, and I would get home about midnight and re-start the day, getting up at seven, going out. So I never really spent any time with them. And then on the weekends, I was busy catching up with my friends, going for dinners, occasionally seeing my parents on Sunday and that's about it. So I felt like time was passing me by (Jessica, Australia).

While these stories may appear to belong to a younger self, one that is now in the past for some of the university students we interviewed, the challenge of juggling or accommodating the demands of study, work or preparation for work is one that some of our interviewees are still experiencing in the present. Morgane explains:

> I mean, that's a basic student's life day: we do studies, we work, there is a part-time time to pay off studies or to live. Like, this year, I am studying my Master's and I have a [part-time] job until May .... Sometimes I am also struggling to plan things in the short-term, especially during the weekend: 'oh, my God, how am I going to organise my work and my homework for university?' ... I have a lot of friends who are in the same situation (Morgane, France).

Rose gives a similar example of her own inability to plan around her new casual job, a situation which, once again, is a source of some anxiety:

> ... sometimes they would call me and say, 'oh, we need you to come in today'. And you think, wow, my life is not in my hands. Are they allowed to do that? Can they do that? ... I feel frustrated with that because, I don't know, as me, I like to have control of what I do with my time. ... as a sort of person who is already so anxious about what's going to happen, and has this generalised anxiety about everything, it is really tough when someone just gives you a call last minute, and you are on public transport and you are going to take one hour to just reach there (Rose, Australia).

As Tyler also observes from Australia, the nature of the youth labour market means that 'you have less bargaining power, essentially. You essentially take what you get'. One of his concerns is that 'that probably has a negative impact on social lives, which has more far-reaching impacts'. This is certainly a current issue for Ninon and Irina, both of whom face difficulties in planning their social lives. For Ninon in France, this is less because of her own commitments than because her friends are either caught up in current work or in trying to secure their future employability: 'even planning a weekend or a vacation, it's actually kind of complicated because everyone around me is actually either having a job or is studying or internship'. While Irina in Australia is content working as a casual sales assistant while studying at university, she describes a similar challenge:

> I like the salary and I like it that I work flexible hours and I like it that I can both work/study … . But at the same time, I sometimes find it difficult to make any plans with my friends - mostly friends because my family is not here. Because I don't know if I will be free or if I will have to work on this same day that we want to plan something (Irina, Australia).

For other young people, the case is much more serious than this. While Grace in France is 'very hopeful' for her own future, she describes the uncertainty that besets many of her school peers, and the difficulty that they face in imagining a future at all:

> I know a lot of young people, the people that I went to school with, after they graduated, they started taking up small jobs. So maybe they work in fast foods, retail and everything fast-foods, and they struggle to think about the future, to think ahead, or imagine that they would be able to buy a house or to plan the future as well because they just work all these small jobs. They really don't know how to get out of it (Grace, France).

For such young people, as Grace goes on to explain, the need to work may colonise or undermine the ability to study, despite the prospect that study might offer a pathway to better work:

> I have a friend [who] ended up living on her own, since high school. And she wanted to go to college/university, but she couldn't because she found a job, a small job and she couldn't live and go to university because then, again, she wouldn't be able to pay for her house and afford her living conditions. So she was stuck … she can't really think about the future. She's just living with the time (Grace, France).

Even having a higher education degree is no assurance of the capacity to plan for key personal goals such as owning a home. As Becky explains, working on casual or temporary professional contracts can also affect young people's ability to realise their hopes:

> I think any young person that starts off on a career that is casual, which most of them are now, you can't get a decent contract like you used to, you kind of have to start at zero - planning is really tough. I think mentally it has an effect on you. If you can't plan in the future, you feel uncertain. You feel like a lack of control over your life, at which point then you start to think, oh, God, what am I actually doing? I feel lost. Where am I going with this, kind of thing?
>
> For me, having regular hours is so important - for mental health, for security in life. … I was teaching – because I was on agency pay – we went to get a mortgage and my other half is self-employed. We earn really good money together. We have been paying our rent for sort of three years, previous, quite a bit of money per month. They wouldn't give us a mortgage because on paper we looked inconsistent (Becky, UK).

Becky also describes the structural economic conditions that prevent growing numbers of young people from planning their lives in the present, let alone working to realise an imagined future:

> For me, it was another thing for coming to university. I want something where I get a wage. People know exactly how much I make, so I can go to a bank and go, 'this is exactly how

much I make. I am secure. I am safe. You can rely on me', kind of thing. And I think a lot of young people struggle with that … . Zero hour contracts in the UK are horrific. You know, they leave people literally in the lurch because you don't know one month to the next, or even one week to the next, what hours you are getting, how much money you are getting. How can anyone plan a life, plan what food they want to buy, what clothes they have got, going out, seeing their friends, you know, having a relationship – how can you do any of that, when you don't even know what hours you are working? (Becky, UK).

For Alice, too, life is lived mainly in the short-term:

I don't really have a sort of steady/stable routine or anything. … I am applying for a lot of [music] festivals at the moment but [job] applications are like six to eight months in advance. It's like, I don't know what I am doing in eight months. I don't know what I am doing in three months. So, yeah, it is kind of hard to plan (Alice, Australia).

Irina's uncertainty is of a different nature. As we discussed in Chap. 3, she is studying in Australia through a scholarship provided by the Russian government. There are requirements attached to this scholarship: she has to return to Russia once she completes her degree to work in her field of study for three years. While there is potentially more work in Moscow (where Irina has friends) and in St. Petersburg, both cities are highly competitive because there is a quota imposed on how many positions are available. She may have to work in another city or go back to her home town, where 'there's no opportunities and it is very hard to find a good job there'. Her father has actively encouraged Irina to leave Russia 'because this country won't give you anything good.' She would like to return to Australia after meeting her obligations to the Russian government, but is 'really anxious' about whether this will be possible:

… I hope that this education, this degree that I am getting here now, will help me with it in the future. But I am still nervous about what if it doesn't? … What will happen then? (Irina, Australia).

Homo Promptus Is not Tethered to a Single Place

A recent analysis of European youth mobilities has concluded that youth in the contemporary era is 'a life stage of enhanced geographic mobility' (King 2018, p. 9). In Chap. 2, we introduced the strong discursive and practical relationship that is drawn between higher education and geographic mobility. International mobility, in particular, is both one of the promised products of higher education and a prerequisite for the successful attainment of graduates' personal and professional goals. It is also frequently a necessary step to ensure access to higher education in the first place. Many of our interviewees have relocated or travelled far from their homes to go to university. They also envisage that they will travel in the future. In 10 years, for example, Ninon imagines that she 'will have a stable job. I like to work abroad like, in the US or the UK … I want to travel a lot' (Ninon, France).

Even those of our interviewees who already have children are contemplating geographic mobility in order to secure a better future for themselves and their families.

Becky from the UK has great hopes of migrating to Australia with her partner and young daughter. She and her partner have already visited both New Zealand and Australia to ascertain which country offers the best and most achievable prospects for them. They are actively investigating the available visa options and are doing all they can to progress their case in the lead-up to a formal application.

Others are more tethered to place, but must leave home in order to one day come back to work there. As we have flagged earlier, Abi has come to Australia from Indonesia to take up university study. Although his scholarship would help cover the costs of bringing his wife and daughter to Australia with him, this is impossible: 'unfortunately, I could not bring my family here because my wife is a civil servant so she need to work in Indonesia. So, every semester I go back to Indonesia'. His life is lived across geographic contexts, and is forcibly mobile due to the gravitational pull factor of study opportunities. He hopes that these will in turn allow him to pursue his preferred career in West Borneo as well as to be with his family. At the same time, he is actively considering relocating his family to other Indonesian cities in search of desirable work.

For most of our other interviewees, mobility is not such a serious prospect. Instead, it is a desirable and enriching experience, one that is explicitly connected to being young, as Sophia explains:

> ... what makes youth is travelling, what makes youth is different experiences. If you are not letting people do these experiences, then where is the fun? Also, they are not going to be curious anymore, they are not going to think anymore. I mean, it's just going to do what other people want them to do, which is grow up, have an occasion, get a job, get married, boom, that's it - the end. At age 27, *the end!* [laughs]. And that is just sad. [Sophia's preference is to rather] take your time, go outside and do some things and go to raves and festivals and travel around - go to Europe, go to Asia and see other things (Sophia, France).

For Juliane, too, and for her friends in her home nation of Germany, travel and mobility are an assumed and natural part of life:

> ... my family ... are based in Germany, as well. They always say I am crazy because I am going everywhere. However, in Berlin, all my friends do the same ... it is totally normal (Juliane, France).

This is quite different to the 'vision of education and life' that is held by her French friends and fostered by the French educational system:

> I think we [in Germany] are more liberal, a little bit hippy. We are like: 'okay, we do high school and then maybe we go away for one year and then we do the Bachelor and then we go away again and then we go into here and we do that'. Like, we just float around a little bit and travel and maybe: 'oh, we don't do that study. Okay, do the next one' ... whereas in France, they are really strict. You already have to focus on a subject when you are 16 (Juliane, France).

Especially for the French cohort, higher education has already brought travel opportunities, which many imagine will continue in future. For Zaynab, for example, the freedom to be mobile currently outweighs other normative priorities such as buying a home: 'most of us have had experience or easier access to studies abroad [and] work abroad, so we would tend to be less attached to one place'. Still in France,

Morgane agrees that 'every young person wants to travel', but she also recognises that the desire for work and work experience may be drivers of this youth mobility. She is undertaking international studies and hopes to gain an internship with the BBC: 'I started to look for jobs in London—trying to get there before Brexit [laughs]'. For Juliette, the link between travel and work is equally strong. She has already relocated within France to attend university, and moving back to her family town is one possible future, but she also wants 'to see the world': 'I like to either be able to travel, thanks to my job, or live abroad and work as a correspondent. And then, maybe, I go back south'.

For Grace, too, seeing the world is a priority. She wants to 'go outside of France, to broaden horizons, to live on my own and to meet other people, to have different cultures and meet new cultures'. Her imagined future career is an important aspect of these travel plans: 'I would like to work maybe at an embassy but in different countries. ... I don't want to stay in one place for too long'. Grace is particularly interested in living 'somewhere that I have never been, somewhere, like, a culture that I am not familiar with, and then just establish my life from there, from the new place and build my life from there'. Once again, this imagined future mobility is strongly linked to more pragmatic career and financial considerations:

> Everyone says that Canada is a really nice country: they are very open. In terms of jobs, there's more opportunities there. And it is a bit like the United States but a better version of the United States with less political dramas, without issues, I guess (Grace, France).

Earlier, we suggested that homo promptus is expected to plan for both the immediate and long-term future despite the barriers that may make this impossible. Partly because of its association with the formation of future plans and decisions, travel may also be attached to uncertainty, as Juliane explains. She recognises that it is 'a freedom that you have but, also, it is stressing me a little bit':

> [As of] September this year, I don't know what I am going to do. I can still stay enrolled as a student but I don't know when I will be going back to Berlin or maybe travel in Asia for three months .... I think a lot of young people are feeling like this, floating around a little bit. Maybe more in Germany than in France because they are more into their planning and everything (Juliane, France).

At the same time, as Kim acknowledges, opportunities for travel are not available to all by choice:

> I can imagine that 50 years ago, or even 100 years ago, you were born in a certain family. You knew where you would end [up]. Today, you are born in a certain family but you can go wherever you want, almost - not always, of course. Of course, it's more difficult for ... refugees or people in [my city] who don't have a lot of money, like, also depending on the area where you live (Kim, France).

We have suggested earlier that homo promptus is both strategic and flexible. The link between mobility and adaptability is a recurring theme across our interviews. Both Zaynab and George describe the mobile, flexible self to which they and their peers aspire:

... I don't think 'stable and secure' is common anymore or realistic anymore. So flexibility, that's something that I enjoy, that's something that I think a lot of young people can offer ... . Down the line it could be teaching, teaching foreign languages, but it could be working in the private sector, companies, international, multi-national companies, things like that, that would allow that flexibility (Zaynab, France).

... my generation is very much empowered by the idea that we have that flexibility, that independence to an extent: we are not tied down to one place (George, UK).

These ideas of mobility also cross cultural lines. For Rose, they represent a desire to break with the past, a desire that she attributes to many other young people in her country of birth:

Young people in India don't like their culture. They don't like the collectivism. They are very frustrated with what the society demands of them and they want to break free of it. Because of that, there is a movement towards cities, the metros and just because you want to live on your own terms and you don't want to be tied down by the society. That is the future - moving towards a westernised way of living, taking your own decisions, having more freedom, which means having more responsibility and sort of a disconnection with your previous generation because they don't understand you as well now. Yeah, that is the future. And that is even the present – that's what's happening even now (Rose, Australia).

Homo Promptus Is Permanently in 'Situational' Mode

We have suggested that homo promptus is responsive and entrepreneurial, creating plans for the future where circumstances allow. Returning to Peou and Zinn's (2015) typology, there is also an aspect of homo promptus which sees the future as 'mainly unknowable'. This arises chiefly from the uncertainty attached to the changing youth labour markets which we have described in the previous chapter. 'I think it is difficult', Juliette reflects from France, 'because we have to fight to get a job. ... I think to fight for what we want to do is really hard'. It is also connected to the severing of the opportunity bargain of higher education for many young people. One survey of 5,300 young people found that only 42% of young people in Germany, Greece, Italy, Portugal, Spain and Sweden believed that post-secondary education would improve their employment opportunities, compared to 50% of those in the global survey. For those young people in the UK, it was even lower (40%), while in France it was lower still (35%) (Mourshed et al. 2017). Ninon describes the emotional effects of this erosion of core assumptions about what university qualifications will lead to:

... it's really depressing because you are doing four/five years of studying and you actually think it is going to be for nothing, at the end, or you can also feel that you are being ... *dévalorisé* (undervalued or made to feel worthless) (Ninon, France).

In Chap. 3, we observed that our three cohorts of young university students shared a strong hope for stable and secure professional employment. Despite the strength of this common hope, a number of our interviewees challenge the very idea of a stable career plan or career security. In Australia, Alice asks:

What does 'security' mean? Does it even exist? I think there's this myth that certainly my parents buy into that you can get this big, fat corporate job and climb the ladder and become a partner and get all these benefits - you know, they will look after you and all this. I don't think it is real. Maybe it used to be but I don't think it's real now, and I think people get made redundant whenever it suits the company. If they need to make more profits or whatever, they won't think twice: they'll just get rid of you (Alice, Australia).

Sophia goes a step further, characterising her generation as 'the lost generation' and the 'disillusioned generation':

… our dreams are being crushed all the time. Well, from what I have heard, it's basically that we grew up with TV shows and movies and music/artists and artists of different genres and politicians and everything that is around us, telling us that we can do whatever we want, we can do whatever job we want, and then we just realised later - mmm, nope, I cannot do that (Sophia, France).

Following on from Sophia's comments, it comes as little surprise that a 2017 UK survey of 2,215 people aged 16–25 found declining levels of happiness and confidence, with emotional health decreasing to its lowest level to date compared to previous years. The authors of the survey suggest that 'many young people feel that they have no control over their lives, are full of self-doubt and feel trapped by their circumstances' (The Prince's Trust 2017, p. 2). Just over a third of those surveyed (36%) felt that they had no control over their job prospects, 18% felt that they had no ability to change their circumstances, and 16% felt that their lives would amount to nothing, no matter how hard they tried. The 2018 iteration of the survey shows that these figures have further declined, with 39% of young people feeling that their lives are beyond their ability to control (The Prince's Trust 2018).

An important aspect of this loss of faith in the future is linked to employment status: those young people who are in some form of education, training or work are more likely to be happy and have self-belief and confident compared to those who are not (The Prince's Trust 2017). Another aspect is linked to issues of power and the current political climate in the UK. In 2017, a significant proportion of the young people surveyed (58%) expressed anxiety about how recent political events might affect their future (The Prince's Trust 2017). These figures have stayed stable within the 2018 study, a theme to which we will return in this chapter.

Young people's anxiety or loss of faith in the future is not limited to the UK, of course. Another survey of almost 8,000 young people across 30 countries who had a college or university degree and were working full-time (mainly in private-sector organizations) found pervasive feelings of pessimism about the economy (Deloitte 2017). In Chap. 5, we described the emergence of the gig economy as the latest phase of the individualisation of the labour market. Perceptions of uncertainty in global markets are making graduates risk averse, with some expressing a reluctance to take their chances in the gig economy as freelancers or consultants, preferring instead to stay in their current jobs. As the report notes, 'in a period of great uncertainty, stability is appealing' (Deloitte 2017, p. 1). Another survey came up with similar findings, concluding that 'today's risk averse younger generation are drawn to working for large or medium sized companies that can offer stability, training and progression. On average, less than one in 10 want to work for a start up' (Infosys 2016, p. 4). This is at odds with the entrepreneurial dimension of homo promptus, and is one of many conflicting messages sent to young people about the value of their higher education study in securing future (stable) work.

Homo Promptus Lives in Waithood

Earlier in this book, we described how young people are experiencing elongated trajectories to financial security and other conventional markers of adulthood, such as owning a home, in a period which we have previously described as waithood. The deferral (or disappearance) of home ownership may be one of the clearest markers of this prolongation of youth. While we have discussed this at length in Chap. 4, it also warrants consideration here in the context of the dispositions which homo promptus is expected to demonstrate.

The transition to adulthood is conventionally characterised by five key experiences: leaving the parental home; completing formal education; beginning full-time employment; marrying or partnering; and becoming a parent. The acquisition of a home—whether purchased or securely rented—can be considered a sixth marker of this transition (Berngruber 2015; Krahn et al. 2018), yet according to a survey commissioned by the Citi Foundation (2017), only 48% of the 7,000 respondents aged 18–24 in developed economies are optimistic about their ability to afford a home relative to their parents at their age. While this may reflect the continued effects of the GFC and escalating property and living costs, it is also indicative of the wider circumstances within which many young people are trying to forge their imagined futures. In the UK, for example, the so-called 'Generation Rent' represents a growing proportion of people forced to rent privately for longer periods of their lives, reinforcing generational differences in housing access and opportunities (Hoolachan et al. 2017). In Australia, too, despite the relatively high disposable incomes of many young people, the dream of owning a home is increasingly out of reach (Taylor 2018). As Ben Phillips from the Australian National University's Centre for Social Research suggests:

> I think it's quite clear that older Australians have done very well out of the property boom [...] Their house prices have doubled or tripled or quadrupled over the last 20 or so years, whereas younger people obviously find it much more difficult to even get into the housing market (cited in Taylor 2018).

This combination of push and pull factors means that homo promptus may be caught in a crossfire, desiring mobility and independence on the one hand while being subject to rising costs of living on the other that compel their dependence on parents and carers. It also has real implications for their future economic prospects and, by extension, for their ability to realise their hopes for the future. One recent study notes that young people's participation in the gig economy prevents them from being able to borrow money to enter the housing market: 'Those people who are inside the gig economy … the people who have missed super [-annuated pension], or missed the opportunity to participate in it, are going to suffer' (Inwood cited in Taylor 2018). John Daley from the Grattan Institute has also observed that:

> ... it used to be that, as a young person, whether you owned your own home or not, essentially your income didn't matter ... Whereas today, society is very highly divided. ... Those on higher incomes ... are much much more likely to own their own home. ... So the average older household in Australia effectively was getting a wealth boost every year of about $60,000, and that's a free kick the younger generation will not get. ... Instead they're part of a generation where, if they want to be wealthy, they basically need to have rich parents (cited in Taylor 2018).

It is not surprising that in Australia, Cynthia is just starting to explore home ownership options but finds the cost daunting:

> ... just the other day when I was looking prospectively – oh, how much would it actually cost for a house deposit – and it does shock you now. Like, you are pretty much paying the same price ... for a much smaller place or even just rent compared to your parents ... with that same amount of money ... . And it is a big fear. And even just from working hard this year and last year, just to earn a car, it takes a long time, just to earn a certain amount of money. And you really have to work hard (Cynthia, Australia).

Mel expresses a similar view:

> I have friends who, you know, would love to get a house in a few years but they genuinely cannot afford it and things like that ... . As for others things: getting a stable job and all that is still – like, there's still markers of 'adult', like entering adulthood, that kind of thing – but I think there's also more competition. So, we have family friends who have done Bachelor of Science for three/four years and they come out, they can't get a job (Mel, Australia).

This is not solely an Australian story, though. For Zaynab in France, '[the] overall prospects in buying a house at a certain age ... is not the same as it used to be'. For Becky in the UK, the disappearing dream of home ownership is just one of the grim circumstances that make up her imagined future for young people more widely:

> For me, that's why it is so bleak for young people. They might not even know it's bleak, but the future is. The next 10 years - in fact, the next 30 years, if we are going by the predicted standard - the next 30 years is really, really not good financially and everything else, because we are going to have no job prospects, no prospects of buying a home, no job security, government that is going to come in and start a war with God knows who, and God knows where. Everything is kind of apart, really (Becky, UK).

Being 'Precarious People'

We noted in the Introduction that contemporary young people are encouraged to maintain a degree of hope or optimism for the future that belies the effects and impacts of uncertainty. In light of the trends outlined above and in the previous chapter, one could anticipate that more of our interviewees would be pessimistic about the future. Certainly, there have been abundant warnings since the GFC that young people are losing hope, particularly in the economic future (Muižnieks 2014), yet what we have found overall in the accounts of our young interviewees is a more complex affective mixture of hope, optimism, pessimism and anxiety. This complexity has been previously observed by Woodman, who proposes that young people 'concurrently mix multiple, and sometimes seemingly contradictory, orientations to the future' (2011, p. 112). It emerges with particular clarity in regards to how they imagine the future by comparison with their parents' lives.

In Chap. 2, we noted the suggestion by Hardgrove and her colleagues that youth studies may have had too strong a focus on 'generational "rupture" and sharp breaks between the lived experiences and values of this generation and those of their parents and grandparents' (2015, p. 164). We acknowledge the importance of recognising the continuity of aspects of young people's lives with those of previous generations, but we also maintain, with numerous scholars, that fundamental changes have taken place. Let's look at some of the recent data that describes how young people themselves perceive these changes.

In 2015, Leach and Hanton argued that 'the idea of each new generation being better off than the previous generation has been shattered' (2015, p. 5). The erosion of this idea also shows itself in the empirical findings of recent studies and surveys. A UK study of five generations found that 66% of young people born after 1995 were optimistic about being able to form a family of their own and 55% were confident of securing successful, well-paid work. But fewer than two in five (37%) expected life to be better overall than it has been for their parents. These figures are striking compared to the views of the older cohorts in the study. 42% of Generation Y participants (the generation born during the 1980s and early 1990s) thought they would have a better life than their parents. For the generation before them (those born between 1965 and 1984), this figure grew to 60%, while 70% of Baby Boomers (born between 1946 and 1964) and 79% of people born before World War II felt that their generation had had a better life than the one before it. Pessimism about the future has clearly grown with each UK generation (NCB 2014).

This pessimism was mirrored in another study of 20 countries. In Australia, 42% of respondents believed that today's youth will have had a worse life than their parents' generation (versus 30% who thought they would have a better life). In the UK, 54% of respondents felt they would be worse off (compared to 20% who thought the opposite). In France, 69% stated that they would be worse off: only 7% believed that young people had better prospects than their parents. Survey respondents aged under 30 were more pessimistic for their generation than the survey population as whole, with only 16% in France thinking their life will be better than their parents. In the UK, 22% gave the same response compared with 36% of the whole population (Ipsos MORI 2014).

By contrast, young people in rapidly growing economies such as China and India are more optimistic that their generation will be better off than that of their parents (Ipsos 2018). The question of whether this optimism will be rewarded is one to which we return in the Conclusion: meanwhile, the Ipsos data echoes the findings of the Citi Foundation survey cited earlier (Citi Foundation 2017). This recorded a higher level of optimism amongst young people in developing cities compared to developed cities. Eight in ten (79%) of young people in developing markets believe they will find opportunities to succeed in their preferred career as compared to 64% of their counterparts in developed markets (Citi Foundation 2017, p. 3).

On the back of this data, we put a similar question to our interviewees: do you think that your generation will be better or worse off than that of your parents? Reflecting on the impact of the credential inflation which we describe earlier, Tyler thinks that the Baby Boomers 'were just perfectly placed', but that members of his generation will have less economic success and less ability to convert their educational achievement into work and financial security:

> We are obviously better educated, probably, so there is one positive. But ... I guess the bar is getting higher. The percentage of people that had Bachelor degrees when my parents were being educated was probably ... under 10 per cent or something like that. And now I believe it's reached something like 60 per cent or something like that. ... even a PhD doesn't guarantee you a job anymore. ... you know, our parents instilled in us a respect for education, I guess, which is a really good thing, but now it's so saturated that it doesn't necessarily automatically—you know, I think me, I will be fine, but I can see other people in my generation, the unskilled jobs are being automated and the education system is flooded. So, essentially, it is, which way do you go? (Tyler, Australia).

Tyler also feels that there have been deeper economic changes since his parents were his age, changes that he fears will have a marked impact on his generation:

> I would be quite confident in saying that there is rising inequality, and I think that is probably one of the largest factors in why our generation won't be as well-off as the previous generation. I think probably inequality wasn't as bad 30/40 years ago.

Still in Australia, Jessica shares a similar view. She thinks that her parents 'may have had it better because these days we are brought up go to university, go to work, pretty much, become financially stable'. For Lyr in France, there is no equivocation or doubt. He is firmly of the belief that his generation will be worse off:

> ... we already are. ... When I talk to my parents, I tell them, 'but we are not in the same conditions. We don't have enough employment security, much more precarious people' ... You know, then we are thinking even with we retire or something, problems as simple as we don't make as many children, so there's not going to be as many people heading to retirement. So it is problems that are pending, be a much bigger problem, once we get there ... So, yeah, I don't such have an optimistic view of my future (Lyr, France).

Paloma's outlook echoes Lyr's:

> There are no jobs. The unemployment in young people is rising, exponentially ... we are going to be less well-off than our parents. ... That is depressing (Paloma, France).

But not all of our interviewees feel the same way. Still in France, Ines hearkens back to the mobility and flexibility which we have suggested are characteristic of homo promptus, suggesting that 'some elements will be better than our parents—because we have more freedom, we have more choices, maybe'. Juliette agrees that her generation is better off than her parents', while acknowledging the challenge of making such a comparison:

> But, yes, I think we would be better off than our parents. But time's changed. It is not the same. ... Because of those changes, we can't compare, really, because people before were living with all their family in the same place, in small villages or big cities .... They didn't travel a lot. Nowadays, young people travel. They want to see the world, and it's in every country. It is not just in France - it is also in Africa, it is also in Asia: people want to travel and see the world, and that was not before. Yeah, for this reason, I would say we are better off, because we have more options (Juliette, France).

Conclusion

In this chapter, we have described the emergence of homo promptus, a form of youth selfhood that is fostered by the discourses of higher education and the labour market. Echoing Vingaard Johansson and his colleagues (2017), we believe that homo promptus is a 'seismograph' of the future, one that signals social change. At the same time, and as we acknowledge in Chap. 2, there are strong elements of continuity in young people's experience, including their feelings that the future is risky and uncertain (Furlong and Cartmel 1997). Over half a century ago, Connell, Francis and Skilbeck made this observation about the 'problematic future' of young people in the Australian city of Sydney that could have been written today:

> The Sydney adolescent of the present day, therefore, finds himself in a situation whose stability is suspect, and the duration is uncertain. To learn how to cope with the insecurity of the present and with the problematic future involves him in the difficult task of learning not only knowledge, principles of present value, but also, and probably more importantly, the means and techniques whereby knowledge appropriate to new situations is acquired, and principles are modified, jettisoned, or adhered to, in the light of changing circumstances (1957, p. 207).

Some changes seem indisputable, however. Young people's relationship to work certainly appears to be changing. Previously assumed truths of youth such as the role of higher education as a stable path to career are being questioned. Transitions to secure work are also taking longer. This elongation or prolongation of youth transitions affirms the need that we noted in Chap. 2 to rethink static definitions of youth and young people.

An education-to-work transition is typically defined as 'the transition as the length of time between the exit from education (either upon graduation or early exit without completion) to the first entry into fixed-term employment', but the meaning of 'fixed-term employment', and consequently its measurement, varies from country to country (Matsumoto and Elder 2010, p. 3). The end point of transition is often defined as 'the first moment of employment in any job', while others define it as the 'first fixed-term job (measured by contract type)' or 'a job that meets a very basic criteria of "decency", namely a permanency that can provide the worker with a sense of security (e.g. a permanent contract), or a job that the worker feels personally satisfied with' (Matsumoto and Elder 2010, p. 3). This latter definition seeks to improve on the previous two, but it also poses additional dimensions. For example, while financial security is indeed seen to be desirable by many young people, the job they secure might not be desirable in and of itself. If the promise of higher education is desirable work and not just security, then arguably the 'transition' to work has not taken place. This has deeper implications for how we understand youth as a concept.

In Chap. 2, we noted that notions of youth vary or gain meaning according to 'their social, cultural, political, institutional, locational, governmental, and economic contexts' (Wyn 2015, p. 5). We also introduced Honwana's notion of waithood, a term which describes the prolongation of youth as a time when young people are 'negotiating personal identity and financial independence' (2014, p. 23). Although Honwana writes in relation to young people in Africa whose socioeconomic and cultural conditions vary vastly from those of our interviewees, this characterisation is also applicable to young people in Australia, France and the UK. Being entrepreneurial, cultivating personal brands, and seeking both paid and unpaid opportunities for professional experience and personal development are some of the ways that young people seek to enhance their perceived employability, but these take place within dynamics arising from the hegemonies of money and power that drive the globalised, deregulated labour market economies of the current era.

Waithood would seem to have negative connotations. In itself, it might be characterised as a 'failed transition, a form of deviance, or a pathology from which young people suffer' (Honwana 2014, p. 24), yet it can also constitute 'a period of experimentation, of improvisation and of great creativity as young [people] adopt a range of survival strategies to cope with the daily challenges in their lives' (Honwana 2014, p. 24). Homo promptus is a way of navigating life in the contemporary global economy. It is also an affective response to the complexities of that economy.

When young people imagine their working futures, they do so in an affective way. Some maintain hope and optimism, as they are encouraged to do by the prevalent discourses of this time. Some are pessimistic or fearful about their own prospects and about the trend of wider national and global events. Others recall Leccardi's depiction of 'hyper-activist' individuals who 'embrace unpredictability', and seek 'to conquer new spaces of freedom and experimentation' (2014, p. 49). Sometimes, these feelings and responses are combined. Young people may harbour a deep concern about their long-term futures and the forces beyond their control that are shaping those futures, yet feel optimistic as to what lies ahead in the more manageable, personal and accessible short-term future (Cook 2015). They may also feel able to influence aspects of those short-term futures. We explore these themes in the next chapter by critically investigating how the dispositions and behaviours of homo promptus manifest themselves in young people's current and imagined future lives as political actors.

References

Bauman, Z. (2000). *Liquid modernity*. Cambridge: Polity Press.
Berngruber, A. (2015). 'Generation boomerang' in Germany? Returning to the parental home in young adulthood. *Journal of Youth Studies, 18*(10), 1274–1290. https://doi.org/10.1080/13676261.2015.1039969.

Brooks, R. (2017). The construction of higher education students in English policy documents. *British Journal of Sociology of Education, 39*(6), 745–761. https://doi.org/10.1080/01425692.2017.1406339.

Budd, R. (2017). Undergraduate orientations towards higher education in Germany and England: Problematizing the notion of 'student as customer'. *Higher Education, 73*(1), 23–37. https://doi.org/10.1007/s10734-015-9977-4.

Citi Foundation. (2017). *Pathways to progress global youth survey 2017: Economic prospects & expectations*. Retrieved August 13, 2018, from https://www.citigroup.com/citi/foundation/data/p2p_global_youth_survey_full_data.pdf.

Connell, W. F., Francis, E., & Skilbeck, E. (1957). *Growing up in an Australian city: A study of adolescents in Sydney*. Melbourne: ACER.

Cook, J. (2015). Young adults' hopes for the long-term future: From re-enchantment with technology to faith in humanity. *Journal of Youth Studies, 19*(4), 517–532. https://doi.org/10.1080/13676261.2015.1083959.

Deloitte. (2017). *The 2017 Deloitte millennial survey. Apprehensive millennials: seeking stability and opportunities in an uncertain world*. Retrieved September 20, 2018, from https://www2.deloitte.com/content/dam/Deloitte/global/Documents/About-Deloitte/gx-deloitte-millennial-survey-2017-executive-summary.pdf.

Furlong, A., & Cartmel, F. (1997). *Young people and social change: New perspectives*. Maidenhead, UK: Open University Press.

Hardgrove, A., Rootham, E., & McDowell, L. (2015). Possible selves in a precarious labour market: Youth, imagined futures, and transitions to work in the UK. *Geoforum, 60,* 163–171. https://doi.org/10.1016/j.geoforum.2015.01.014.

Hoolachan, J., McKee, K., Moore, T., & Soaita, A. M. (2017). 'Generation rent' and the ability to 'settle down': Economic and geographical variation in young people's housing transitions. *Journal of Youth Studies, 20*(1), 63–78. https://doi.org/10.1080/13676261.2016.1184241.

Honwana, A. (2014). Waithood: Youth transitions and social change. In D. Foeken, T. Dietz, L. Haan, and L. Johnson (Eds.), *Development and equity: An interdisciplinary exploration by ten scholars from Africa, Asia and Latin America* (pp. 28–40). Brill Online.

Infosys. (2016). *Amplifying human potential: Education and skills for the fourth industrial revolution*. Retrieved May 25, 2017, from http://www.experienceinfosys.com/humanpotential.

Ipsos MORI. (2014). *Global Trends 2014. Navigating the New*. Retrieved November 15, 2018, from https://www.ipsos.com/sites/default/files/publication/1970-01/ipsos-mori-global-trends-2014.pdf.

Ipsos. (2108). *Goalkeepers Global Youth Outlook Poll*. Retrieved September 27, 2018, from https://www.ipsos.com/en-us/news-polls/Gates-goalkeepers-youth-optimism.

King, R. (2018). Theorising new European youth mobilities. *Population, Space and Place, 24*(1), 1–12. https://doi.org/10.1002/psp.2117.

Krahn, H. J., Chai, C.-A., Fang, S., Galambos, N. L., & Johnson, M. D. (2018). Quick, uncertain, and delayed adults: timing, sequencing and duration of youth-adult transitions in Canada. *Journal of Youth Studies, 21*(7), 905–921. https://doi.org/10.1080/13676261.2017.1421750.

Leach, J., & Hanton, A. (2015). *Intergenerational fairness index 2015*. London: The Intergenerational Foundation.

Leccardi, C. (2014). Young people and the new semantics of the future. *SocietàMutamentoPolitica, 5*(10), 41–54. https://doi.org/10.13128/SMP-15404.

Matsumoto, M., & Elder, S. (2010). *Characterizing the school-to-work transitions of young men and women: Evidence from the ILO school-to-work transition surveys*. ILO Working Papers 994572743402676. Geneva: International Labour Organization.

Mourshed, M., Patel, J., & Suder, K. (2017). *Education to employment: Getting Europe's youth into work*. McKinsey Center for Government. Retrieved June 2, 2018, from http://egdcfoundation.org/work/assets/McKinsey-Education-to-Employment-Europe.pdf.

References

Muižnieks, N. (2014). *Youth human rights at risk during the crisis*. Council of Europe. Retrieved June 25, 2017, from https://www.coe.int/en/web/commissioner/-/youth-human-rights-at-risk-during-the-crisis.

National Children's Bureau [NCB]. (2014). *Who is generation next?*. London: National Children's Bureau.

Peou, C., & Zinn, J. (2015). Cambodian youth managing expectations and uncertainties of the life course—A typology of biographical management. *Journal of Youth Studies, 18*(6), 726–742. https://doi.org/10.1080/13676261.2014.992328.

The Foundation for Young Australians [FYA]. (2017). *The new work smarts: Thriving in the new work order*. Retrieved July 11, 2017, from https://www.fya.org.au/wp-content/uploads/2017/07/FYA_TheNewWorkSmarts_July2017.pdf.

The Prince's Trust. (2017). The Prince's Trust Macquarie Youth Index 2017. Retrieved November 13, 2017, from https://www.princes-trust.org.uk/Youth-Index-2017-report.pdf.

The Prince's Trust. (2018). The Prince's Trust Macquarie Youth Index 2018. Retrieved September 22, 2018, from https://www.princes-trust.org.uk/about-the-trust/news-views/macquarie-youth-index-2018-annual-report.

Taylor, D. (2018, May 25). Older and younger Australians face different worlds due to intergeneration gap, experts say. *ABC News*. Retrieved June 23, 2018, from http://www.abc.net.au/news/2018-05-25/younger-generation-doing-better-than-any-other-australia/9797616.

Vingaard Johansen, U., Knudsen, F. B., Engelbrecht Kristoffersen, C., Stellfeld Rasmussen, J., Saaby Steffen, E., & Sund, K. J. (2017). Political discourse on higher education in Denmark: from enlightened citizen to homo economicus. *Studies in Higher Education, 42*(2), 264–277. https://doi.org/10.1080/03075079.2015.1045477.

Woodman, D. (2011). Young people and the future: Multiple temporal orientations shaped in interaction with significant others. *Young, 19*(2), 111–128. https://doi.org/10.1177/110330881001900201.

Wyn, J. (2015). Thinking about childhood and youth. In J. Wyn & H. Cahill (Eds.), *Handbook of children and youth studies* (pp. 3–20). Singapore: Springer.

Chapter 7
Making the Future: Homo Promptus and the Political

> People distrust media now and they distrust politicians. … I feel at least in my circle of friends, and my acquaintances and people that I meet all the time and I know, I feel there's a feeling of distrust. … we never talk about politics because it feels like it doesn't concern us anymore (Sophia, France).

Introduction

Many of the economic trends we have discussed in our previous chapters are also entwined with political change, of which Brexit and the election of US President Donald Trump are two of the most recent and most dramatic examples. This change is adding to the destabilisation of political orthodoxies in ways that have immediate implications for the mobility and security of many young people and that exacerbate the growing distance between young people and political representatives that we have explored in our previous book (Walsh and Black 2018b). The emergence of post-truth politics is further adding to this destabilisation, unsettling the very foundations of public discourse and the ability of governments (and citizens) to respond to pressing changes. It is also fostering a complex environment of hyperbole which brings into sharp focus the role of affect in contemporary politics and young people's response to them.

In Chap. 6, we introduced our idea of homo promptus to describe the entrepreneurial youth selfhood that is produced by education and labour market forces and discourses, but that is also actively cultivated by young people themselves in response to these forces and discourses and as a means of engaging with uncertainty as it manifests across the various aspects of their lives. In this chapter, we turn to the political dimension of those lives. We draw on our interviews with 30 young university students in France, the UK and Australia and our review of the recent international literature to consider how young university students understand themselves as political actors.

We recognise that for some young people, the existing political system offers the democratic opportunities they seek. We also recognise that an increasing number of others engage as political actors in ways that reflect the values and behaviours of homo promptus: they are sceptical of conventional political processes and information sources; their preferred modes of political action are extra-institutional, affective and flexible and often based on the pursuit of issues and causes that are personally meaningful and connected to their local or social networks; and they rely on 'gut-feelings' in making sense of political discourses.

The Politics of Uncertainty

We return first to the political themes and contexts raised at the start of this book. When discussing the impact of current political developments on their imagined futures, our interviewees raise a number of concerns including the influence of Russian President Vladimir Putin over global affairs, the rise of right wing populist movements, austerity politics in the UK, the election of Trump and the implications and effects of Brexit on the fabric of British and European life. These latter two events are a particular point of focus for many: as we have seen in our earlier chapters, they serve as touchstones of uncertainty and instability.

This uncertainty arguably began during both the Trump and Brexit campaigns. The outcome of the so-called Brexit advisory referendum held in June 2016, in which 52% of Britons voted for the UK's withdrawal from the EU, was partly predicated on a perception that such a departure would restore migration and economic control, despite concerns that it would divide the UK in the process (Castle 2016). The exit campaign controversially drew on misleading data (Stone 2017). During his campaign for US President across the Atlantic, Republican nominee Donald Trump promised that his policies would be 'Brexit plus plus plus!' (Erlanger 2016), using a similar language of isolationism and a return to nation-state control as well as misleading information and rhetoric.

Polling suggests that the majority of young people in the US were in favour of neither of these political outcomes: 55% of young people aged 18–29 voted for Democrat candidate Hillary Clinton compared to 37% for Trump (New York Times 2016). This also echoes the UK experience, where young people expressed concern about how Brexit would affect their mobility and education (Stefanou 2016) and where polling suggests that only 19% of people aged 18 to 24 voted to leave compared to 59% of old age pensioners (Shuster 2016). Such concerns were repeated by many of our interviewees from France and the UK, which we will continue to explore in the conclusion to this book. In this chapter, meanwhile, we suggest that these developments are linked to deeper concerns about certain epistemological aspects of contemporary politics: namely, young people's attitudes towards the emergence of fake news and post-truth politics.

These attitudes are perhaps best understood in the context of recent research into young people's political engagement, and the ways in which manifestations of this engagement are described by public and policy discourses. The past decades have seen a well-documented explosion of concern amongst governments and public institutions regarding young people's engagement in the democratic process and their willingness and ability to contribute to the political and civic fabric. This concern has led to a proliferation of strategies and interventions by supranational agencies such as the OECD, UNESCO and the EU, as well as by local education jurisdictions and individual schools and universities. It has been particularly strong across the UK, Europe and Australia, following a marked overall decline in young people's electoral and formal political involvement (Cammaerts et al. 2014; Henn and Oldfield 2016; Martin 2014). It has also contributed to a persistent deficit discourse which portrays young people as democratically disconnected, disenchanted, disaffected and disengaged. This truth of youth associates youth as a category with democratic risk and uncertainty, with the weakening of the democratic political system and even with the death of democracy as a system.

The more objective truth is that young people's declining political engagement is part of a wider demographic trend across developed nations that has seen a fall in commitment by people of all ages to national political systems and mainstream political parties, including a drop in electoral participation and party and trade union membership. There is also evidence of an even deeper disengagement. A survey of just over 18,000 people aged 16–64 across 23 countries found consistent agreement with the proposition that politicians don't care about people like them. In Australia, 75% of respondents agreed with this statement, followed by 73% in France and 72% in the UK (Ipsos 2017).

This disengagement and disaffection may be attributable to a lack of knowledge or understanding about politics and how governments work. In a recent survey of 15 countries, including the UK and Australia, the more than 40,000 respondents aged 12 and up were divided as to whether or not they were knowledgeable about politics and the nature of government. On average, the young people surveyed felt less likely to know much about government and the political process than older participants: 36% overall felt that they were knowledgeable while 38% felt that they were not. 42% of young Australian respondents disagreed with the statement 'I'm knowledgeable about politics and government, while 48% and 43% respectively of young French and UK respondents disagreed, although the figures across the three countries had all softened since the 2014 iteration of the survey (Ipsos 2018).

But something deeper is going on here than can be addressed by questions of simple political knowledge and familiarity. Despite what we have said above, young people's commitment to political institutions does remain consistently weaker than that of older citizens. In a recent international survey, two thirds of young people felt that their government did not care about them (IYF 2017) while the annual independent Lowy Institute poll shows a consistently low level of support amongst young Australians for the idea of democracy itself. In 2012, only 39% of Australians aged 18–29 agreed that democracy was preferable to any other kind of government compared to 60% of Australians aged 60 years and over (Hanson 2012). In 2017, these figures had grown to 52% of young people and 70% of older people, but the gap between younger and older cohorts remained (Oliver 2017a).

Losing Trust in Politics

There are a number of explanations for this trend. One suggests that there is a dissonance between the concerns of political institutions and those of young people, particularly those who have grown up in uncertain socioeconomic contexts aggravated by the introduction of austerity policies, such as in the UK. Another—not unrelated to the first—attributes young people's disengagement from institutionalised politics to conditions such as precarious employment and the associated extended transitions into adulthood which we have considered at various points across this book. For example, a recent study of young people's political participation in Eastern Europe draws a clear causal link between the unprecedented austerity-driven levels of youth unemployment in the nations that comprise the study and young people's declining political engagement across those nations (Kovacic and Dolenec 2018). There are also concerns emerging from Norway, which has been free of austerity measures and largely immune to the issues we have just considered, that young people's trust in political institutions is declining in line with the growth of economic inequality (Seippel and Strandbu 2017).

There is a feeling shared by many young people that the 'existing political offer' is simply inadequate (Cammaerts et al. 2014, p. 645). Many feel that they have been overlooked or marginalised by professional politicians (Henn et al. 2017), that those politicians have little interest in or commitment to championing young people's interests or concerns (Henn and Foard 2014), or even that politicians and the political process are unjust, deceitful or corrupt (Pilkington and Pollock 2015). As Pickard and Bessant put it, many are critical of what they see as 'a failure on the part of governments and other power elites to do their job; namely, to develop a political agenda and policies that are supportive of young people's aspirations to live a good life' (2018, pp. 3–4).

This critical view certainly emerges from our discussions with our three cohorts of young university students and acts as a kind of push factor for their lack of trust in the aspects of the contemporary political machine. This distrust is particularly directed at political parties and leadership. In the UK, Becky's description of Trump conveys little trust either in his integrity as a leader or in the electoral process that enabled him to come to power: 'he's a bigot, he's a racist, he's a businessman, he's not a presidential candidate, realistically. He's not a leader; he's a man who had a lot of money'. A similar view is held by most of our French interviewees, as Juliane explains:

> I remember watching the inauguration with my flatmates and I was just sitting there. I was numb, like 'this is not happening'. And then you see these big headlines of things he has said or tweeted and you are like, 'it is not a president'. It's like, I don't know, a joke. ... it is very alarming (Juliane, France).

Turning to the recent UK elections, Mark highlights what he sees as the divisive nature of contemporary politics, even within the same political party:

> ... there's always a ... hidden agenda to them all. ... And there's always that minor aspect of majority parties are against themselves within their own parties. So in the Labour Party, a majority of [its members] are against Jeremy Corbyn but there's another aspect who support him. Same thing with [British Prime Minister] Theresa May: the majority party members aren't fully supportive of her (Mark, UK).

For most of our interviewees, neither individual politicians nor political parties inspire much faith or desire to become engaged as political actors. The following observations also point to a deeper disenchantment, one that stems from a loss of faith in the integrity of politicians and the political process and the veracity and reliability of the statements issuing from the political space. This concern about the nature of truth in contemporary politics raises issues to which we return in our Conclusion:

> ... I don't think I could trust politicians. But I feel like we do – we can shape policies for our choice on the ballot. But in terms of trusting a political party to act in favour of your interests, no, I wouldn't say I trust them (Zaynab, France).
>
> ... I feel like [politicians] have an agenda so they try to - I don't know, they have their own agenda. They do their things to try to please people but, I don't know, I just don't understand politics and don't want to understand politics. I just don't trust it (Grace, France).
>
> I think a lot of young people have really lost faith, to be honest. There aren't really any very appealing leaders, overly (Alice, UK).
>
> If you ask me who was in charge of the government right now, I would guess. I have never voted in any country. ... I always got taught and told never to trust politician because whilst they might say something that's true, it could be true to them [but] twisted – like a twisted statement (Jessica, Australia).
>
> I don't believe a word that comes out of any of their mouths. I take it with a pinch of salt (Becky, UK).

This lack or loss of faith and subsequent withdrawal from conventional political processes is not an abstract stance: for many of our interviewees, it is a direct response to their experience of the political process in their own home nations. Isabella has come to the UK from Italy, where up to 40% of young people abstained from voting in the recent election (Giuffrida 2018). Like them, she finds the political system alienating:

> The big problem is that, especially in Italy, no-one knows what's going on, really, and that is the problem with politics. They, like, use all these big words, they use all these big things, but they don't connect to the people, and it is the people who should be making politics – not just the small party or the government (Isabella, UK).

In France, some of our interviewees expressed relief that Emmanuel Macron had become President rather than Marie Le Pen, but when we asked whether his election had given them more hope for the future, Paloma responded in the negative:

> First of all, I don't like him. And no, I don't get more hope for the future because even if he does something nice for women in Parliament and access to culture, he's still the president for rich people (Paloma, France).

Paloma's statement echoes a 2016 survey of over 17,780 adults across 22 countries, which found strong agreement with the statement that 'The economy of my country is rigged to advantage the rich and powerful', including strong agreement across the three nations of our study: 76% of UK respondents and 75% of French and Australian respondents agreed with this statement (Ipsos 2017). In another Ipsos survey, respondents in 14 out of 22 nations felt that their country was in decline. In Australia, this figure was 49%, while the UK was higher at 57% and France stood at even greater 69% (Ipsos 2016). This pattern is also reflected in studies of young people's political views. One European study found strong agreement by young French people in particular to the statements such as:

- The only person you can count on in life is yourself
- Money is given too much importance in today's society
- One of life's golden rule is - you either fuck or get fucked
- The gap between the rich and the poor is widening in France
- Politicians are corrupt (EBU n.d.).

Trump and Macron are not the only political figures about whom our interviewees express alarm or disappointment. For Irina, who has come from Russia to study in Australia, Russian President Vladimir Putin represents an almost immovable force ('he's been a president almost my whole life'), but not one who inspires any faith in the political process:

> … when it comes to whatever is happening within Russia, it is always so bad because bad things keep happening, like a lot of corruption, crime and everything. And he doesn't seem to be doing anything about it and that's what I don't like. … when it comes to our lives, the lives of his people, he doesn't do anything about it. He doesn't do anything to change it. … So, yeah, I don't trust politics (Irina, Australia).

This does not necessarily mean that these young people have turned their backs on the political process, however. For a number of them, electoral participation is still an important principle and political act:

> I, personally, wouldn't say that I am politically very engaged. … But I go and vote because that's pretty much not the only way, but a very important way to participate (Juliane, France).

> But, yeah, I vote. I have never not voted, because I think it's important. … I tended to consider not voting is like giving up on the political life and that's what I see around me - all the people who don't go to vote is because they think it's going to be useless (Ninon, France).

> I don't do any other political things. I don't have any engagement. But I think it's important to vote because I know some people who are against voting because they think it won't change anything. But if you don't vote, it won't change anything either (Kim, France).

I vote regularly whenever we get the opportunity because it seems something important. Yeah, you could not vote and it may not affect it. But in the end, one vote can always make a difference (Mark, UK).

These snapshots provide a glimpse into the ambivalence of some young people towards politics, an ambivalence that resists neat simplifications and stereotypes. Our small pool of interviewees reveals a diversity of political attitudes and activities that defy neat categorisation. Some of their accounts are pervaded by a palpable political malaise. As such, they could be seen as reinforcement for the deficit discourse that we mention earlier. Other accounts reflect a belief in the importance of maintaining some kind of political participation. As such, they also reflect a degree of hope in the possibility of affecting political or social change.

The Comfort of the Familiar

It is not our intention here to add to the hyperbole about young people's political engagement, which is, like so much else in their lives, already subject to numerous crude and erroneous binaries: 'formal or informal, conventional or unconventional, representative or identity, collective or lifestyle, macro or micro, and geographical or digital' (Coe et al. 2016, p. 1322). As we have previously cautioned (Walsh and Black 2018a), there is little to be gained either by perpetuating the discourse that links young people with political risk, or by creating new romantic narratives of 'autonomous, innate and pure forms of youth protest and rebellion' (Sukarieh and Tannock 2014, p. 109). The reality of young people's political action is more nuanced than any discourse can capture. It may combine both engagement and disengagement (Farthing 2010). It may bring also draw upon both 'old' and 'new' modes of political action (Coe et al. 2016).

There is ample evidence, for example, that many young people are willing to engage in traditional institutional politics in order to express their views and exert influence (Brooks et al. 2015). A large-scale study of young people in the UK, France, Spain, Austria, Finland and Hungary has found that many retain a strong desire to participate in democratic life even though this desire is not well supported or recognised by existing political institutions and discourses. The researchers conclude that 'nonparticipation is by no means the same as a lack of interest in politics or a general feeling of apathy' (Cammaerts et al. 2014, p. 662). In Norway, young people have been found to demonstrate a high degree of trust in political institutions, in line with the views of the general population (Seippel and Strandbu 2017). Along similar lines, a study of 1,355 young people in the US found that many are still comfortable and engaged with familiar forms of political expression such as donations to political parties, communications with elected officials or even party membership (Gotlieb and Thorson 2017).

The evidence is, then, that many young people want to see the existing democratic system become stronger and more responsive. They want to be taken more seriously by their political representatives, to have greater contact with those representatives, and to see their priorities better represented by them. This has been borne out in recent years by unexpected levels of youth participation in key voting processes, especially in single-issue referenda where the issue is clearly of concern to young people. In the UK, for example, 75% of 16 and 17 year olds voted at the 2014 Scottish Independence Referendum and an estimated 64% of 18–24 year olds cast a ballot at the 2016 referendum on EU membership (Henn et al. 2017). The 2016 referendum also showed a marked growth in young people's participation: where the 2015 general election saw a difference of 16% in turnout levels between those under and over the age of 45, this gap shrank to less than 3% during the referendum. This pattern was further reinforced by the 2017 general election, when an estimated 72% of eligible young people voted (mostly for Jeremy Corbyn), more than in any of the previous six elections (Banaji and Mejias 2017). Corbyn's 2015 election as leader of the Labour party had already been credited with drawing large numbers of young people into politics, but this 'youthquake' provides more solid proof of young people's willingness to engage when they feel that their interests and values are reflected in that process (Birch 2016).

A similar pattern emerged during 2018 in the mass return to Ireland of young people deeply concerned to have their voices counted in the abortion referendum. Cambridge, Oxford, London and Nottingham universities all set up bursaries to help students fly home for this historic poll (O'Carroll and Baker 2018). As in the elections and referenda we have already discussed, there was a massive surge in enrolment to vote in Ireland in the lead-up to the referendum, and many of these newly-registered voters were young people (Catholic News Agency 2018). The result was an overturn of the abortion ban by a vote of 66.4%.

A similar trend has also been seen in the southern hemisphere. The 2017 New Zealand general election saw young people turn out to vote in record numbers, possibly due to the popularity of Labour leader Jacinda Ardern. In Australia, the controversial and highly emotive voluntary same-sex marriage survey of 2017 (the Australian Marriage Law Postal Survey, to use its formal title) acted in a similar way to engage unprecedented numbers of young people in the electoral process. It attracted a participation rate amongst 18–19 year olds—78.2%—that was almost as high as that of the population as a whole. By comparison, only 66% of eligible 18–19 year olds had voted at the previous federal election. This was despite the survey's reliance on an 'old-school' postal vote, a mode of participation predicted to discourage many young people (Oliver 2017b). Young people's widespread engagement in the survey also has significance because of the fact that they had to register to vote before they could participate. An enormous enrolment surge between the announcement of the survey and the registration deadline saw over 98,000 Australians enrol to vote for the first time: of these 66%, or over 65,000, were aged between 18 and 24 (Reynolds 2017).

This is all part of a trend which has been captured by the term we used earlier. 'Youthquake', defined as 'a significant cultural, political, or social change arising from the actions or influence of young people', was selected by Oxford Dictionaries as the 2017 word of the year (following the selection of 'post-truth' a year earlier). It suggests that many young people retain 'an immense political appetite' coupled with strong ideals about the nature of the democratic process and their own involvement in it (Cammaerts et al. 2014, p. 661). Even in the UK, where young people's political disengagement has previously been particularly great, young people may be averse to the practices of their politicians and lack confidence in the political system yet remain strongly interested in politics in its broadest sense (Henn and Foard 2014). One of our UK interviewees, George, has joined the British Labour Party 'because I want to one day get involved'. This imagined involvement could include running for office or, at the least, supporting someone else running for office. He explains his motivations in these terms:

> ... I think for about 10 years I have been interested in politics. I can remember [former US President] Obama coming through in 2008 and the hope of that message really struck me. And then to a lesser extent, 2010/2012, I started getting interested in British politics as well (George, UK).

This observation highlights the international influence and permeability of politics: what happens in one country shapes others, and their constituents, in myriad ways. While George is the only one of our interviewees who is actively involved in the formal political system, he is not the only interviewee who is interested in the political process. Abi's Indonesian family includes an uncle and a cousin who are politicians. Abi himself has been enthusiastically engaged in the electoral and wider political process since he was eligible to vote:

> Since I was 18, ... I joined to be a voter in some elections: regional election, national elections. I participate, I watch out about the process of the elections, how each party tried to make some coalitions/group, to present their candidates in the elections. I also like to join some conversations about politics. ... Sometimes I listen to [my uncle and cousin] talk about ... the reason why they try to support these candidates and why they do not choose to support these parties (Abi, Australia).

Abi's political engagement is to some extent shaped by familial connections. This reinforces our earlier suggestion that for many young people, it is the politics of the familiar (and the familial) that are the most attractive and engaging. This is a theme that has emerged from our previous research (Walsh and Black 2018a, b). It also points to a set of political behaviours that align with the values and preferences of what we have called homo promptus.

Homo Promptus as a Political Actor

Numerous studies suggest that young people are not simply disengaged from politics but are sceptical of conventional forms of political expression which they see as 'formal, rational, controlling, hierarchical (top–down), future-oriented and focused on the preservation of the social order' (Andersson 2015, pp. 2–3). They are gravitating instead towards modes of political participation that are informal, local, extra-institutional and horizontal in their processes (Alteri et al. 2017; Soler-i-Martí 2015) These modes are also strongly affective in nature: they are based on the pursuit of issues and causes that are personally meaningful and connected to young people's communities and social networks (Alteri et al. 2017; Andersson 2015; Sloam 2016). They may include political consumerism or so-called 'lifestyle politics' that are expressed through boycotts or blockades. They may also include 'repertories of contention' (Tilly 2004, p. 29) such as civil disobedience, marches, occupations, 'flash mob' protests, walk-outs and sit-ins, online petitions and 'clicktivism' as well as the use of digital media to coordinate any of these repertoires (Henn et al. 2017; Monticelli and Bassoli 2017; Rheingans and Hollands 2013).

Discussing political issues with family, friends or others in their social networks can also enable young people to become political actors in the private sphere of their own lives (Amnå and Ekman 2014). Particularly where they share their political concerns with online or digitally-enabled communities, this sharing can also raise their participation to the next level: it can 'transform individual concerns into collective concerns, and extend participation from the private spheres of everyday life into the public sphere' (Gotlieb and Thorson 2017, p. 1044).

This transformation was most observable in the unprecedented youth vote in the 2017 UK election to which we refer earlier, one that has been chiefly attributed to the work of Corbyn supporters and the Momentum movement in creating, curating and editing a vast amount of online content directed chiefly at young people. One video that warned young people about the perils of life in 'Tory UK 2030' reached over a quarter of the UK Facebook population, with more than 7 million views (Banaji and Mejias 2017). Momentum as a political movement also captures many of the attributes that characterise homo promptus as a political actor: its non-hierarchical, grassroots nature means that it functions like a 'horizontal social movement', a mode of 'doing politics' which is clearly attractive to many young people (Pickard 2018, p. 128).

Some scholars argue that this movement from 'palace democracy' to 'street democracy' (Martelli 2013) represents a strengthening and an enlargement of the democratic process and of mechanisms for citizens' involvement in that process. Amnå and Ekman, for example, mount an argument for the democratic importance of young 'standby' citizens: those who do not necessarily engage in regular formal politics but who 'stay alert, keep themselves informed about politics by bringing up political issues in everyday life contexts, and are willing and able to participate if needed' (2014, p. 262). This reflexive and flexible political stance is one that Zaynab also describes as her own:

> I don't see myself taking part in a political movement or belonging to a political party or seeking membership or anything. But on precise topics or issues, I would probably get involved (Zaynab, France).

For other interviewees such as Juliette, Ninon and Ines, more substantial political change is needed. Sitting with us in the 16th century café described in Chap. 2, these three young people consciously evoke the language of revolution that remains a legacy of the history of the city in which they are studying. Their call to arms requires a deeper level of commitment from young political actors, although it is not clear just how Juliette and Ninon see their own role in this:

> … when it comes to politics, there's certain laws that need to be respected. … But I think breaking the rules in the way that it will help change a country for the better. I don't see any reason why it shouldn't be broken (Juliette, France).
>
> … we have this kind of revolution background/history and … we always think that we have to elect someone who is going to change everything and make everything better, and really be a turning point in the political space (Ninon, France).
>
> I think that we have to break some rules because we cannot just obey the government and be okay with everything (Ines, France).

For Ines, as well as for Paloma, political change is not enough in itself. Both have grown up in the disadvantaged suburbs that surround the city where they are studying. Both are strongly motivated to make a difference for other young people in those suburbs. Their imagined futures as political actors is geographically grounded. It also bears a strong resemblance to the preferred political modes of homo promptus. It takes place outside formal political institutions; it is affectively driven; and it is based on the pursuit of issues and causes that are personally meaningful and connected to their local networks:

> I am more passionate in human rights, social actions, associations, things like that. I'm not very optimistic about politics because, for me, politicians just talk and they have their suits and things like that. But I prefer a person who helps going directly, helping people. … the suburbs are very left aside by the government. The majority of politicians never went to the suburbs. They talk about that, but they don't know what it looks like. And that's why I think it's important to lead actions in the suburbs (Ines, France).
>
> I try to make a difference for me and I would love to make a difference for other people … if you live in the suburb, like mine, where criminality is always a bit high, for children who have less privileges than me, I think they don't get any kind of good role models (Paloma, France).

Lyr, too, embodies the political preferences and modes of homo promptus. His studies are themselves a political act. They are also a way of fostering other young people's future engagement in the project of social improvement and political change, a way of fostering the hope of change:

> I feel like, by doing what I do with the studies and pursuing – trying to push a particular field of study, trying to push at least in my own circle ideologies about feminism or gay rights or … animal rights and everything, ecology – I feel like I am doing something. And my field of studies as well, I mean, I am also doing it because I want to educate people better: you know, provide better education for young people because, I mean, I have this idea that it is not adults or old people that are going to change things. We might as well wait for them to leave [laughs] … And at that time we need to be ready and educated to do it. … I really hope to be not just a teacher but someone who makes a difference (Lyr, France).

In Chap. 2, we discussed the focus in youth studies on 'ordinary' young people and youth experiences and made a case for the continued importance of this focus. Lyr's comments reaffirm the fact that the political for many young people is not restricted to the formal or distant institutions of power: rather, it is something very close to hand, both geographically and in relationship to their everyday practices such as study. It is a personal project, one to which their higher education enables them to contribute.

Young Political Actors in a Post-truth World

In the first two chapters of this book, we highlighted the role of emotion and the affective turn in recent youth scholarship. In Chap. 2, we suggested that a focus on affect can yield new insights into the 'everyday details and embodied experiences' (McLeod 2016, p. 277) of young lives. A focus on affect can also provide insight into young people's relationships to political systems in ways that go beyond tired binaries of engagement and disengagement. Specific affective manifestations such as hope, optimism or anxiety provide a prism through which to view these relationships, which have a direct bearing on young people's present and future political lives.

Recent political events have highlighted the powerful and troubling dominance of certain affective dimensions of contemporary democracy which are intimately linked to the explosive growth of social media. Many young people are either experiencing or observing a distance not only from political systems and representatives, as we discussed earlier, but from the use of fact-based evidence to drive political deliberation and critical public and policy discourse. This has not been helped by the Brexit campaign or by Trump's disregard of facts and evidence and promotion of fake news and post-truth politics. These phenomena have added to the degradation of political authority and a widespread erosion of trust in the ways we speak about politics itself.

When we asked our interviewees to consider the question of whether we were living in a post-truth world, the subsequent discussion evoked a range of strongly felt responses. Some express keen concerns about the weakening of the reliability of political statements and what they see as the manipulation of the truth for solely political ends:

> … there are huge issues at the moment with the authority … that a person speaks with. … In terms of Trump, for example, he can literally be pointed out on things that he says are … false, yet his followers … will explain what Trump meant: 'he didn't actually mean that. He meant this'. So they are his interpretation service (Tyler, Australia).
>
> … politics, political people, it is really about communication and telling people what they want to hear. Yes, it's really a war with words and ideas (Ninon, France).

For George in the UK, who is actively involved in the formal political system, this manipulation of the truth is, to some degree, an inescapable aspect of the political process. When we ask whether he trusts politicians and political processes, he replies:

> Trust is a strong word. Honestly, it depends what they are saying. … I appreciate there are times when they do need to deceive us, be it national security or whatever, but there are times when they abuse those powers, equally, to keep themselves in power (George, UK).

Even for George, though, this pragmatic attitude is tempered by a concern about the degree to which politicians and the political process knowingly mislead their constituents: 'I accept the world is not perfect and you sometimes need to tell lies, basically. But, equally, I think it's abused too much as well'. For some of our other interviewees, the line between the political system and the public media have been blurred to the degree that neither can be trusted any longer. In Australia, Mel is concerned that 'we live in an age where it's very, very difficult to tell what is true and what is false'. Her response is to focus instead on what is closer to hand: 'so I kind of focus on my own little life and just what I need to achieve'. For both Mel and Cynthia, this mutability and unreliability of the public and political discourse have much to do with what they see as the vested interests of the media:

> Like, if you have money, you have power, especially in the media, and because of that, like, I don't really trust anything that I see. ... I don't have the time to go around researching, you know, questioning databases to see, like, you know, who said what, you know, what actually happened. Because of that ... I try to detach myself from a lot of the media stuff, social media, politics, and all that (Mel, Australia).

> I feel like more and more people are sort of getting manipulated by what they read and not really thinking is that really true, is that not true? That's why a lot of things, as such, whenever there are big incidents like bombings and stuff, there's always so much news. A lot of it is actually debunked as being fake and they're just to make headlines and that. And Donald Trump isn't wrong: there is fake news. Although the way he was referring to it, it is just any news that he didn't like about himself. But it is definitely a thing that goes on, and the way that the media and how it's portrayed to try and manipulate how you think and not really giving you - not really providing just news and letting you be able to think for yourself about how to interpret it (Cynthia, Australia).

Zaynab and Ines express very similar and strongly felt concerns about the unreliability of the media and the erosion of evidence-based policy and politics, both in the UK and in France:

> ... it's just incredible the sort of lies and exaggerations the British press sells to the British public – *frightening*! And I was especially shocked by that Brexit - not just the vote but the sort of social movement and sort of reactionary movement against the EU and against numbers and facts and figures (Zaynab, France).

> I think in France, it is a big problem because people are educated by the TV. They watch TV all day and they think that the truth is on TV and they don't need to question that. So politicians, I think, are to the contrary: people don't have any trust in politicians (Ines, France).

In a similar vein, Rose highlights the loss of reliable truths in public and social life. She also points to the powerful role of social media in creating false relationships, suggesting that

> ... we as a society ... have lost the ability to be neutral and to look at something without the coloured lens of how it really is. I mean, we always like to sometimes put in 'what am I getting out of this and how do I see this', instead of seeing how it really is.... if you go on Facebook today, you think you have a thousand friends but you don't, you know. So we are very far from the truth (Rose, Australia).

These observations go a long way to explaining the youth disenchantment with politics which we described earlier, as well as the preference of the young person as homo promptus for modes of political action that are more localised and ethically transparent. They also capture many young people's deep concern about the dissolution of accepted public and policy truths and the uncertainty that this brings. Ines speaks for many of her peers when she says 'what is evident today—what is true today—can change tomorrow'.

Post-truth Politics and Affect

In the Introduction, we reflected on Enfield's (2017) argument that the post-truth discourse is attended by a suspicion of specialists, experts and previously trusted sources of information as well as 'an erosion of trust in the fundamental norms around people's accountability for the things we say'. For many of the young people we have interviewed, the effect of post-truth politics has been to make them 'much more sceptical about everything', as Morgane explains from France. A number of our French interviewees, in particular, believe that this scepticism or questioning of accepted truths is an important response to the nature of contemporary politics and the media:

> We are questioning every single law of society, you know. Like, even last year, I had a friend in America who was questioning everything I was believing in – everything. Like, for instance, the European Union. He was also questioning faith, religions being peaceful - you can think which one he was talking about. He was also questioning … the ability of French people to make right decisions. Yeah, he was questioning everything - everything! And he got me to question everything as well (Morgane, France).
>
> … I have personally the need to question everything, question everything I have heard, question everything that I see. That's why it's important to do study for me, because our teachers always told us that we don't have to be 100 per cent sure of what people told us, either TV/media, and you have to question everything (Ines, France).

For some of our interviewees, this scepticism about politics and the media goes far beyond interrogation. Speaking from France, Juliane believes that we have entered post-truth times in which 'everyone has their own truth,… their own beliefs [and] their own reality'. Her suggestion that 'maybe there's no reality' is one that is also taken up by Becky and Sophia:

> So unconsciously, I think people are then: well, let's follow another moral compass. Let's go with our feelings over here. [Trump is] doing the right thing for his country. No, he's not. Let's be honest. And I think that's where it comes from. I believe that we are in a post-truth world, whatever the hell that means. It is ridiculous to think - as scientists, as researchers, how the hell can we not be in a non-evidence-based world? It beggars belief (Becky, UK).
>
> … I feel like everyone can change their mind in less of a second, just by scrolling the feed on Facebook and seeing facts, news, believing them, and then feeling outraged or feeling happy or feeling, I don't know, political for a second. I mean, there's fake news [and] it is outrageous, the amount of people believing in stuff and just blindly believing in them, without even trying to see the other side, without even trying to see if that's true, without even trying to make sure that the source is a relevant source. And it is absolutely mad. It's an insane job to do, to make sure all the time that what you read is correct and what you read is actually true (Sophia, France).

All of these observations are affectively framed. They convey a deep concern about the nature of post-truth politics. Some of our interviewees also describe a wider malaise which highlights the affective aspect of the post-truth zeitgeist. In the Introduction, we described the ways in which post-truth politics appeal to personal subjectivities and privilege emotion over evidence. We also discussed the greater concern for many observers that emotion and personal belief have effectively subsumed or replaced people's trust in the solidity of objective facts. Speaking from Australia, for example, Mel thinks that

> we live in an age where it's very, very difficult to tell what is true and what is false.... if I focus on all that, I think I would just have depression or something [laughs].

A number of our interviewees describe the same trend away from faith in facts and evidence that is taking place across Europe. In the UK, Becky says: 'I believe that people, human-beings, are governed by their feelings. If people don't like the evidence, they are going to look for something else to guide them'. Zaynab makes a similar observation from France: 'at the moment, feelings are definitely winning over facts'. In Australia, Tyler and Jessica also point to the challenge of navigating the affective post-truth landscape:

> I can't speak to before my time, but I have a feeling that people have always been more swayed by feelings. I think the difference now is, you know, as ridiculous as it is, social media has completely changed the landscape of, say, our discourse. I think that there's more information available to people and people have different skill-sets in terms of evaluating that information. And I think that probably what we need to be doing better is helping people critically analyse things (Tyler, Australia).

> And then that puts the whole society in disarray as you don't know who to question, who to look to. With regards to the political side of it, you don't know who to trust either, because you have got your president telling you one thing, and then you are reading this other stuff that completely contradicts what he's saying (Jessica, Australia).

For both Paloma and Morgane, the culpability for this public erosion of trust in the idea of the truth lies squarely with politicians and the current political process:

> ... I think a lot of people are mainly focussing on what they feel. But we can't really blame them because usually those are people who are not very well-off and not very wealthy. Like, I am thinking about Trump's elections. Most of his voters were poor white people. Same thing happened last week in Italy. We had a big majority for far right and neo-fascists candidates. And the voters were people who lived in the south of Italy, where a lot of refugees arrived, and there are already no jobs in Italy and it doesn't help the situation. So I think they are really voting on what they feel and not what they know or can do, et cetera. But we can't really blame them for that. We should blame the politicians who take advantage of this, to get more votes (Paloma, France).

> ... people tend to vote by their feelings, today, and politicians are taking advantage of this. ... they are no longer trying to seize people's attention by ... giving them possibilities to solve things. ... Today, they are trying to rise emotions in them. Marie Le Pen [in France], she was telling people, 'yeah, you are being invaded. Your jobs are being stolen.' You know, the way she was saying it, the people she was stressing to were people were in distress and easy to get them emotional. And same with the extreme left [which] was doing the same thing. So, yeah, I noticed that everywhere in the world – even with Trump – he was doing the same thing (Morgane, France).

Both Allysa and Ellie are concerned about the social implications of this dissolution of regard for evidence and provable facts, including the implications for young people in particular:

> ... I think it's kind of sad to think that now people believe in things that they feel like they want to believe in, rather than actually see what's happening, rather than actually seeing the facts. But it is also kind of difficult to say which one is fake or not, if there is this issue called fake news. Like, we can never tell whether this fact is real or not (Allysa, Australia).
>
> ... we are deciding on futures – not only our futures but future generations – and it is based on lies. It does make you question your place in society then because all this stuff about fake news, Trump may be making it up, I don't know, but it does make you start questioning things. Is what I am reading true? Is what my lecturer is telling me true? Or are they twisting things? Or is what my parents telling me, true? It does make you start to question it, and it is not a nice place to be (Ellie, UK).

Conclusion

Many of our interviewees share a deep concern about the nature of contemporary politics, the response of citizens to those politics, and the future for young people in post-truth times. These concerns are part of a widespread malaise about politics that is particularly evident in developed economies. This does not mean, of course, that young people have no hope in the collective and political future. Despite the apparent prevalence of the post-truth zeitgeist, some of our interviewees maintain a degree of tempered hope or dark optimism that they and other young people will be able to navigate this zeitgeist to forge a more secure relationship to trust, evidence and the political process. In Australia, Rose equates the idea of hope with 'seeing things as they are'. In France, Zaynab frames her hopes for a better future in terms of a return to 'a more normalised state of things' where 'truth will prevail. Yep, facts will prevail, hopefully'.

We began this chapter by acknowledging that some young people are comfortable with existing political systems and offerings. We also suggested that an increasing number are seeking or creating modes of political engagement that reflect the values and behaviours of homo promptus. Our interviewees' accounts straddle these two youth positions. They highlight the complex interplay of feelings that many young people are experiencing about the political present and its possible future. They combine scepticism, a deep concern for the integrity of the political process, a sense of outrage about the damage being done to the democratic fabric by post-truth politics, and the tempered hope that we have just described.

Hope may be, as Janet Newman points out, 'an ambiguous political construct' (2015), but it is also an essential resource in uncertain political times. While it needs to be 'more than a fantasy, a vague sense of optimism', hope offers a 'collective sensibility', one that speaks to 'wider cultural and political—as well as personal—futures' (2015). The relative resilience of young people's optimism and hope for a renewed political and social contract is something to which we will return in the next chapter, the conclusion to this book.

References

Alteri, L., Leccardi, C., & Raffini, L. (2017). Youth and the reinvention of politics. New forms of participation in the age of individualization and presentification. *Partecipazione e Conflitto, 9*(3), 717–747. https://doi.org/10.1285/i20356609v9i3p717.

Amnå, E., & Ekman, J. (2014). Standby citizens: Diverse faces of political passivity. *European Political Science Review, 6*(2), 261–281. https://doi.org/10.1177/0010414012453441.

Andersson, E. (2015). Situational political socialization: A normative approach to young people's adoption and acquisition of political preferences and skills. *Journal of Youth Studies, 18*(8), 967–983. https://doi.org/10.1080/13676261.2015.1020926.

Banaji, S., & Mejias, S. (2017, June 27). Story of a vote unforetold: Young people, youth activism and the UK general election. *Polis*. Retrieved 5 July 2017, from http://blogs.lse.ac.uk/polis/2017/06/27/story-of-a-vote-unforetold-young-people-youth-activism-and-the-uk-general-election/.

Birch, S. (2016). Our new voters: Brexit, political mobilisation and the emerging electoral cleavage. *Juncture, 23*(2), 107–110. https://doi.org/10.1111/newe.12003.

Brooks, R., Byford, K., & Sela, K. (2015). The changing role of students' unions within contemporary higher education. *Journal of Education Policy, 30*(2), 165–181. https://doi.org/10.1080/02680939.2014.924562.

Cammaerts, B., Bruter, M., Banaji, S., Harrison, S., & Anstead, N. (2014). The myth of youth apathy: Young Europeans' critical attitudes toward democratic life. *American Behavioral Scientist, 58*(5), 645–664. https://doi.org/10.1177/0002764213515992.

Castle, S. (2016, June 6). Choosing 'Brexit' could leave the Kingdom less united. *New York Times*. Retrieved July 7, 2016, from http://www.nytimes.com/2016/06/18/world/europe/britain-referendum-european-union-brexit.html?_r=0.

Catholic News Agency. (2018, May 22). 125,000 additional Irish register to vote on abortion referendum. *Crux*. Retrieved May 30, 2018, from https://cruxnow.com/church-in-uk-and-ireland/2018/05/22/125000-additional-irish-register-to-vote-on-abortion-referendum/.

Coe, A.-B., Wiklund, M., Uttjek, M., & Nygren, L. (2016). Youth politics as multiple processes: How teenagers construct political action in Sweden. *Journal of Youth Studies, 19*(10), 1321–1337. https://doi.org/10.1080/13676261.2016.1166191.

EBU. (n.d.). *Generation what? Young people and optimism: A pan-European view*. Geneva: EBU.

Enfield, N. (2017, November 17). We're in a post-truth world with eroding trust and accountability. It can't end well. *The Guardian*. Retrieved November 19, 2017, from https://www.theguardian.com/commentisfree/2017/nov/17/were-in-a-post-truth-world-with-eroding-trust-and-accountability-it-cant-end-well.

Erlanger, S. (2016, November 10). 'Brexit' proved to be sign of things to come in U.S. *New York Times*. Retrieved November 15, 2017, from https://www.nytimes.com/2016/11/10/world/europe/for-us-brexit-was-a-sign-of-things-to-come.html.

Farthing, R. (2010). The politics of youthful antipolitics: Representing the 'issue' of youth participation in politics. *Journal of Youth Studies, 13*(2), 181–195. https://doi.org/10.1080/13676260903233696.

Giuffrida, A. (2018, February 27). 'There is no long-term vision': young Italians lose faith in politics. *The Guardian*. Retrieved March 3, 2018, from https://www.theguardian.com/world/2018/feb/27/there-is-no-long-term-vision-young-italians-lose-faith-in-politics?CMP=Share_iOSApp_Other.

Gotlieb, M. R., & Thorson, K. (2017). Connected political consumers: Transforming personalized politics among youth into broader repertoires of action. *Journal of Youth Studies, 20*(8), 1044–1061. https://doi.org/10.1080/13676261.2017.1305101.

Hanson, F. (2012). *The Lowy Institute Poll 2012. Australia and New Zealand in the World: Public Opinion and Foreign Policy*. Retrieved December 3, 2017, from https://archive.lowyinstitute.org/publications/lowy-institute-poll-2012-public-opinion-and-foreign-policy.

Henn, M., & Foard, N. (2014). Social differentiation in young people's political participation: The impact of social and educational factors on youth political engagement in Britain. *Journal of Youth Studies, 17*(3), 360–380. https://doi.org/10.1080/13676261.2013.830704.

Henn, M., & Oldfield, B. (2016). Cajoling or coercing: Would electoral engineering resolve the young citizen–state disconnect? *Journal of Youth Studies, 19*(9), 1259–1280. https://doi.org/10.1080/13676261.2016.1154935.

Henn, M., Oldfield, B., & Hart, J. (2017). Postmaterialism and young people's political participation in a time of austerity. *The British Journal of Sociology, 69*(3), 712–737. https://doi.org/10.1111/1468-4446.12309.

Ipsos (2016). *Is the system broken? International views*. IPSOS Game Changers December 2016. Retrieved October 11, 2018, from https://www.ipsos.com/sites/default/files/migrations/en-uk/files/Assets/Docs/Polls/global-advisor-political-uncertainty-dec-2016-slides.pdf.

Ipsos. (2017). *Ipsos 2017 Global Trends: Fragmentation, cohesion and uncertainty*. Retrieved October 11, 2018, from https://www.ipsos.com/sites/default/files/2017-07/Ipsos%20Global%20Trends%202017%20report.pdf.

Ipsos. (2018). *Goalkeepers global youth outlook poll*. Retrieved September 27, 2018, from https://www.ipsos.com/sites/default/files/ct/news/documents/2018-09/gates_ipsos_topline_report_09_24_2018.pdf.

International Youth Foundation [IYF]. (2017). *2017 global youth wellbeing index*. Retrieved March 3, 2018, from https://www.iyfnet.org/library/2017-global-youth-wellbeing-index.

Kovacic, M., & Dolenec, D. (2018). Youth participation in eastern Europe in the age of austerity. In S. Pickard & J. Bessant (Eds.), *Young people re-generating politics in times of crises* (pp. 375–394). Cham: Springer International Publishing.

Martelli, A. (2013). The debate on young people and participatory citizenship. Questions and research prospects. *International Review of Sociology, 23*(2), 421–437.

Martin, A. (2014). *Political engagement among the young in Australia*. Papers on Parliament, 60. Retrieved November 19, 2017, from http://www.aph.gov.au/sitecore/content/Home/About_Parliament/Senate/Powers_practice_n_procedures/pops/pop60/c03.

McLeod, J. (2016). Memory, affective practice and teacher narratives: Researching emotion in oral histories of educational and personal change. In M. Zembylas & P. A. Schutz (Eds.), *Methodological advances in research on emotion and education* (pp. 273–284). Cham, Switzerland: Springer.

Monticelli, L., & Bassoli, M. (2017). Precarious voices? Types of "political citizens" and repertoires of action among European youth. *Partecipazione e Conflitto, 9*(3), 824–856. https://doi.org/10.1285/i20356609v9i3p824.

New York Times. (2016, November 8). Election 2016: Exit polls. *New York Times*. Retrieved November 28, 2016, from http://www.nytimes.com/interactive/2016/11/08/us/politics/election-exit-polls.html?_r=1.

Newman, J. (2015, June 3). Austerity, aspiration and the politics of hope. *Compass*. Retrieved February 23, 2017, from http://www.compassonline.org.uk/austerity-aspiration-and-the-politics-of-hope/.

O'Carroll, L., & Baker, S. (2018, May 21). Irish abortion referendum: voters on both sides prepare to head home. *The Guardian*. Retrieved May 31, 2018, from https://www.theguardian.com/world/2018/may/21/irish-abortion-referendum-expats-both-sides-head-home-vote.

Oliver, A. (2017a). *The Lowy Institute poll 2017: Understanding Australian attitudes to the world*. Retrieved March 1, 2018, from https://www.lowyinstitute.org/publications/2017-lowy-institute-poll.

Oliver, A. (2017b). *Same-sex marriage survey: Gen Y got involved and the pollsters got it right*. Retrieved March 1, 2018, from https://www.lowyinstitute.org/the-interpreter/same-sex-marriage-survey-gen-y-got-involved-and-pollsters-got-it-right.

Pickard, S. (2018). Momentum and the movementist 'Corbynistas': Young people regenerating the labour party in Britain. In S. Pickard & J. Bessant (Eds.), *Young people re-generating politics in times of crises* (pp. 115–137). Cham: Springer International Publishing.

Pickard, S., & Bessant, J. (2018). Introduction. In S. Pickard & J. Bessant (Eds.), *Young people re-generating politics in times of crises* (pp. 1–17). Cham: Springer International Publishing.

References

Pilkington, H., & Pollock, G. (2015). 'Politics are bollocks': Youth, politics and activism in contemporary Europe. *The Sociological Review, 63*(2_suppl), 1–35.

Reynolds, E. (2017, October 3). Women and youth drive same-sex marriage vote. *news.com.au*. Retrieved October 7, 2017, from http://www.news.com.au/lifestyle/gay-marriage/women-and-youth-drive-samesex-marriage-vote/news-story/ca2d75afe82aacd644a123c4a2a4edfe.

Rheingans, R., & Hollands, R. (2013). 'There is no alternative?': Challenging dominant understandings of youth politics in late modernity through a case study of the 2010 UK student occupation movement. *Journal of Youth Studies, 16*(4), 546–564. https://doi.org/10.1080/13676261.2012.733811.

Seippel, Ø., & Strandbu, Å. (2017). Populist political right opinions and political trust among Norwegian youth. *Journal of Youth Studies, 20*(4), 415–429. https://doi.org/10.1080/13676261.2016.1241863.

Shuster, S. (2016, June 26). The U.K.'s old decided for the young in the Brexit vote. *Time Magazine*. Retrieved November 28 2016, from http://time.com/4381878/brexit-generation-gap-older-younger-voters/.

Sloam, J. (2016). Diversity and voice: The political participation of young people in the European Union. *The British Journal of Politics and International Relations, 18*(3), 521–537. https://doi.org/10.1177/1369148116647176.

Soler-i-Martí, R. (2015). Youth political involvement update: Measuring the role of cause-oriented political interest in young people's activism. *Journal of Youth Studies, 18*(3), 396–416. https://doi.org/10.1080/13676261.2014.963538.

Stefanou, E. (2016, June 25). 'What do young people think about Brexit?'. *The Guardian*. Retrieved December 3, 2016, from https://www.theguardian.com/uk-news/video/2016/jun/24/what-do-young-people-think-about-brexit-video.

Stone, J. (2017, December 17). Brexit lies: The demonstrably false claims of the EU referendum campaign. *The Independent* 2017. Retrieved March 2, 2018, from https://www.independent.co.uk/infact/brexit-second-referendum-false-claims-eu-referendum-campaign-lies-fake-news-a8113381.html.

Sukarieh, M., & Tannock, S. (2014). *Youth rising?: The politics of youth in the global economy*. New York: Routledge.

Tilly, C. (2004). *Contention and democracy in Europe, 1650–2000*. Cambridge: Cambridge University Press.

Walsh, L., & Black, R. (2018a). Off the radar democracy: young people's alternate acts of citizenship in Australia. In S. Pickard & J. Bessant (Eds.), *Youth politics in crisis: New forms of political participation in the austerity era* (pp. 217–232). Basingstoke: Palgrave Macmillan.

Walsh, L., & Black, R. (2018b). *Rethinking youth citizenship after the age of entitlement*. London: Bloomsbury.

Chapter 8
Conclusion—What Is the Future of Youth?

> I think the society we are in at the moment, the community in the future, looks negative, and that is making young people disengaged. But I don't think that's true for everyone. I am still hopeful and I am still determined that I am not going to let a negative society determine where I am. I think if you ask a lot of young people, they would feel the same. It is easy to have the off comments about 'oh, we don't care, we are supported by our government. Past generations are ruining it for us and we are the ones that are going to have to live it'. But people still have hope. I don't think it completely gets rid of that (Ellie, UK).

Introduction

This book has considered the hopes, plans and concerns of three cohorts of young university students in relation to their current and imagined future lives as family members, workers and political actors. The perspectives of our interviewees are varied, reflecting the nuance and complexities of young people's lives in general. One common theme to emerge, however, has been the uncertainty experienced by all across these three areas of their lives. This uncertainty manifests itself in feelings that range from caution, anxiety and even fear, to a tempered hope or dark optimism.

We have previously suggested that these feelings—and the experiences and prospects which prompt them—provide the foundation for thinking about the university student as homo promptus: that is, as an entrepreneurial and strategic individual, a 'standby' citizen who is expected to constantly plan for the future while living life in the short-term. We have suggested that homo promptus is not tethered to a single place, is permanently in 'situational' mode, and lives in waithood. While not all interviewees display these characteristics, all acknowledge the ways that the uncertainty which gives rise to homo promptus permeates various aspects of their lives.

Towards the end of our discussions with them, we invited our interviewees to reflect further on this uncertainty by asking a final question: are the conventional markers of youth and adulthood changing? This question builds on our discussion across the book of the contemporary prolongation of youth and the deferral of what have traditionally been considered the markers of adulthood in many cultures. It recognises that young people's experience of these markers has become complex: as Valentine argued some years ago, they 'may be or may not be connected and may occur simultaneously, serially or not at all' (2003, p. 48). It also reflects our desire, one that has informed this book as a whole, to do three things: to interrogate those commonly accepted truths of youth which we have described in the Introduction and subsequent chapters; to determine how young people understand the new – and perhaps untold – truths that may be emerging from uncertainty; and to meet Wood's call for 'deeper insights into what it means to *live* and to *be* a young citizen in times of flux and change, rupture as well as continuity' (2017, p. 3, original emphases).

For this reason, we present our interviewees' responses to our final question at length and mostly unmediated, to let them tell their stories. As youth scholars, we recognise what Mayes has called 'the impossibility of "extracting" a "raw voice" that "speaks for itself"' (2018, p. 3). At the same time, we believe that there is much to be gained by allowing our interviewees to close this book with their own extended reflections on some of the themes that have emerged across our discussion.

We then seek to bring together the various themes of the book by proposing a tripartite framework through which young people's imagined futures might be understood, including their feelings about these futures and the strategies they employ to navigate and negotiate them. We have developed this framework to provide what we see as a missing piece in the way in which young people's imagined futures are conceived, a piece that recognises both the spatial and the temporal dimensions of those futures. In Chap. 2, we discussed the temporal turn within youth studies and its efforts to achieve a more nuanced understanding of young people's interaction with 'the messy, moving relations between past, present and future' (McLeod 2017, p. 13). We also reviewed some of the typologies that have been developed to promote that understanding.

Our framework offers a further way in which we might conceptualise young people's temporal orientations. As we also noted in Chap. 2, our discussion in this book is primarily located within the large body of youth scholarship that is concerned with how young people imagine their personal futures, rather than how they envisage large scale or macro social, political and environmental futures. At the same time, we have argued that personal youth futures are inextricably bound up with wider forces and discourses. Our framework brings this relationship into stronger focus. It proposes that young people's imagined futures can be understood within three temporal and spatial scales: the microfuture, which encompasses those aspects of the future that are potentially within young people's capacity to shape and that arise directly from their own immediate social, economic and geographic life-worlds; the mesofuture, which concerns those forces and events that are within the visible horizons of young people's lives but which may not be in their immediate grasp and which they may feel little or no agency to influence; and the macrofuture, which comprises global future forces and widespread change beyond the scope of individual lives.

Whether or not these futures are within the scope of young people's control, they each have the potential to influence young people's lives. Later in this chapter, we consider how each of these futures may make itself felt in the hopes and plans of our interviewees. We describe them separately, but we also propose that there can be a complex relationship between them. As Longo argues, 'temporal dimensions are built simultaneously; there is a constant remodeling of the past and projections by the actual situation, and by present conditions' (2018, p. 395). Labour market change, for example, may affect all three types of future. The tightening of local job markets may constrain young people's microfutures by limiting their immediate work prospects and heightening the need for the competitive strategies we discussed in Chaps. 3 and 5. Developments such as Brexit may have an impact on their mesofutures by curtailing their ability to craft regionally mobile careers, while macrofutures such as the growth of the gig economy and the automation of labour form an unsteady basis upon which their trajectories to work are imagined and negotiated. Finally, we conclude with a series of reflections and questions about what hope might mean for young people navigating the post-truth world and its 'colliding temporalities' (Harootunian 2007, p. 478), how that hope might be sustained, and what role key institutions might play in creating a climate in which sustained hope and its realisation might be possible.

Rethinking the Truths of Youth

In the Introduction to this book, we introduced Kelly's reference to the 'truths of youth' (e.g. 2000, 2011) to describe certain persistent constructions and depictions of young people within contexts of uncertainty. Writing further about the conventional truths of youth promoted by government, the NGO sector and other organisations, Kelly notes that

> None of these [truths] are a sham. Indeed, they should be read in ways that allow space for the irony and ambiguity that they provoke. Such ideas about the person ... emerge from, and give shape to the fields of possibilities in which we contrive to fashion a life – and they should be critiqued to explore their limitations and possibilities (2014, p. 41).

He then goes on to propose three key questions for young people seeking to navigate the contemporary globalised world:

> Who can I become in such a world where the meanings and limits of the subject are set out in advance for me? By what means am I constrained as I begin to ask what I may become? What happens when I begin to become that for which there is no place in the given regime of truth? (p. 47).

These questions are all salient to our proposal that young university students can best be understood as homo promptus: individualised young subjects who are created and cultivated by the current neoliberal regime. They are also salient to our concern that, as Leccardi puts it, uncertainty has removed or 'uncoupled' the capacity of educational and other institutions from their previous roles as 'guarantors of individual and collective continuity' (2014, p. 85). As she writes:

... young people tend not to receive support from the institutions in regard to their entry into adulthood. In other words, key social institutions like the school, work, or the family no longer guarantee the success of that transition. Whatever the level of individual commitment may be, the outcome is uncertain. Young people must individually negotiate the manner and timing of their entry into adulthood (Leccardi 2014, p. 85).

In Chap. 2, we argued that the prolongation of youth that has been described by so many youth scholars is inextricably associated with uncertainty, one that affects both the experience of the present and the imagined future. Following this line of thought, we asked our interviewees if they felt that the markers and meanings of youth and adulthood are changing. Tyler from Australia is firm and quick in his response:

Absolutely. I got married and bought a house in the same year. I would say that is a rarity amongst most people I know. In fact, ... amongst my friendship group, after me, the next marriage wasn't for almost another four years, and that person doesn't own a home - still lives with his parents, as do many people in my friendship group: they still live with their parents. Some of them even have full-time professional jobs, and they still live with their parents. So they are not necessarily not making a lot of money. It is just that - particularly if buying a house is a marker of "adulthood" – I would have to challenge that in this day and age because the cost of housing has risen so substantially. So even having a well-paying job is sometimes not enough, particularly if you might be single or something like that, if you don't have a second income.

Tyler describes how he

was lucky in terms of buying my home. While I only got married a few years ago, I had been in a relationship since I was 17. So my wife is a midwife and she's been working for a number of years, whereas I have been studying, so in terms of saving for a home and things like that. We also have quite generous in-laws and stuff like that, that allowed us to live at their house while we saved and things like that. Some people don't have that. So, essentially, you are stuck in this loop of renting a home for the rest of your life. I certainly wouldn't believe that buying a house is a marker of adulthood. I'm not even sure getting married anymore would be either, given that a lot of people elect not to (Tyler, Australia).

Where Tyler challenges the conventional definition of adulthood and the markers or milestones on which it relies, both Zaynab and Ines in France feel that elements of this definition still have some validity:

I think an adult is someone who is independent enough to make their own decisions on how to shape their own lives, to the best of their ability, and someone who tries to improve their own life, whether it be through studies or through work progression ...So you are a legal adult at 18, so I would say that notion of independence is important because you are responsible for your own future. Obviously, circumstances can affect you and your life but I would say that notion of independence and responsibility that comes with finding your own way in life, through studies or work (Zaynab, France).

[to be an adult] is to be independent, financially. I think it's when you can take care of yourself without anybody. You can take care of yourself for your health issues, for your financial situation, for your psychologic state. You don't need your mother/father to be here to tell what you to do. [to be young] is on the contrary: having a kind of dependence. It is not negative, but dependence – you need someone to be by your side and support you. But when you are an adult, also, but it is different, I think. I felt it for myself. When you are young, I think that your choices/decisions ... have less consequence than when you are an adult. ... But now, some decisions [that young people make] can have some really serious consequences. I think that is the difference (Ines, France).

At the same time, Ines describes the changing relationship of many young people to these established markers of adulthood. For her and for Alice, too, the established construction of adulthood is either an abstract imposition or else makes little sense in light of their own experience. Both describe this experience in terms that are consistent with the idea of waithood which we have suggested is a central aspect of the young university student as homo promptus:

> I think that young people tend to study more and do more long studies. So some people start to work at 30, maybe 25, so it's very late compared to before. I think people have children very late, also, because they want to have fun, they want to study. So I think that adulthood trend is more advanced than before ... It's complicated because I face responsibilities, because I work, I have to pay myself. But on the other hand, I am 20 years old and I live with my parents' house. So for some people, it can look like I am still a child with that (Ines, France).

> I feel like I am still an adolescent, to be honest. I am still going through a lot of the transitions that normally, on paper, it says that you are going through when you are 16/17. So I don't know – and I question all this stuff all the time. I have always questioned the whole idea of the dream lifestyle: getting married, having a house and two cars and becoming a corporate lawyer or whatever, and working nine till 10, or whatever it is these days, like, nine till six/seven, until you die or you get old and then you retire and then your life can start. What the hell? Where does that make sense? I don't know. So adulthood for me is a socially constructed thing that I don't necessarily agree with (Alice, Australia).

For Morgane, the world is in a state of flux, particularly when it comes to the prospect of achieving the milestone of stable, qualified work. When she imagines her working future, it is as one that is far less knowable and subject to planning and control than it was for her parents. It is clear that her parents share her view that achieving the accepted markers of adulthood and financial independence has become much more difficult for young people in France:

> We are evolving in a changing world .... Some of us might do something good with our lives but I don't see that people of my generation being as happy as my parents were, at our age. ... my parents' generation started to make life in the '80s/'90s. And compared to our time, those years were more peaceful – to me easier ... while for us, we have to get a job, go through lot of things, go through more competition. Society is expecting more things from us.

> Like, for instance, when you are working in journalism, you cannot specify yourself in one field. You have to be good at many fields today. ... And it does apply to many jobs, to many things in life. Also, we have more troubles in society, I think, than our parents have. ... I'm not really optimistic about the world right now. I don't know how it's going to evolve; but ... it does make me more pessimistic, for sure. Because with my parents, we talked about it. Every time they say 'we wouldn't like to be here in your time' or they often say, 'you know, when I was your age, it was so easy to get a job. I don't understand why you have to do all these studies'. Like my mother never went to university and today she's working for an administration academy ... and she's earning very well. My dad didn't go to university, neither, and he's an engineer. Today, to do that, you have to go to a grade school, you have to work a lot, get internships (Morgane, France).

For Juliane and Zaynab, also in France, it is not only the markers of adulthood that have changed, but the whole climate in which young people's decisions have to be made. They describe these changes in terms that evoke the individualised pressures and expectations to which homo promptus is subject. They raise questions about what the future may look like for young people in a world where accepted definitions and markers of youth and adulthood are in flux. At the same time, they raise the possibility that the weakening of these previous truths and assumptions enable greater degree of flexibility and freedom in relation to their options and choices:

> Well, psychologically, I think that the life choices that you had in the past were maybe more narrow, but maybe that made your life easier as well. My dad said, oh, I could pick from three apprenticeships that I could do and that was it. And for some people that might be harder for them: for some people, it might be a relief. When I graduated from my high school, I was like - cool, I had 12,000 study courses to choose from in Germany. And that is only Germany. I really don't know what to do. So that's a little bit overwhelming. It's a freedom, but it is also overwhelming (Juliane, France).

> … we are growing in a totally different world. I don't think it's fair to say – because I have heard this argument before – that it's hard to get a secure job, as you don't have as many responsibilities as young has before, in another age for another generation. But another argument is: it's more difficult to do everything, so you have no other choice but to sort of handle everything on your own quicker (Zaynab, France).

Both Juliane and Zaynab's statements evoke the core sensibility of homo promptus. They describe the strategic, entrepreneurial decision-making that is intrinsic to this youth selfhood. They also highlight the affective burden which accompanies the individualised responsibility of self-creation that rests with homo promptus.

Engaging the Microfuture: 'My Biggest Worry … Is Outside of Myself'

These perceived changes to the markers and meanings of adulthood may bring a sense of entrepreneurial possibility. For the young university student as homo promptus, they may be an opportunity for a welcome self-curation and exploration of options. Alternately, they may contribute to the uncertainty and contingency which young people face, and which is clearly a source of anxiety for many. For these young people, focusing primarily on the microfuture may bring some sense of "knowability" and a perception (at least) of control over the kind of flux and change which Morgane and others describe. As we propose above, the microfuture encapsulates young people's hopes, plans and concerns about the imagined future that arises directly from their immediate life-worlds. For our interviewees, it has both material and ontological dimensions. It is dynamically shaped by the barriers, opportunities and disruptions that may befall them directly. It is geographically fluid but may also at times be anchored to place, such as the places where their families reside.

One example comes from Becky's hopes and concerns for the microfuture. We have previously described Becky's hopes of migrating to Australia with her partner and their young daughter. These hopes are accompanied by a fear that this opportunity for mobility may be closing, as other young people in the UK compete for avenues of escape from what many feel to be a grim economic future. She feels the pressure not only to realise her plans, but to do so quickly:

> You know, obviously, the older we get as well, already the less [migration visa] points we have to get in. So it is kind of, you have got to be quick with it. I know a lot of people that have talked about immigrating into Canada, Australia, New Zealand. We wanted to get in there first. You know, get in before they close it, basically, because I can see it going that way …. [Australia is] already changing what's on the skill job list [to qualify for migration], constantly. … the visas are getting harder to get, so it's really competitive (Becky, UK).

Rose has already moved to Australia from India in order to study. She is also concerned that a lack of desirable work, whether in Australia or India, will necessitate her further mobility:

> If I don't get a job after I graduate because maybe an organisation doesn't like what I have to offer: maybe they are looking for something else. And through that process, if I don't get a job, how will I stay here? Because your parents, they cannot pay for your rent and everything forever. Beyond a point, you have to take responsibility for it, and we hope that 'okay, I am going to get a job and be more independent'. But what if you don't? That's my biggest worry, which is outside of myself (Rose, Australia).

Both Becky and Rose are engaged in strategies and attempts to shape their own microfutures as far as circumstances allow. Becky hopes to migrate to Australia. Rose hopes to secure stable employment. These imagined microfutures concern acts and choices that are only partly within their scope of influence: they also ultimately depend on mediating forces outside themselves, forces that are economic and political and that operate in time and space.

Imagining the Mesofuture: 'I just Don't Know What the Future Might Bring'

Another manifestation of our interviewees' concerns about the future relates to the mesofuture. This incorporates events and phenomena that are visible on the horizons of young people's lives but which may also be beyond their immediate capacity to influence. Geopolitical change is an active source of concern for several of our interviewees. While Becky worries about the tightening of Australian migration rules, Lyr reflects on the geopolitical implications of Trump's presidency both within the US and in relation to the wider 'political atmosphere', expressing the dark optimism that we have described earlier:

> … when I look at America, for instance, and I am thinking, it's been a year with Trump. We have four more to go. It's not going to go well, is it? It is going to take a while to recover from that. So, in a way, the future is not going to be that good for them. … I was thinking about Trump earlier, and I feel like there is definitely concerted backlash happening. I don't know if it is going to be counter-balanced soon. I don't know if it is going to end, or it is going to be pursued until it finally bursts. … I usually try to keep optimistic about it, so it doesn't worry me too much. But I guess the political atmosphere, mostly, is really worrying (Lyr, France).

For other interviewees, geopolitical change and uncertainty in Europe, in particular, means that the mesofuture is more than just worrying. Irina is committed to returning to Russia once she completes her studies in Australia, but this prospect is a source of real anxiety as she contemplates the political instability – and possible conflict—that may affect her own personal future:

> ... everything that's happening in the sphere of international relations now seems a bit frightening for me, because I feel like with every year, Russia keeps getting more and more enemies and I don't like it. Because I don't know what happens. I mean, what if another war is about to happen? ... I just don't know what the future might bring (Irina, Australia).

In France, Paloma 'would like to be optimist' about the mesofuture. She believes that France will stay in the EU, but fears the consequences if it does not:

> Clearly, it would be a disaster if Europe came to crumbling because ... Europe is the basis, the Eurozone and European economic centre: it is the basis of our society/economy. I don't want it to crumble because this would be hell (Paloma, France).

For Ines, too, the mesofuture is one that has been made much more precarious by recent events. As we have already flagged, Brexit has a potential impact on the mesofutures of both our UK and European interviewees. In France, Ines explains that the uncertainty of Brexit is generating real anxiety about the future:

> Brexit [is] a very dangerous thing. But maybe because I am French ... I am scared about all the extra missed ideas, in Europe/Italy, for example. Sometimes we tend to think that we [in Europe] are advanced, that some progress has been done. But sometimes I think that we are going to go back in time (Ines, France).

Similar concerns prey on the minds of our UK interviewees. At the time of our interviews, some British ministers were signalling an end to austerity in the UK (BBC 2018), but our interviewees were ambivalent about the likelihood of this. Becky's views about the emerging mesofuture are laced with the political mistrust and scepticism which we described in Chap. 7:

> I think the fact that people are even saying that austerity is over and it is not necessary is ridiculous, because you only need to look at the landscape to figure out that they are using that as a political tactic, to try and undermine the previous government. So that's all they are trying to do is to undermine everybody. ... I think it is a very clever tactic ... God, you can just feed people whatever they want to hear, can't you? We know that our wages are going down, yet the cost of the living is going up: the police service have got no funds to do what they need to do. The NHS [National Health System] have got nothing. And yet, all of this is broadly clear of people going 'yeah, but no, austerity is over. It's all good'. No, it's really not, is it? Like, come on: it is absurd (Becky, UK).

Not all of our interviewees share the same assumptions about the role or effects of austerity, though. George has a different view about the context for austerity policies in the UK, and about the mesofutures they may have seeded:

> I think we had austerity for the rich in many ways. So by that, we saw public services cut quite heavily and people on the lowest breadline hurt. But when you are bailing out banks that have deceived people and you are bailing out corporations that have deceived people, I think it's tough to kind of turn to the [people who must] provide for their family and say, by the way, can you not have a pay-rise for the next 10 years, or whatever. So I am [unsure] how much austerity we ever really had. ... It's just been basically a freeze on wages, and

then a general kind of freeze on public spending. But for the most part, I don't think it ever went too deep.

Now, obviously, I should stress that I have not known anyone too closely that's been affected by it. I am sure there's people who have genuine horror stories. But, yeah, my view is: we had austerity but not to the extent that people are making out, but that doesn't mean they don't cause any damage. And I think ... people keep saying it was a political choice. I think we needed both. We needed to invest in certain areas but we definitely needed to cut back where cutbacks could be made because I think it's clear that there are unnecessary bureaucracies in certain places and unnecessary red tape, even though I do believe in market regulation (George, UK).

Navigating the Macrofuture: 'There's Something Weird Happening'

If the microfuture and the mesofuture are within the visible horizons of young people's lives, macrofutures appear in their imaginaries as more abstract phenomena, such as the global changes in technology and automation which we described in Chap. 5. Technological innovation may have 'the power to improve our lives, raising productivity, living standards and average life span, and freeing people to focus on personal fulfilment', but it also brings the risk of social and political unrest if its advantages are not accessible to all (PWC 2017, p. 7). For some of our interviewees, the macrofuture and how young lives may be affected by technological innovation is a source of concern:

... a lot of things are going to be very technologically driven. Like, the youth of today and even myself, really, like you are constantly on different social media platforms. I think more things will be driven through that. Maybe there will be more social rebellions through social media. I think it's getting increasingly difficult, to be honest. I think young people do face a lot of challenges now [in] uncertain futures (Alice, UK).

... people are starting to feel overwhelmed about the effect of big populations and crimes today; not only for danger it can bring but, also, we are overwhelmed with the social networks; being constantly connected to people without having a break. So I tend to be more hopeful when I am just alone, with only a few people around me. ... And I can see more and more people of my age think the same (Morgane, France).

For others, such as Lila, technological change is a positive thing, with hopeful implications for youth futures at the macro level:

I think absolutely for young people now, in the future it's really, really hopeful, like, really bright for them. For example, I use internet: we can check all the information through Google and they have different types of response. We have got YouTube video and we can everything that we want to know ... . We have also got internet and we can internet connect people around the world, and all the people have different thoughts/ideas, help us to increase our own knowledge as well and improve the whole knowledge of the society (Lila, Australia).

Global labour market uncertainty and rolling economic volatility is another macrofuture that is omnipresent but which is also sometimes perceived to be far beyond our interviewees' ability to influence. This is another source of anxiety, as Kim explains:

... 50 to 60 years ago, Germany had its own economy – maybe more than 100 years ago, but every country had its own economy and they were not really linked, which means that when one country goes or went bankrupt, the other countries weren't affected by this. But today, because of the stock market, if one country goes bankrupt, the others will have problems, too (Kim, France).

This pervasive anxiety about world events and their potential repercussions for their own more immediate microfutures is one that is shared by a number of our interviewees. When we asked her what the future looks like for young people, Becky replied in considerable depth:

It is a bit bleak. I will be honest ... world-wide, I think the bleakness comes from the wars that are happening and the future wars that are going to happen - they are inevitable. [The] war on terrorism: I hate that term but it is a real war, whether there is a real threat or not, where there's an enemy. I don't believe there's actually an enemy but they are creating something and realistically, it is only the perception that needs to be there, for it to become a war. That is terrifying because what that will do is – well, it creates an imminent threat. The young people growing up now, you ask anybody, especially in Britain ... feel scared for their life when they go to London. ... Why do we feel scared for our lives? We shouldn't do.

And then on top of that, because then they feel scared for their life, they are not thinking too far ahead in future. They are not thinking about buying property, they are not thinking about career paths. They are thinking day-to-day - okay, well, what's happening now? Are we going to be blown up? Are we going to be shot at? You know, I don't think that is unique to Britain: I think that's across the world, especially with what's just happened in America, with the school shootings and whatnot. Young people now are being sucked into this big war that's the making of ... the government. You know, they have created this whole frenzy. Now, the young people are being sucked into it and they don't really know: they are malleable enough that people are now telling them what they should think and how they should behave. And that's a terrifying thought, for me. ... You know, it is quite scary.

... I know friends and family who are young, that go, 'ooh, I am going into town today. I am a bit nervous about it'. Why are you nervous? There's no more threat now, than there was 15/20 years, you know. For our whole lives, there's been exactly the same amount of threat. But because now we are being told to be fearful of it, they are creating this, like, frenzy of it. To see how that affects a young person is scary, because that will affect everything - all the choices they make in their life now, political as well, because in the next – let's just say we have got a 16 year old. Next two years, they are going to be eligible to vote. By the time they get to that point, they would have heard so much crap. The person that comes in ... who has fed them that crap, is then going to prey on that and say exactly what they want them to hear, so that they vote for them and they are in power. It's clever. It is very manipulative and very clever, but it is terrifying. And you can't tell a young person because they are stubborn and they think they know everything and they are right and that's it. They are going to make mistakes but they are going to make mistakes for the whole country (Becky, UK).

We have shared Becky's anxieties about the prospect of war earlier in this book, as well as Irina's very real concerns about the likelihood of conflict involving her home nation of Russia. Concerns about security and the spectre of an imminent terrorist attack are also on the minds of a number of our other interviewees in ways that have real implications for their own possible microfutures. Becky reflects on young people's inability to consider their careers or property purchases in the face of the 'big war that's the making of ... the government'. She draws a link between widespread insecurity and the choices which young people 'make in their life now'.

Alice draws a similar link, describing her partner's difficulty in obtaining work at a time of 'constant anxiety':

> So many things are uncertain now. Because we have left the EU, we don't know what jobs there's going to be. Like a lot of companies are going to leave. It was already difficult, like, getting a job here anyway. Like, my partner's found it really difficult. Just getting onto [university] grad schemes, there's so much competition. And everything is just really underfunded. Increasingly, you see stuff about young people with mental health issues as well. And I think that all leads back to constant anxiety that you have all the time. I know one of the things in the back of my head is also about, like, security, feeling safe. With all the terrorism stuff as well, you are always sometimes a bit on edge. There just seems there's so many different things that you don't know what's going to happen next (Alice, UK).

In France, too, there is real anxiety about 'what's going to happen next', especially in relation to what are felt to be the looming dangers of terror. Sophia, for example, feels

> more and more unsafe in Paris - not because there is something particularly that's happening right now, but I have heard more and more conversations with people in bars/cafés, saying such as: in a year or two, there's going to be something huge happening in Paris/France, and it is going to be very, very serious. ... I don't really try to think about that too much because, as most people say, it would [mean that the] terrorists ... would have won, if we start being terrified of living in our own city, living our lives and just doing what we are used to, that we have been doing for hundreds of years in a free country. ... I don't feel like I want to go far, far away and to leave France because there are many, many people that I love here, and I love this place. But it is just there's something weird happening. I feel that. And I just hope that it is not (Sophia, France).

Some aspects of this imagined and risky macrofuture may also have a direct role in shaping young people's decisions about their microfutures, as Becky's story illustrates. As we have already explained, she wants her family to move from the UK to Australia. This intended move is not solely motivated by economic hopes: it is also an attempt to remove the family from a geographic environment which seems to be rapidly becoming more volatile and unsafe:

> Terror threat is a big one in Europe at the moment and people are getting scared, which means that people are trying to find ways to get out of where they think the hot zone is. For us, over this side of the world, we see Australia/New Zealand as fairly cut-off, and it is quite a safe kind of place (Becky, UK).

Climate change emerged during our interviews as another example of an issue that is located in the macrofuture but that preys on the minds of some of our interviewees. For Tyler, this unknown and apparently uncontrollable future is a little abstract:

> The reality is, even if the environment gets worse, the earth won't end [but] it might impact humans. So I guess part of that is where you live geographically, how badly that impacts your life and stuff like that, and whether it will. You know, that could happen over decades, it could happen over centuries (Tyler, Australia).

For Lyr, however, the prospect of significant climate change is a source of anxiety. He is clear about its potential personal as well as its global implications:

... well, in 10 years, it might not be a problem. But in 20/30 years, there might be some huge issues coming. You know, what I have planned for my life, might not be able to happen, because the world will be too different, or drastically changed by some very important things (Lyr, France).

Imagining the Future in Post-truth Times

That climate change has emerged as a source of concern for some of our interviews brings us back to one of the key themes of our discussion across this book. It has been a touchstone of the book that in the current zeitgeist of the post-truth world, those threads of the social fabric that are based on scientific and journalistic claims to fact-based evidence are unravelling. This attitudinal shift can be seen in claims such as this: 'we are now living in a connected, post-truth world where the default for many consumers is suspicion, not acceptance' (Kantor TNS 2017). It is also evident from recent surveys such as the Ipsos 2017 Global Trends Survey cited elsewhere in this book, which put the following proposition to younger and older participants: 'Even the scientists don't really know what they are talking about on environmental issues'. 40% of respondents from the UK, 42% of Australians, and 46% of the respondents in France agreed with this statement (Ipsos 2017). This challenge to the reliability of scientific knowledge may reflect a deeper questioning of the epistemological foundations of modernity and even the enlightenment period.

We began this book by discussing the affective aspect of this post-truth zeitgeist as a cautionary note. We, and our some of our interviewees, have expressed our concern about the ways in which appeals to emotion and personal belief have superseded the status of fact-based evidence across the political and public domains. We have noted the (sometimes dark) hope of some of our interviewees that they and other young people will able to navigate this zeitgeist to forge a more secure relationship to trust, evidence and the political process. We have argued for the need to understand young people's hopes, plans and concerns for their imagined future lives in post-truth times. We have also suggested that affect can be a powerful resource for young people navigating uncertainty.

In Chap. 2, for example, we noted the arguments of previous scholarship that hope can be a form of youth capital, especially where other forms of capital may be limited. In Chap. 3, we suggested that taking up higher qualifications may be in itself an important exercise in hope. In Chap. 4, we described the affective resource that is the family, and its continued importance in supporting young people's efforts to realise their hopes and plans. In Chap. 6, we noted that what emerges from the accounts of our young interviewees is a complex affective mixture in which a dark optimism persists despite the current and future conditions they must navigate. In Chap. 7, we reflected on the resilience of young people's optimism and hope for a renewed political contract, one that could counter the widespread loss of faith in facts and evidence that is central to the post-truth era.

At a time when many young people globally are experiencing 'the dimming of imagined futures' (Cairns et al. 2014, p. 1058), the possibilities of optimism and hope are critical. One young Australian journalist has summed up the affective state of the current generation of young people in this way: 'we're here, we're living in fear and we refuse to get used to it' (Robertson 2014). Hope is an important antidote to some of the more persistent youth imaginings that have emerged from recent studies and social media. In 2017, for example, Kelly quoted some of the contributions from young people to a Tumblr page called 'We are the 99%', which included this grim portrayal of both the present and the future:

I am 20
I earned a culinary degree
I had to move back w/my parents
I have $$$$ in student loans
I make and have never made more than $9.50/hr
I vow never to have children, for I fear for their future like I fear for my own
I feel this life is almost not worth living …]
I live 4 change
I AM THE 99%
#OCCUPYWS (p. 61).

Studies of hope and optimism suggest variances between countries, but with some recurring themes overall. The 2018 UK Youth Index released by The Prince's Trust shows that young people's overall levels of happiness, optimism and wellbeing are at their lowest levels since the study was first commissioned in 2009. More than half (59%) of the survey participants say that what they see as an unpredictable political climate makes them anxious about the future. The number who do not feel in control of their lives has increased by more than one third since the 2017 Index, from 28 to 39% (The Prince's Trust 2018).

This is a contrast to the findings of the 2018 Ipsos study which we cited earlier in the book. This extensive study was conducted in 15 countries and included more than 40,000 interviews with young people from age 12 and upwards. It found that while there are differences between nations, young people overall are more optimistic about their own future, the future of their country and the future of the world than older cohorts: France was the only nation in which young people were less optimistic about the future of the world than older people. Across the study, young people are also more likely to believe that 'their generation will have a more positive impact than the previous one' (Ipsos 2018, p. 4). Perhaps as a reflection of this, 50% believe that they can make a difference in how their country is governed.

This does not mean, of course, that these young people have no concerns or anxieties about the future: across the 15 nations of the study, the three issues that most concern young people are, in descending order of importance: security, education and unemployment. It is no coincidence that these anxieties mirror the youth concerns identified by the previous studies we have discussed throughout this book, as well as the concerns of our interviewees. It may also be no coincidence that the top issue about which young people want to see global political leadership and action is improving education: this was ranked even more highly than ending poverty.

Concluding Thoughts for a Hopeful Future

Despite the strongly felt youth fears, anxieties and concerns which we have discussed in this conclusion, we feel that there are grounds for concluding this book on a hopeful note. Virtually all of our interviewees have expressed some degree of hope or optimism for the future: for their own personal microfutures but also for wider meso and macrofutures. While Ninon in France recognises that it 'is a really pessimistic context that we are living in', for example, she also feels that this is not a permanent condition:

> … it is more like a period of time that's going to pass. What I see around me and what I actually feel, I don't feel like this is such a terrible time to live in and I don't see – I don't think that the future is going to be so dark with migrants everywhere, or countries that are going to lose their power, their sovereignty. I don't really feel that at all (Ninon, France).

Zaynab, too, feels hopeful that the democratic and social fabric of France and other democratic nations will prove resilient to the machinations of these post-truth times. She also believes that there is a critical mass of citizens who will be able to resist and perhaps challenge these forces:

> … I don't want to believe that we are in a post-truth world because I feel like there's enough of us that see Trump for who he is, and how he panics every time someone brings him down on a topic. I think a lot of people are seeing how Brexit is being dealt with by [British Prime Minister] Theresa May and her government, and how the government's own assessment shows that there's no way the economy will be better off with Brexit. So there is hope in that (Zaynab, France).

Change and uncertainty are destabilising influences in relation to how people feel about the future. In a 2017 Ipsos Global Trends Survey of 23 countries, a majority of 18,180 respondents aged 16–64 agreed that 'The world is changing too fast' (79%). Of these, 60% were in the UK, 72% in Australia and 78% in France (Ipsos 2017). By contrast, hope is—at least in part—a function of feelings of security. It can be nurtured and fostered by political and economic stability. One European study suggests that 'the current younger generation has grown up with crises', but it also argues that 'If the political and legal systems manage to provide a stable foundation for young people, this has a direct impact on their optimism' (EBU n.d., p. 6). This raises essential questions about the role and responsibility of such systems, questions to which we return shortly.

The findings of this book are not just reflections of a small group of young people navigating their lives within and beyond university: they also have salience for policymakers, educators and practitioners seeking to improve the lives and trajectories of young people in general, now and in the future. Some key concluding questions for this book are therefore:

- What role should be played by key institutions, including political and educational institutions, in creating a climate in which young people can generate and maintain a viable hope for the future?
- Borrowing from Bessant and her colleagues, how might we forge 'a new intergenerational contract', one that is 'based on a clear view of what constitutes a good life and what is required to sustain such a life' (2017, p. 184)?

The costs of not answering these questions are high. The uncertainty and contingency which characterises the post-truth era, and which is promoting the rise of homo promptus, has rendered the future fundamentally unknowable for the current generation of young people. It is, nonetheless, something in which many continue to invest hope, a hope that may be tempered by other concerns but which needs to be nurtured, nonetheless. We have suggested that educational and other institutions have a responsibility in nurturing that hope. At the same time, we are concerned about the way in which these institutions employ strategies that focus on young people as though they are crafting their present and future lives in isolation from the wider forces we have described across this book. The sociology of youth (and education) 'speaks to and anticipates a future' (McLeod 2017, p. 15), but the responsibility for that future does not and cannot rest on young people alone.

We have focused across this book on three cohorts of young university students, all living and learning in nations facing the effects of uncertainty. We have considered their current and imagined future lives as family members, workers and political actors in order to reflect on and provoke thought about the effects of uncertainty in such young people's lives and what a climate of viable hope might look like. As we have noted earlier, such students are too often positioned within contemporary policies and discourses as 'a resource for others, for future economic growth and global competition' (Nikunen 2017, p. 673). Like other young people, they are also too often positioned as individual actors who are responsible for their own success (Alteri et al. 2017; Woodman and Wyn 2014), who can engage with uncertainty 'as a challenge and opportunity' (O'Malley 2013, p. 191) and who are able to translate this uncertainty into hope—for themselves, their communities and society as a whole (Black 2018).

This individualisation and responsibilisation of hope is an extension of the wider individualisation of youth on which we have touched many times in this book, one that represents the young person and their choices 'as a *deus ex machina* in regard to external difficulties' (Leccardi 2014, p. 47, original emphasis). It is also one of the most pervasive truths of contemporary youth, one that obscures the multiple forces and factors that influence young people's imagined and actual journeys through and beyond higher education in uncertain times, and which leaves young people largely unsupported in the difficult work of maintaining faith in the future. To quote Furlong:

> While young people are resourceful and often develop imaginative solutions to create fulfilling lives under trying circumstances, there is clear evidence that their lack of control over key aspects of their lives results in anxiety and stress and impacts on their psychological health. There is also evidence that policies that respect and facilitate personal choice and autonomy, which avoid the temptation to penalise young people who are unsuccessfully negotiating difficult circumstances, help increase well-being among young people (2014, p. xi).

That the 2017 Oxford Dictionaries word of the year, 'youthquake', followed the selection of 'post-truth' in 2016 is probably just a coincidence, but we also read it as a sign of the persistence of hope and the possibility for political and social change. In the time of homo promptus, young people face both familiar and changing landscapes that require a nuanced understanding of the contemporary truths of youth futures. This starts by listening to young people themselves, but it must also go beyond that. We began Chap. 2 with a reference to ant tribes, a term coined in recent years to describe the vast number of young university graduates living in crammed, cramped and impoverished conditions on the outskirts of large Chinese cities and commuting long hours to the city centre to compete fiercely for low-paid casual jobs in the hope of securing stable employment.

The ant tribe is considered one of the most disadvantaged social groups in the contemporary Chinese economy: instead of enjoying the security that higher education traditionally promises, their situation is as precarious as migrant workers and the traditionally disadvantaged peasant class. Many come from rural families, in fact, lured by the promise of education and a career. Their families often endure significant hardship to support them through their studies, investing them with their own hopes of a better future. These hopes for the future are in fact what drives most "ants". They are summed up by the popular Ant Tribe song, which has been translated as saying: 'Going ahead with determination, I walk against the wind, although the road is far ahead, I will hold up the sky washed clear by the rain. They are also captured by this quote from one recent graduate:

> Although I work and live in such a way, I believe everything will change through my efforts, and I can see the future that I am building by my own hands. … I am still young and I am glad that I have a dream to fight for (Qiwei 2015).

This individualised optimism echoes that of many young people in emerging economies such as India and China, something that we noted in the previous chapter. Recent surveys by both Citi Foundation (2017) and Ipsos (2018) have found a stronger belief amongst such young people that their generation will be better off than that of their parents, a belief that is particularly prevalent in developing cities such as those to which the ant tribes are flocking in pursuit of their dreams. At the same time, an earlier survey by Ipsos MORI, which we mentioned previously, reminds us of the risks of promoting homogenous understandings of how young people in specific circumstances view the future. It also raises the question, one which we asked earlier, about the likelihood that the ant tribes and similar cohorts of young people will be able to realise the dreams that drive them:

> we need to be careful to avoid a view of unbridled hope in emerging economies – as our data makes clear, beyond China, there are significant minorities who think the future will be worse. Young people (and their parents) see the coming pressures from growth and the scramble to get on, which will leave many behind (one million young people in India will enter the labour market each month for the next 20 years) (Ipsos MORI 2014, p. 51).

For the subjects of this book, these individualised hopes cannot be the only prospect that they take forward into the future. Throughout our discussion, we have explored a confluence of global and local trends, discourses and phenomena that are shaping and unsettling the lives of young people—from technological disruption and geopolitical change to economic fluctuations, labour market change and the financial pressures placed on young university students and the families supporting them. The dark optimism of some of our interviewees suggests a dual awareness of possibility and pessimism as they, too, 'walk against the wind' of uncertainty. Our concern is that as the opportunity bargain of higher education erodes, so too will hope and, along with it, all that these young people—indeed, all young people—have to offer. Our purpose as university educators is not merely to develop homo promptus—the young self that is able to adapt and react to change—but to provide the best possibilities for young people to actively critique, shape and change their futures at micro-, meso- and macro-levels. This responsibility also rests with universities, policymakers and other groups seeking to support young people, their families and their communities to understand and grapple with the enormous personal, social and existential challenges facing us all. This cannot be achieved at an individual level alone.

We conclude with some thoughts from Rose in Australia, which we feel capture the complex and affective relationship which many young people have with the imagined future in uncertain times:

> … if I don't get what I hope to achieve, I don't think I would be that distressed inside. … As humans, it is a natural tendency to want a better future because we like to believe that if this is the struggle I am going through today, then it must have a purpose. You know, I am going through something and going to achieve something better. But for example, if that doesn't happen, there's no point in crying about it, that 'this is what I hoped for'. So, yes, I have hopes, but my sense of self is not tied to 'if I can't do this or if good things don't happen to me, then there's something wrong with me or maybe there's something wrong with the universe that nothing is working out'. It is what it is (Rose, Australia).

References

Alteri, L., Leccardi, C., & Raffini, L. (2017). Youth and the reinvention of politics. New forms of participation in the age of individualization and presentification. *Partecipazione e Conflitto, 9*(3), 717–747.

BBC. (2018, March 11). We're not out of austerity tunnel yet—Chancellor Philip Hammond. *BBC*. Retrieved May 10, 2018, from http://www.bbc.com/news/uk-politics-43363167.

Bessant, J., Farthing, R., & Watts, R. (2017). *The precarious generation: A political economy of young people*. Abingdon: Routledge.

Black, R. (2018). Making the hopeful citizen in precarious times. In P. Campbell, L. Harrison, C. Hickey, & P. Kelly, (Eds.), *Young people and the politics of outrage and hope* (pp. 128–139). Amsterdam: Brill.

Cairns, D., Growiec, K., & de Almeida Alves, N. (2014). Another 'missing middle'? The marginalised majority of tertiary-educated youth in Portugal during the economic crisis. *Journal of Youth Studies, 17*(8), 1046–1060. https://doi.org/10.1080/13676261.2013.878789.

Citi Foundation. (2017). *Pathways to progress global youth survey 2017: Economic prospects & expectations*. Retrieved August 13, 2018, from https://www.citigroup.com/citi/foundation/data/p2p_global_youth_survey_full_data.pdf.

EBU. (n.d.). *Generation what? Young people and optimism: A pan-European view*. Geneva: EBU.

Furlong, A. (2014). Foreword. In L. Antonucci, M. Hamilton, & S. Roberts (Eds.), *Young people and social policy in Europe: Dealing with risk, inequality and precarity in times of crisis* (pp. x–xi). London: Palgrave Macmillan UK.

Harootunian, H. (2007). Remembering the historical present. *Critical Inquiry, 33*(3), 471–494. https://doi.org/10.1086/513523.

Ipsos MORI. (2014). *Global trends 2014. Navigating the new*. Retrieved November 15, 2018, from https://www.ipsos.com/sites/default/files/publication/1970-01/ipsos-mori-global-trends-2014.pdf.

Ipsos. (2017). *Ipsos 2017 Global trends: Fragmentation, cohesion and uncertainty*. Ipsos MORI. Retrieved October 11, 2018, from https://www.ipsos.com/sites/default/files/2017-07/Ipsos%20Global%20Trends%202017%20report.pdf.

Ipsos. (2018). *Goalkeepers global youth outlook poll*. Retrieved September 27, 2018, from https://www.ipsos.com/en-us/news-polls/Gates-goalkeepers-youth-optimism.

Kantor TNS. (2017). *The consumer trust divide for brands online*. Retrieved March 22, 2018, from http://www.tnsglobal.com/press-release/connected-life-2017-press-release.

Kelly, P. (2000). Youth as an artefact of expertise: Problematizing the practice of youth studies in an age of uncertainty. *Journal of Youth Studies, 3*(3), 301–315. https://doi.org/10.1080/713684381.

Kelly, P. (2011). Breath and the truths of youth at risk: Allegory and the social scientific imagination. *Journal of Youth Studies, 14*(4), 431–447. https://doi.org/10.1080/13676261.2010.543668.

Kelly, P. (2014). *The self as enterprise: Foucault and the spirit of 21st century capitalism*. VT Gower: Farnham Burlington.

Kelly, P. (2017). Growing up after the GFC: Responsibilisation and mortgaged futures. *Discourse: Studies in the Cultural Politics of Education, 38*(1), 57–69. https://doi.org/10.1080/01596306.2015.1104852.

Leccardi, C. (2014). Young people and the new semantics of the future. *SocietàMutamentoPolitica, 5*(10), 41–54. https://doi.org/10.13128/SMP-15404.

Longo, M. E. (2018). Youth temporalities and uncertainty: Understanding variations in young Argentinians' professional careers. *Time & Society, 27*(3), 389–414. https://doi.org/10.1177/0961463X15609828.

O'Malley, P. (2013). Uncertain governance and resilient subjects in the risk society. *Oñati Socio-legal Series, 3*(2), 180–195.

Mayes, E. (2018). Student voice in an age of 'security'? *Critical Studies in Education*, 1–18. https://doi.org/10.1080/17508487.2018.145572.

McLeod, J. (2017). Marking time, making methods: Temporality and untimely dilemmas in the sociology of youth and educational change. *British Journal of Sociology of Education, 38*(1), 13–25. https://doi.org/10.1080/01425692.2016.1254541.

Nikunen, M. (2017). Young people, future hopes and concerns in Finland and the European Union: Classed and gendered expectations in policy documents. *Journal of Youth Studies, 20*(6), 661–676. https://doi.org/10.1080/13676261.2016.1260693.

PWC. (2017). *Workforce of the future: The competing forces shaping 2030*. Retrieved March 5, 2018, from https://www.pwc.com/gx/en/services/people-organisation/publications/workforce-of-the-future.html.

Qiwei, W. (2015, July 6). Ant Tribe: Between dreams and reality. *GB Times*. Retrieved November 9, 2018, from https://gbtimes.com/ant-tribe-between-dreams-and-reality.

Robertson, E. (2014, October 17). Generation Y didn't go crazy in a vacuum. How can we enjoy life when our future is so uncertain? *The Guardian*. Retrieved September 13, 2017, from https://www.theguardian.com/commentisfree/2014/oct/17/generation-y-didnt-go-crazy-in-a-vacuum-how-can-we-enjoy-life-when-our-future-is-so-uncertain.

The Prince's Trust. (2018). *The Prince's Trust Macquarie Youth Index 2018*. Retrieved September 22, 2018, from https://www.princes-trust.org.uk/about-the-trust/news-views/macquarie-youth-index-2018-annual-report.

Valentine, G. (2003). Boundary crossings: Transitions from childhood to adulthood. *Children's Geographies, 1*(1), 37–52. https://doi.org/10.1080/14733280302186.

Wood, B. E. (2017). Youth studies, citizenship and transitions: Towards a new research agenda. *Journal of Youth Studies, 20*(9), 1176–1190. https://doi.org/10.1080/13676261.2017.1316363.

Woodman, D., & Wyn, J. (2014). *Youth and generation: Rethinking change and inequality in the lives of young people*. London: Sage.